THIS BOOK BELONGS TO

_____

_____
DATE

The OLD TESTAMENT
FAMILY READER

Other
FAMILY READERS

The Book of Mormon Family Reader

The New Testament Family Reader

The Doctrine and Covenants Family Reader

The Book of Mormon Family Reader—Spanish Edition

The OLD TESTAMENT
FAMILY READER

EDITED BY

Tyler McKellar and
Stephanie McKellar

ILLUSTRATED BY
Dan Burr

DESERET
BOOK

SALT LAKE CITY, UTAH

Library of Congress Cataloging-in-Publication Data

(CIP data on file)

ISBN 978-1-62972-946-6

Printed in China

RR Donnelley, Dongguan, China

10 9 8 7 6 5 4 3 2 1

Editors' Introduction

The Old Testament Family Reader was created to help children, youth, and families discover and discuss important doctrines and principles found throughout the Old Testament.

From our own experience, we know that reading the scriptures as a family can be challenging—for parents and children alike. Time is often short. Attention spans are even shorter. And many of the cultural and historic references in the Old Testament can be challenging for young readers in particular. This book is an effort to help families spend what limited study time they have on the Old Testament's most doctrinally relevant passages.

We are not scholars or professional teachers. And it is not our intention to diminish in any way the portions of the Old Testament that are not included in this book. In deciding which passages to include, we followed the same pattern used to create *The Book of Mormon Family Reader*, *The New Testament Family Reader*, and *The Doctrine and Covenants Family Reader* by considering three factors: the doctrines we want our six children to understand, our own impressions from repeated readings of the Old Testament, and the doctrines currently emphasized by latter-day prophets. With these factors in mind and through prayerful consideration, we made our best effort to organize this book. Even so, we acknowledge the subjectivity of this undertaking.

The Old Testament Family Reader divides the content of the Old Testament into 145 sections. Each section is designed to be read and discussed in about five to ten minutes, providing families a simple, consistent method for discovering and exploring the doctrines taught in the Old Testament. The sections contain the following:

- A title that identifies who is speaking or writing and the doctrine or event being discussed.

- A short introduction that reminds readers what is going on in the overall narrative and explains the background specific to the events being discussed.

- Selected scriptural verses from the Old Testament and the Pearl of Great Price, presented verbatim. While some verses are omitted to enable short scripture study opportunities, the verses that are included are unaltered from how they are found in the Old Testament and the Pearl of Great Price. (Please note the purpose for including portions of the Pearl of Great Price as explained in "How Did the Old Testament Come to Be?" on the following pages.)

- A few follow-up questions at the end of each section that offer suggestions for discussing that section. Some questions focus on understanding the teachings of a specific chapter. Others focus on how to apply those teachings to our own lives. These questions are, of course, merely suggestions. Guided by experience and the Spirit, parents will know the questions that best encourage discussion and understanding tailored to the unique needs of their families.

- Over 80 illustrations featured throughout the book that bring the people, events, and doctrinal topics of the Old Testament to life. Your experiences with this book will be made more vivid and memorable through the artistry of our friend Dan Burr.

Dividing the Old Testament into brief, sequential chapters presents some unique challenges. In an effort to ensure this book is accessible to all readers (especially children) without losing the potency of the Old Testament's inspiring words and events, the following considerations have been made:

- In the chapter introductions, we have attempted to explain only the most pertinent cultural and doctrinal references.

- Though the focus of this book is specifically on the doctrinally significant passages of the Old Testament, we have also included some passages that are not necessarily doctrinally pertinent but do help connect the overarching narrative of the Old Testament and illuminate iconic people and events of the era.

- Though designed for daily use by families, this book might also be beneficial in personal study, family home evening lessons, and Primary and youth lessons. However it is used, it is our hope that the pivotal doctrines taught in the Old Testament will be more clearly understood and easily discussed.

Included, where applicable, are the corrections and additions to the Old Testament text as revealed to Joseph Smith. The presence of these additions (known as the Joseph Smith Translation or JST) are noted in the introduction of the sections where they appear. The Lord inspired the Prophet Joseph Smith to restore truths to the King James Bible text that had become lost or changed over time. These truths often help readers more clearly understand doctrines taught in the scripture. As in the Latter-day Saint King James Version of the Old Testament, the JST portions of the scriptural text are presented in italic type.

We are grateful for the words of God and His prophets that have been carefully recorded in the Old Testament. We take courage from the men and women of that era who showed faith and humility in obeying God through all manner of challenges. The words they were taught have been lovingly preserved for our day—teachings and prophecies that speak of God's role as our Father, the reality of Jesus Christ's atoning sacrifice, and the eternal rewards offered to those who repent and covenant with God. It is our hope that this book will help families and individuals more fully understand and apply these eternal truths.

Stephanie and Tyler McKellar
Tetonia, Idaho
2021

How Did the Old Testament Come to Be?

The Old Testament is a collection of thirty-nine books that recount events, prophecies, laws, commandments, and revelations that occurred from about 4000 B.C. to 400 B.C. Together, the Old Testament and the New Testament form the Holy Bible. The word *testament* means "covenant." God first made covenants with Adam and Eve, as recounted in Genesis, the Old Testament's first book. Among many descriptions of the Old Testament, the Church has stated the following:

> The Old Testament gives an account of the Creation, the Fall of Adam and Eve, the great flood in the days of Noah, and the establishment of God's covenant with Abraham, Isaac, and Jacob, whom the Lord renamed Israel. It records the history of God's covenant people, the descendants of Jacob, who are called "the house of Israel" or "the children of Israel." It states how God delivered the children of Israel from Egyptian bondage through the prophet Moses and led them to a promised land. The Old Testament also contains the prophecies and warnings of the Lord's ancient prophets, whom He called to preach repentance to the children of Israel. Through His prophets, the Lord gave the Israelites laws, covenants, and doctrines to prepare them for His coming and teach them how to return to God and how to live in God's presence. For Latter-day Saints, the Bible stands alongside the Book of Mormon, Doctrine and Covenants, and Pearl of Great Price as holy scripture.[1]

Latter-day revelation confirms that the first five books of the Old Testament were written by (or under the direction of) Moses. The remaining books are named after the prophets or kings central to the events described, though who exactly recorded the words thousands of years ago is impossible to know. These books were recorded on scrolls made of animal skins and papyrus and were carefully preserved by Jewish leaders who passed them down through four millennia to the time of Christ. During His mortal ministry, Jesus Christ read aloud from physical copies of these records as He publicly declared His role as the Messiah. Later, while recording their own testimonies of Jesus Christ, the writers of many New Testament books quoted extensively from prophecies, history, and law from these same Old Testament records.

In the first century following Jesus Christ's Resurrection, as the Jewish and Christian faiths became increasingly divergent, the compilation of today's Old Testament record began to take shape. Jewish leaders—having rejected Christianity—wanted to ensure consistency of the scriptural record. Their decisions ultimately led to the content and order of today's Old Testament, accepted by both Jewish and Christian audiences.[2]

Acknowledging the understandable mistakes that can occur when copying and translating a collection of records over a period of 4,000 years, The Church of Jesus Christ of Latter-day Saints has declared, "We believe the Bible to be the word of God, as far as it is translated correctly" (Articles of Faith 1:8).

---

1. "Welcome to the Old Testament," *Old Testament Study Guide for Home-Study Seminary Students* (2015).
2. See Lenet H. Read, "How the Bible Came to Be: Part 2, The Word Is Preserved," *Ensign*, February 1982.

Some omissions and mistranslations in the Old Testament were corrected by the Prophet Joseph Smith, as directed by God. In 1830, Joseph Smith dictated a new revelation of part of the book of Genesis, which was then titled the book of Moses. From 1835 to 1842, after coming into possession of ancient Egyptian records, Joseph Smith received the book of Abraham by the gift and power of God. Both of these books— which greatly illuminate pivotal events of the Old Testament—are contained in a volume of canonized scripture called the Pearl of Great Price. These two books are also used alongside Old Testament scriptures in this family reader.

It's a mesmerizing thing to consider: Here in the twenty-first century we have access to words that God and His prophets spoke as far back as 6,000 years ago—a surviving record testifying of God's intentions, works, and words. Indeed, this is the comfort and guidance the Old Testament offers: God is our Father in Heaven. We lived with Him before we came to earth. He loves us, desires that we return to Him, and has a plan of redemption that makes that possible. A Savior has been prepared from the beginning. Prophets are called to teach these truths. Obedience is required. Repentance is possible. Eternal covenants that will bless us eternally are freely available to all God's children. These truths are taught on earth today. And in the Old Testament, we find record of them being taught before the world was even created.

MAP #1
ISRAEL'S EXODUS FROM EGYPT AND ENTRY INTO CANAAN

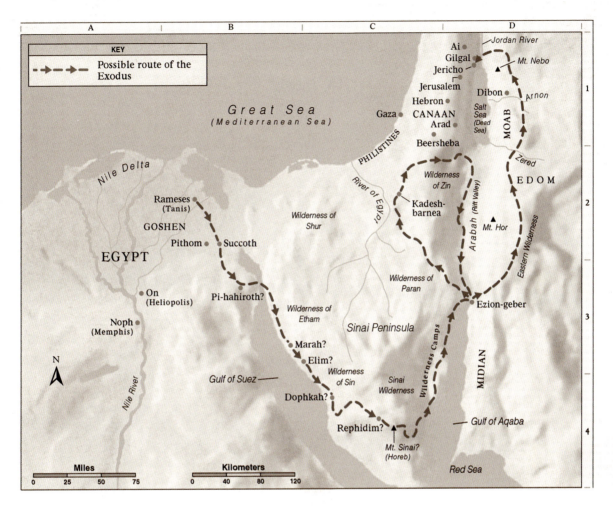

MAP #2
THE DIVISION OF THE 12 TRIBES

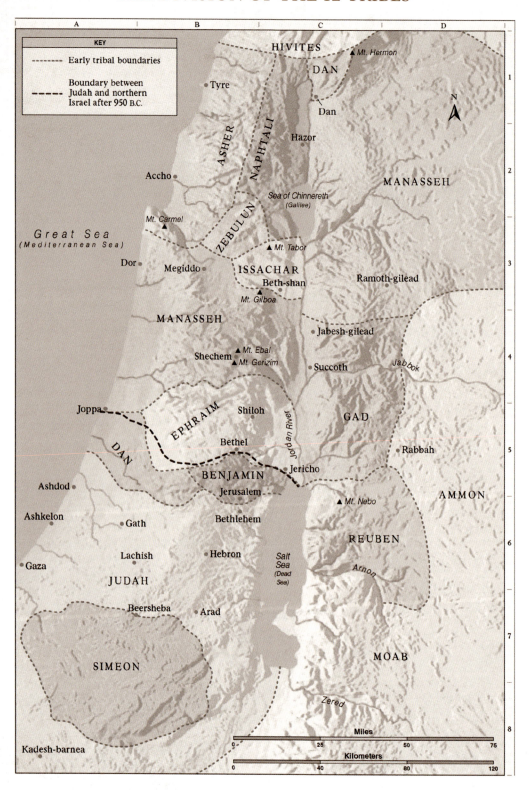

KEY
- - - - - Early tribal boundaries
- – – – Boundary between Judah and northern Israel after 950 B.C.

HIVITES

DAN

▲ Mt. Hermon

N

Tyre

Dan

ASHER

NAPHTALI

Hazor

Accho

MANASSEH

Sea of Chinnereth
(Galilee)

ZEBULUN

Mt. Carmel ▲

Great Sea
(Mediterranean Sea)

▲ Mt. Tabor

Dor

Megiddo

ISSACHAR

Beth-shan

Ramoth-gilead

Mt. Gilboa

MANASSEH

Jabesh-gilead

Shechem ▲ Mt. Ebal
▲ Mt. Gerizim

Succoth

Jabbok

Joppa

EPHRAIM

Shiloh

Jordan River

GAD

DAN

Bethel

Rabbah

Ashdod

Jericho

BENJAMIN

Jerusalem

▲ Mt. Nebo

AMMON

Ashkelon

Gath

Bethlehem

Lachish

Hebron

Salt
Sea
(Dead
Sea)

REUBEN

Gaza

Arnon

JUDAH

Beersheba

Arad

MOAB

SIMEON

Zered

Kadesh-barnea

Miles

0   25   50   75

Kilometers

0   40   80   120

MAP #3
THE EMPIRE OF DAVID AND SOLOMON

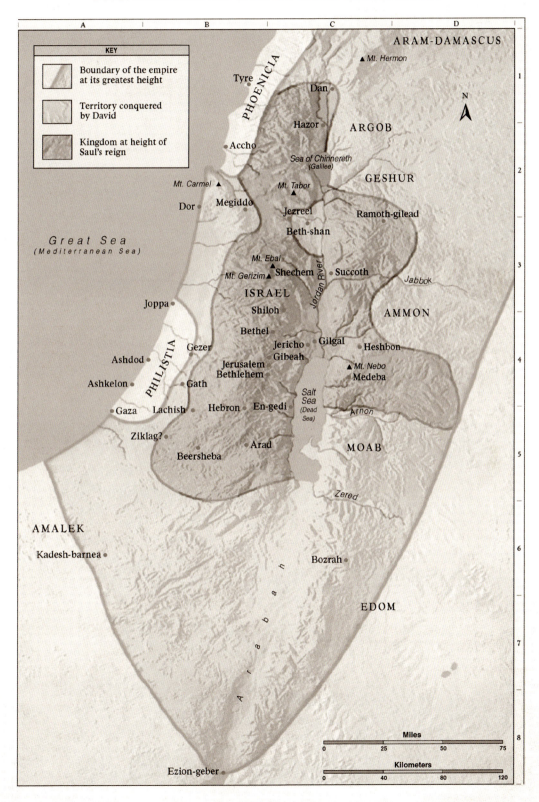

KEY

☐ Boundary of the empire at its greatest height

☐ Territory conquered by David

☐ Kingdom at height of Saul's reign

ARAM-DAMASCUS

▲ Mt. Hermon

N

PHOENICIA

Tyre

Dan

Hazor

ARGOB

Accho

Sea of Chinnereth (Galilee)

GESHUR

Mt. Carmel ▲

Mt. Tabor ▲

Dor

Megiddo

Jezreel

Ramoth-gilead

Beth-shan

Great Sea
(Mediterranean Sea)

Mt. Ebal ▲

Mt. Gerizim ▲ Shechem

Succoth

Jabbok

ISRAEL

Jordan River

Joppa

Shiloh

Bethel

AMMON

Jericho

Gilgal

Heshbon

Gezer

Gibeah

Ashdod

▲ Mt. Nebo

Jerusalem

Medeba

Ashkelon

PHILISTIA

Gath

Bethlehem

Salt Sea
(Dead Sea)

Gaza

Lachish

Hebron

En-gedi

Arnon

Ziklag?

Arad

MOAB

Beersheba

Zered

AMALEK

Kadesh-barnea

Bozrah

EDOM

Arabah

Miles

0   25   50   75

Kilometers

0   40   80   120

Ezion-geber

MAP #4
THE ASSYRIAN EMPIRE

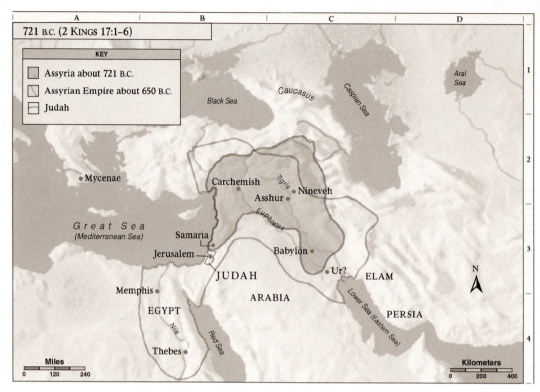

721 B.C. (2 KINGS 17:1–6)

KEY
- Assyria about 721 B.C.
- Assyrian Empire about 650 B.C.
- Judah

Aral Sea

Caucasus

Black Sea

Caspian Sea

Mycenae

Carchemish

Tigris

Nineveh

Asshur

Euphrates

Great Sea
(Mediterranean Sea)

Samaria

Jerusalem

Babylon

Ur?

ELAM

JUDAH

ARABIA

Lower Sea (Eastern Sea)

PERSIA

Memphis

N

EGYPT

Nile

Red Sea

Thebes

Miles
0   120   240

Kilometers
0   200   400

MAP #5
THE PERSIAN EMPIRE

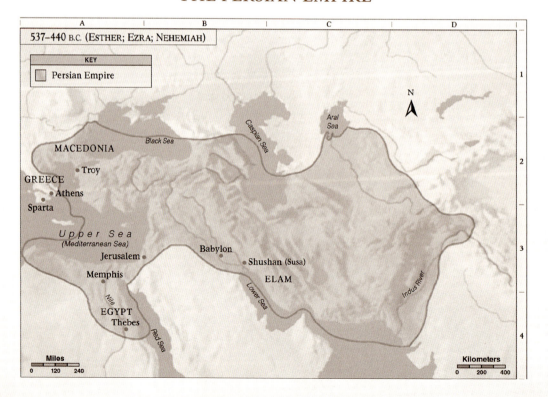

537–440 B.C. (ESTHER; EZRA; NEHEMIAH)

KEY
- Persian Empire

N

Aral Sea

MACEDONIA

Black Sea

Caspian Sea

Troy

GREECE

Athens

Sparta

Upper Sea
(Mediterranean Sea)

Babylon

Jerusalem

Shushan (Susa)

Memphis

ELAM

Indus River

Lower Sea

Nile

EGYPT

Thebes

Red Sea

Miles
0   120   240

Kilometers
0   200   400

GOD TEACHES ABRAHAM THAT THE EARTH WAS CREATED AS A PLACE OF TESTING FOR HIS CHILDREN

Though the Old Testament begins by describing the Creation of the earth, the book of Abraham (found in the Pearl of Great Price) helps us understand the purpose of that Creation. Abraham lived about 2,000 years before the birth of Christ. In his youth he desired to be righteous, but he was persecuted by wicked priests who attempted to sacrifice him to false gods. Abraham's life was saved by Jehovah (the title used to describe Jesus Christ in the Old Testament). After fleeing his homeland, Abraham was personally taught of God's eternal works by God Himself. These verses give us a glimpse of premortal life before the earth was created.

ABRAHAM 3:22–28

Now the Lord had shown unto me, Abraham, the intelligences that were organized before the world was; and among all these there were many of the noble and great ones;

23 And God saw these souls that they were good, and he stood in the midst of them, and he said: These I will make my rulers; for he stood among those that were spirits, and he saw that they were good; and he said unto me: Abraham, thou art one of them; thou wast chosen before thou wast born.

24 And there stood one among them that was like unto God, and he said unto those who were with him: We will go down, for there is space there, and we will take of these materials, and we will make an earth whereon these may dwell;

25 And we will prove them herewith, to see if they will do all things whatsoever the Lord their God shall command them;

26 And they who keep their first estate shall be added upon; and they who keep not their first estate shall not have glory in the same kingdom with those who keep their first estate; and they who keep their second estate shall have glory added upon their heads for ever and ever.

27 And the Lord said: Whom shall I send? And one answered like unto the Son of Man: Here am I, send me. And another answered and said: Here am I, send me. And the Lord said: I will send the first.

28 And the second was angry, and kept not his first estate; and, at that day, many followed after him.

What did Abraham learn about himself in his vision of the premortal world? What does this teach you about yourself? According to verses 24–25, what was the purpose of the earth's creation? What blessings were promised to those who were obedient during their earthly lives? Who else was present in the premortal world, as taught in these verses?

GOD TEACHES MOSES THAT HE IS GOD'S SON AND GOD HAS A WORK FOR HIM TO DO

Moses was a prophet who lived about 1,300 years before Christ was born. He is recognized as the author of the first five books of the Old Testament. In 1830, Joseph Smith was commanded to produce a translation of the Old Testament that restored important details and truths that had been lost. Part of that work resulted in the book of Moses, now found in the Pearl of Great Price. In these verses, Moses is taught of God's endless creations and of His Son Jesus Christ, the Savior of the world. Similar to the verses in the previous section from the book of Abraham, these verses help us understand the purpose of God's work. In these verses, the word "similitude" means to be similar to something or to point to something similar of greater importance.

MOSES 1:1–10

The words of God, which he spake unto Moses at a time when Moses was caught up into an exceedingly high mountain,

2 And he saw God face to face, and he talked with him, and the glory of God was upon Moses; therefore Moses could endure his presence.

3 And God spake unto Moses, saying: Behold, I am the Lord God Almighty, and Endless is my name; for I am without beginning of days or end of years; and is not this endless?

4 And, behold, thou art my son; wherefore look, and I will show thee the workmanship of mine hands; but not all, for my works are without end, and also my words, for they never cease.

5 Wherefore, no man can behold all my works, except he behold all my glory; and no man can behold all my glory, and afterwards remain in the flesh on the earth.

6 And I have a work for thee, Moses, my son; and thou art in the similitude of mine Only Begotten; and mine Only Begotten is and shall be the Savior, for he is full of grace and truth; but there is no God beside me, and all things are present with me, for I know them all.

7 And now, behold, this one thing I show unto thee, Moses, my son, for thou art in the world, and now I show it unto thee.

8 And it came to pass that Moses looked, and beheld the world upon which he was created; and Moses beheld the world and the ends thereof, and all the children of men which are, and which were created; of the same he greatly marveled and wondered.

9 And the presence of God withdrew from Moses, that his glory was not upon Moses; and Moses was left unto himself. And as he was left unto himself, he fell unto the earth.

10 And it came to pass that it was for the space of many hours before Moses did again receive his natural strength like unto man; and he said unto himself: Now, for this cause I know that man is nothing, which thing I never had supposed.

What did Moses learn as he spoke with God? What title did God use in referring to Moses? What descriptions are given of Jesus Christ? What was Moses's reaction to what he saw?

MOSES REJECTS SATAN'S TEMPTATIONS AND DECLARES THAT HE IS A SON OF GOD

Moses had been shown a mighty vision of God's eternal and glorious creations and was taught that Jesus Christ would come to save the world. Following the vision, Moses was left alone and fell to the earth. After many hours, he regained his strength and declared that "man is nothing" (Moses 1:10). His words then continued.

MOSES 1:11–22

But now mine own eyes have beheld God; but not my natural, but my spiritual eyes, for my natural eyes could not have beheld; for I should have withered and died in his presence; but his glory was upon me; and I beheld his face, for I was transfigured before him.

12 And it came to pass that when Moses had said these words, behold, Satan came tempting him, saying: Moses, son of man, worship me.

13 And it came to pass that Moses looked upon Satan and said: Who art thou? For behold, I am a son of God, in the similitude of his Only Begotten; and where is thy glory, that I should worship thee?

14 For behold, I could not look upon God, except his glory should come upon me, and I were transfigured before him. But I can look upon thee in the natural man. Is it not so, surely?

15 Blessed be the name of my God, for his Spirit hath not altogether withdrawn from me, or else where is thy glory, for it is darkness unto me? And I can judge between thee and God; for God said unto me: Worship God, for him only shalt thou serve.

16 Get thee hence, Satan; deceive me not; for God said unto me: Thou art after the similitude of mine Only Begotten.

17 And he also gave me commandments when he called unto me out of the burning bush, saying: Call upon God in the name of mine Only Begotten, and worship me.

18 And again Moses said: I will not cease to call upon God, I have other things to inquire of him: for his glory has been upon me, wherefore I can judge between him and thee. Depart hence, Satan.

19 And now, when Moses had said these words, Satan cried with a loud voice, and ranted upon the earth, and commanded, saying: I am the Only Begotten, worship me.

20 And it came to pass that Moses began to fear exceedingly; and as he began to fear, he saw the bitterness of hell. Nevertheless, calling upon God, he received strength, and he commanded, saying: Depart from me, Satan, for this one God only will I worship, which is the God of glory.

21 And now Satan began to tremble, and the earth shook; and Moses received strength, and called upon God, saying: In the name of the Only Begotten, depart hence, Satan.

22 And it came to pass that Satan cried with a loud voice, with weeping, and wailing, and gnashing of teeth; and he departed hence, even from the presence of Moses, that he beheld him not.

What differences did Moses identify between the appearances of God and of Satan? What did Moses do to stand strong against Satan's temptations? What did Moses do when he was afraid? How can God help you when you are worried or afraid?

3

GOD TEACHES MOSES THAT HIS WORK IS TO BRING TO PASS OUR IMMORTALITY AND ETERNAL LIFE

After Moses's mighty vision of God's eternal and glorious creations, he was visited by Satan. Moses rejected Satan's temptation to worship him and commanded that he depart. Satan cried with a loud voice, trembled, and finally departed. In these verses, Moses learned additional truths about God's immense creations.

MOSES 1:24–40

And it came to pass that when Satan had departed from the presence of Moses, that Moses lifted up his eyes unto heaven, being filled with the Holy Ghost, which beareth record of the Father and the Son;

25 And calling upon the name of God, he beheld his glory again, for it was upon him; and he heard a voice, saying: Blessed art thou, Moses, for I, the Almighty, have chosen thee, and thou shalt be made stronger than many waters; for they shall obey thy command as if thou wert God.

26 And lo, I am with thee, even unto the end of thy days; for thou shalt deliver my people from bondage, even Israel my chosen.

27 And it came to pass, as the voice was still speaking, Moses cast his eyes and beheld the earth, yea, even all of it; and there was not a particle of it which he did not behold, discerning it by the Spirit of God.

28 And he beheld also the inhabitants thereof, and there was not a soul which he beheld not; and he discerned them by the Spirit of God; and their numbers were great, even numberless as the sand upon the sea shore.

29 And he beheld many lands; and each land was called earth, and there were inhabitants on the face thereof.

30 And it came to pass that Moses called upon God, saying: Tell me, I pray thee, why these things are so, and by what thou madest them?

31 And behold, the glory of the Lord was upon Moses, so that Moses stood in the presence of

God, and talked with him face to face. And the Lord God said unto Moses: For mine own purpose have I made these things. Here is wisdom and it remaineth in me.

32 And by the word of my power, have I created them, which is mine Only Begotten Son, who is full of grace and truth.

33 And worlds without number have I created; and I also created them for mine own purpose; and by the Son I created them, which is mine Only Begotten.

34 And the first man of all men have I called Adam, which is many.

35 But only an account of this earth, and the inhabitants thereof, give I unto you. For behold, there are many worlds that have passed away by the word of my power. And there are many that now stand, and innumerable are they unto man; but all things are numbered unto me, for they are mine and I know them.

36 And it came to pass that Moses spake unto the Lord, saying: Be merciful unto thy servant, O God, and tell me concerning this earth, and the inhabitants thereof, and also the heavens, and then thy servant will be content.

37 And the Lord God spake unto Moses, saying: The heavens, they are many, and they cannot be numbered unto man; but they are numbered unto me, for they are mine.

38 And as one earth shall pass away, and the heavens thereof even so shall another come; and there is no end to my works, neither to my words.

39 For behold, this is my work and my glory—to bring to pass the immortality and eternal life of man.

40 And now, Moses, my son, I will speak unto thee concerning this earth upon which thou standest; and thou shalt write the things which I shall speak.

What did God show to Moses in verses 27–29? According to verse 39, what is God's work and glory? How does Heavenly Father bring about our immortality and eternal life?

GOD CREATES THE EARTH AND FILLS IT WITH LIGHT AND LIFE

During their mortal lives, Abraham and Moses were shown mighty visions of God's work before the earth was created. They learned of God's plan to allow His spirit children to become like Him. They were then shown lengthy visions of how the earth was created. Moses's description of his vision is found in the book of Moses and in the Old Testament book of Genesis, which means "origin" or "beginning." Latter-day revelation has clarified that Heavenly Father commanded His firstborn Son Jesus Christ to oversee the Creation of the earth (see Moses 1:33).

GENESIS 1:1–9, 14–18, 20–22, 24–25 (SEE ALSO MOSES 2:3–25)

In the beginning God created the heaven and the earth.

2 And the earth was without form, and void; and darkness was upon the face of the deep. And the Spirit of God moved upon the face of the waters.

3 And God said, Let there be light: and there was light.

4 And God saw the light, that it was good: and God divided the light from the darkness.

5 And God called the light Day, and the darkness he called Night. And the evening and the morning were the first day.

6 And God said, Let there be a firmament in the midst of the waters, and let it divide the waters from the waters.

7 And God made the firmament, and divided the waters which were under the firmament from the waters which were above the firmament: and it was so.

8 And God called the firmament Heaven. And the evening and the morning were the second day.

9 And God said, Let the waters under the heaven be gathered together unto one place, and let the dry land appear: and it was so.

14 And God said, Let there be lights in the firmament of the heaven to divide the day from the night; and let them be for signs, and for seasons, and for days, and years:

15 And let them be for lights in the firmament of the heaven to give light upon the earth: and it was so.

16 And God made two great lights; the greater light to rule the day, and the lesser light to rule the night: he made the stars also.

17 And God set them in the firmament of the heaven to give light upon the earth,

18 And to rule over the day and over the night, and to divide the light from the darkness: and God saw that it was good.

20 And God said, Let the waters bring forth abundantly the moving creature that hath life, and fowl that may fly above the earth in the open firmament of heaven.

21 And God created great whales, and every living creature that moveth, which the waters brought forth abundantly, after their kind, and every winged fowl after his kind: and God saw that it was good.

22 And God blessed them, saying, Be fruitful, and multiply, and fill the waters in the seas, and let fowl multiply in the earth.

24 And God said, Let the earth bring forth the living creature after his kind, cattle, and creeping thing, and beast of the earth after his kind: and it was so.

25 And God made the beast of the earth after his kind, and cattle after their kind, and every thing that creepeth upon the earth after his kind: and God saw that it was good.

After blessing plant and animal life, what did God command those living things to do (see verse 22)? Why do you think God provided Moses such a detailed explanation of how the earth was created?

GOD CREATES MAN AND WOMAN IN HIS IMAGE

In a vision shown to Moses, God created lights in the heavens and plant and animal life on earth, and commanded all living things to multiply after their own kind. God also explained to Moses that He first created all things spiritually before He created them physically (see Moses 3:5). These verses describe the final things God created spiritually before He then created them physically.

GENESIS 1:26–31 (SEE ALSO MOSES 2:26–31)

And God said, Let us make man in our image, after our likeness: and let them have dominion over the fish of the sea, and over the fowl of the air, and over the cattle, and over all the earth, and over every creeping thing that creepeth upon the earth.

27 So God created man in his own image, in the image of God created he him; male and female created he them.

28 And God blessed them, and God said unto them, Be fruitful, and multiply, and replenish the earth, and subdue it: and have dominion over the fish of the sea, and over the fowl of the air, and over every living thing that moveth upon the earth.

29 And God said, Behold, I have given you every herb bearing seed, which is upon the face of all the earth, and every tree, in the which is the fruit of a tree yielding seed; to you it shall be for meat.

30 And to every beast of the earth, and to every fowl of the air, and to every thing that creepeth upon the earth, wherein there is life, I have given every green herb for meat: and it was so.

31 And God saw every thing that he had made, and, behold, it was very good. And the evening and the morning were the sixth day.

MOSES 3:5 (SEE ALSO GENESIS 2:4–5)

5 And every plant of the field before it was in the earth, and every herb of the field before it grew. For I, the Lord God, created all things, of which I have spoken, spiritually, before they were naturally upon the face of the earth. For I, the Lord God, had not caused it to rain upon the face of the earth. And I, the Lord God, had created all the children of men; and not yet a man to till the ground; for in heaven created I them; and there was not yet flesh upon the earth, neither in the water, neither in the air;

What does it mean that we are created in the image of God? After creating man and woman, what did the Lord command them to do?

ADAM AND EVE ARE PLACED IN THE GARDEN OF EDEN AND TEMPTED BY SATAN

In a vision to Moses, God explained that He first created all things spiritually, including the earth and all living things. He then created all things physically and placed the first man and woman on the earth.

GENESIS 2:8, 15–18, 21–25

And the Lord God planted a garden eastward in Eden; and there he put the man whom he had formed.

15 And the Lord God took the man, and put him into the garden of Eden to dress it and to keep it.

16 And the Lord God commanded the man, saying, Of every tree of the garden thou mayest freely eat:

17 But of the tree of the knowledge of good and evil, thou shalt not eat of it: for in the day that thou eatest thereof thou shalt surely die.

18 And the Lord God said, It is not good that the man should be alone; I will make him an help meet for him.

21 And the Lord God caused a deep sleep to fall upon Adam, and he slept: and he took one of his ribs, and closed up the flesh instead thereof;

22 And the rib, which the Lord God had taken from man, made he a woman, and brought her unto the man.

23 And Adam said, This is now bone of my bones, and flesh of my flesh: she shall be called Woman, because she was taken out of Man.

24 Therefore shall a man leave his father and his mother, and shall cleave unto his wife: and they shall be one flesh.

25 And they were both naked, the man and his wife, and were not ashamed.

GENESIS 3:1–7 (SEE ALSO MOSES 3:8, 15–25; 4:5–13)

1 Now the serpent was more subtil than any beast of the field which the Lord God had made. And he said unto the woman, Yea, hath God said, Ye shall not eat of every tree of the garden?

2 And the woman said unto the serpent, We may eat of the fruit of the trees of the garden:

3 But of the fruit of the tree which is in the midst of the garden, God hath said, Ye shall not eat of it, neither shall ye touch it, lest ye die.

4 And the serpent said unto the woman, Ye shall not surely die:

5 For God doth know that in the day ye eat thereof, then your eyes shall be opened, and ye shall be as gods, knowing good and evil.

6 And when the woman saw that the tree was good for food, and that it was pleasant to the eyes, and a tree to be desired to make one wise, she took of the fruit thereof, and did eat, and gave also unto her husband with her; and he did eat.

7 And the eyes of them both were opened, and they knew that they were naked; and they sewed fig leaves together, and made themselves aprons.

What commandment did God give to Adam and Eve in the garden? What would be the consequences if they disobeyed that commandment? What actions did Eve take after being tempted by Satan? According to Genesis 3:6, why was Eve willing to partake of the fruit?

ADAM AND EVE LEARN THE CONSEQUENCES OF EATING THE FORBIDDEN FRUIT AND ARE CAST OUT OF THE GARDEN OF EDEN

God had told Adam and Eve not to partake of the fruit from the tree of knowledge of good and evil. They were warned that the consequence would be death. Satan tempted Eve to eat the fruit, telling her that by eating the fruit they would be as the gods, knowing good and evil. Eve considered the consequences, ate the fruit, and invited Adam to do the same. Their eyes were then opened, they became aware of their nakedness, and they sewed clothing from fig leaves. They then heard God's voice as He taught them the consequences of their actions.

GENESIS 3:8–24 (SEE ALSO MOSES 4:14–31)

And they heard the voice of the Lord God walking in the garden in the cool of the day: and Adam and his wife hid themselves from the presence of the Lord God amongst the trees of the garden.

9 And the Lord God called unto Adam, and said unto him, Where art thou?

10 And he said, I heard thy voice in the garden, and I was afraid, because I was naked; and I hid myself.

11 And he said, Who told thee that thou wast naked? Hast thou eaten of the tree, whereof I commanded thee that thou shouldest not eat?

12 And the man said, The woman whom thou gavest to be with me, she gave me of the tree, and I did eat.

13 And the Lord God said unto the woman, What is this that thou hast done? And the woman said, The serpent beguiled me, and I did eat.

14 And the Lord God said unto the serpent, Because thou hast done this, thou art cursed above all cattle, and above every beast of the field; upon thy belly shalt thou go, and dust shalt thou eat all the days of thy life:

15 And I will put enmity between thee and the woman, and between thy seed and her seed; it shall bruise thy head, and thou shalt bruise his heel.

16 Unto the woman he said, I will greatly multiply thy sorrow and thy conception; in sorrow thou shalt bring forth children; and thy desire shall be to thy husband, and he shall rule over thee.

17 And unto Adam he said, Because thou hast hearkened unto the voice of thy wife, and hast eaten of the tree, of which I commanded thee, saying, Thou shalt not eat of it: cursed is the ground for thy sake; in sorrow shalt thou eat of it all the days of thy life;

18 Thorns also and thistles shall it bring forth to thee; and thou shalt eat the herb of the field;

19 In the sweat of thy face shalt thou eat bread, till thou return unto the ground; for out of it wast thou taken: for dust thou art, and unto dust shalt thou return.

20 And Adam called his wife's name Eve; because she was the mother of all living.

21 Unto Adam also and to his wife did the Lord God make coats of skins, and clothed them.

22 And the Lord God said, Behold, the man is become as one of us, to know good and evil: and now, lest he put forth his hand, and take also of the tree of life, and eat, and live for ever:

23 Therefore the Lord God sent him forth from the garden of Eden, to till the ground from whence he was taken.

24 So he drove out the man; and he placed at the east of the garden of Eden Cherubims, and a flaming sword which turned every way, to keep the way of the tree of life.

What consequences did Adam and Eve face as a result of eating the forbidden fruit? What consequences did their actions bring to all of us? Consider verse 22. What are some examples of good and evil in the world today? How can you know the difference?

AN ANGEL TEACHES ADAM THE PURPOSE OF ANIMAL SACRIFICES

Adam and Eve partook of the forbidden fruit in the Garden of Eden. By doing so, they became aware of good and evil and began to face the consequences of mortal life. God told Eve that giving birth to children would be painful. He told Adam that tilling the earth to bring forth food would be difficult. They were then cast out of the garden. In verse 5, the commandment to "offer the firstlings of their flocks" is a reference to sacrifices in which certain animals were raised specifically to be killed and placed upon an altar as a form of sacred worship before God.

Moses 5:1–8

And it came to pass that after I, the Lord God, had driven them out, that Adam began to till the earth, and to have dominion over all the beasts of the field, and to eat his bread by the sweat of his brow, as I the Lord had commanded him. And Eve, also, his wife, did labor with him.

2 And Adam knew his wife, and she bare unto him sons and daughters, and they began to multiply and to replenish the earth.

3 And from that time forth, the sons and daughters of Adam began to divide two and two in the land, and to till the land, and to tend flocks, and they also begat sons and daughters.

4 And Adam and Eve, his wife, called upon the name of the Lord, and they heard the voice of the Lord from the way toward the Garden of Eden, speaking unto them, and they saw him not; for they were shut out from his presence.

5 And he gave unto them commandments, that they should worship the Lord their God, and should offer the firstlings of their flocks, for an offering unto the Lord. And Adam was obedient unto the commandments of the Lord.

6 And after many days an angel of the Lord appeared unto Adam, saying: Why dost thou offer sacrifices unto the Lord? And Adam said unto him: I know not, save the Lord commanded me.

7 And then the angel spake, saying: This thing is a similitude of the sacrifice of the Only Begotten of the Father, which is full of grace and truth.

8 Wherefore, thou shalt do all that thou doest in the name of the Son, and thou shalt repent and call upon God in the name of the Son forevermore.

Why do you think Adam was commanded to offer the firstborn of his flocks? Adam obeyed the command to offer the firstborn of his flocks, even before he knew the reason for doing so. In what ways can you show obedience, even if you don't fully understand the reason for a commandment?

ADAM AND EVE LEARN OF THE PLAN OF REDEMPTION AND TEACH IT TO THEIR CHILDREN

Adam was obedient to God's commandment to offer animal sacrifices, and he learned that those sacrifices served as a reminder of the atoning sacrifice of Jesus Christ. Adam and Eve and their children were mortal beings, and their path to return to Heavenly Father and become like Him was blocked by sin and death. But their understanding of the plan of redemption and the wisdom of their choice to partake of the forbidden fruit continued to grow.

MOSES 5:9–15

And in that day the Holy Ghost fell upon Adam, which beareth record of the Father and the Son, saying: I am the Only Begotten of the Father from the beginning, henceforth and forever, that as thou hast fallen thou mayest be redeemed, and all mankind, even as many as will.

10 And in that day Adam blessed God and was filled, and began to prophesy concerning all the families of the earth, saying: Blessed be the name of God, for because of my transgression my eyes are opened, and in this life I shall have joy, and again in the flesh I shall see God.

11 And Eve, his wife, heard all these things and was glad, saying: Were it not for our transgression we never should have had seed, and never should have known good and evil, and the joy of our redemption, and the eternal life which God giveth unto all the obedient.

12 And Adam and Eve blessed the name of God, and they made all things known unto their sons and their daughters.

13 And Satan came among them, saying: I am also a son of God; and he commanded them, saying: Believe it not; and they believed it not, and they loved Satan more than God. And men began from that time forth to be carnal, sensual, and devilish.

14 And the Lord God called upon men by the Holy Ghost everywhere and commanded them that they should repent;

15 And as many as believed in the Son, and repented of their sins, should be saved; and as many as believed not and repented not, should be damned; and the words went forth out of the mouth of God in a firm decree; wherefore they must be fulfilled.

According to verse 9, what truth did Adam learn from the Holy Ghost? What did Eve understand and proclaim about the consequences of their choice? What was the promised blessing for believing in the Son of God and repenting of their sins? How do you increase your belief in Jesus Christ? How does belief in Jesus Christ lead you to repent?

CAIN KILLS HIS BROTHER ABEL AND BECOMES CURSED

Adam and Eve taught their children about Jesus Christ and the plan of happiness. But Satan also had influence among them, leading some people away from the truth.

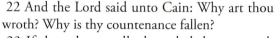

MOSES 5:16–26, 32–35 (SEE ALSO GENESIS 4:1–16)

And Adam and Eve, his wife, ceased not to call upon God. And Adam knew Eve his wife, and she conceived and bare Cain, and said: I have gotten a man from the Lord; wherefore he may not reject his words. But behold, Cain hearkened not, saying: Who is the Lord that I should know him?

17 And she again conceived and bare his brother Abel. And Abel hearkened unto the voice of the Lord. And Abel was a keeper of sheep, but Cain was a tiller of the ground.

18 And Cain loved Satan more than God. And Satan commanded him, saying: Make an offering unto the Lord.

19 And in process of time it came to pass that Cain brought of the fruit of the ground an offering unto the Lord.

20 And Abel, he also brought of the firstlings of his flock, and of the fat thereof. And the Lord had respect unto Abel, and to his offering;

21 But unto Cain, and to his offering, he had not respect. Now Satan knew this, and it pleased him. And Cain was very wroth, and his countenance fell.

22 And the Lord said unto Cain: Why art thou wroth? Why is thy countenance fallen?

23 If thou doest well, thou shalt be accepted. And if thou doest not well, sin lieth at the door, and Satan desireth to have thee; and except thou shalt hearken unto my commandments, I will deliver thee up, and it shall be unto thee according to his desire. And thou shalt rule over him;

24 For from this time forth thou shalt be the father of his lies; thou shalt be called Perdition; for thou wast also before the world.

25 And it shall be said in time to come—That these abominations were had from Cain; for he rejected the greater counsel which was had from God; and this is a cursing which I will put upon thee, except thou repent.

26 And Cain was wroth, and listened not any more to the voice of the Lord, neither to Abel, his brother, who walked in holiness before the Lord.

32 And Cain went into the field, and Cain talked with Abel, his brother. And it came to pass that while they were in the field, Cain rose up against Abel, his brother, and slew him.

33 And Cain gloried in that which he had done, saying: I am free; surely the flocks of my brother falleth into my hands.

34 And the Lord said unto Cain: Where is Abel, thy brother? And he said: I know not. Am I my brother's keeper?

35 And the Lord said: What hast thou done? The voice of thy brother's blood cries unto me from the ground.

Whom did Cain love more than God? What did this lead Cain to do? How can you strengthen your love for God? What blessings have come to you as you have tried to love and serve God?

ADAM AND EVE AND THEIR POSTERITY ARE TAUGHT THAT JESUS CHRIST WILL COME IN THE MERIDIAN OF TIME

Cain had killed Abel and was cursed for it. Adam's children were continually taught the gospel, but Satan's influence was powerful. Some chose righteousness. Many others chose wickedness.

MOSES 5:55–59 (SEE ALSO GENESIS 4:25–26; 5:1–5)

*A*nd thus the works of darkness began to prevail among all the sons of men.

56 And God cursed the earth with a sore curse, and was angry with the wicked, with all the sons of men whom he had made;

57 For they would not hearken unto his voice, nor believe on his Only Begotten Son, even him whom he declared should come in the meridian of time, who was prepared from before the foundation of the world.

58 And thus the Gospel began to be preached, from the beginning, being declared by holy angels sent forth from the presence of God, and by his own voice, and by the gift of the Holy Ghost.

59 And thus all things were confirmed unto Adam, by an holy ordinance, and the Gospel preached, and a decree sent forth, that it should be in the world, until the end thereof; and thus it was. Amen.

MOSES 6:1–12

1 And Adam hearkened unto the voice of God, and called upon his sons to repent.

2 And Adam knew his wife again, and she bare a son, and he called his name Seth. And Adam glorified the name of God; for he said: God hath appointed me another seed, instead of Abel, whom Cain slew.

3 And God revealed himself unto Seth, and he rebelled not, but offered an acceptable sacrifice, like unto his brother Abel. And to him also was born a son, and he called his name Enos.

4 And then began these men to call upon the name of the Lord, and the Lord blessed them;

5 And a book of remembrance was kept, in the which was recorded, in the language of Adam, for it was given unto as many as called upon God to write by the spirit of inspiration;

6 And by them their children were taught to read and write, having a language which was pure and undefiled.

7 Now this same Priesthood, which was in the beginning, shall be in the end of the world also.

8 Now this prophecy Adam spake, as he was moved upon by the Holy Ghost, and a genealogy was kept of the children of God. And this was the book of the generations of Adam, saying: In the day that God created man, in the likeness of God made he him;

9 In the image of his own body, male and female, created he them, and blessed them, and called their name Adam, in the day when they were created and became living souls in the land upon the footstool of God.

10 And Adam lived one hundred and thirty years, and begat a son in his own likeness, after his own image, and called his name Seth.

11 And the days of Adam, after he had begotten Seth, were eight hundred years, and he begat many sons and daughters;

12 And all the days that Adam lived were nine hundred and thirty years, and he died.

In Moses 6:4–6, what did the righteous people do to receive God's blessings for them and their children? Adam and Eve made sure they taught their children the gospel and kept records of their teachings. What can you do in your home to learn and teach the gospel? What records do you have of these truths?

ENOCH IS COMMANDED TO TELL THE PEOPLE TO "CHOOSE . . . THIS DAY, TO SERVE THE LORD GOD"

Adam's son Seth was obedient to God's commandments, but many others were not. Moses recorded that "in those days Satan had great dominion among men, and raged in their hearts; and from thenceforth came wars and bloodshed" (Moses 6:15). While Satan's influence continued to deceive many, Seth's posterity was noted for being "preachers of righteousness" (Moses 6:23). Five generations later, Enoch was born.

MOSES 6:26–27, 31–39

And it came to pass that Enoch journeyed in the land, among the people; and as he journeyed, the Spirit of God descended out of heaven, and abode upon him.

27 And he heard a voice from heaven, saying: Enoch, my son, prophesy unto this people, and say unto them—Repent, for thus saith the Lord: I am angry with this people, and my fierce anger is kindled against them; for their hearts have waxed hard, and their ears are dull of hearing, and their eyes cannot see afar off;

31 And when Enoch had heard these words, he bowed himself to the earth, before the Lord, and spake before the Lord, saying: Why is it that I have found favor in thy sight, and am but a lad, and all the people hate me; for I am slow of speech; wherefore am I thy servant?

32 And the Lord said unto Enoch: Go forth and do as I have commanded thee, and no man shall pierce thee. Open thy mouth, and it shall be filled, and I will give thee utterance, for all flesh is in my hands, and I will do as seemeth me good.

33 Say unto this people: Choose ye this day, to serve the Lord God who made you.

34 Behold my Spirit is upon you, wherefore all thy words will I justify; and the mountains shall flee before you, and the rivers shall turn from their course; and thou shalt abide in me, and I in you; therefore walk with me.

35 And the Lord spake unto Enoch, and said unto him: Anoint thine eyes with clay, and wash them, and thou shalt see. And he did so.

36 And he beheld the spirits that God had created; and he beheld also things which were not visible to the natural eye; and from thenceforth

came the saying abroad in the land: A seer hath the Lord raised up unto his people.

37 And it came to pass that Enoch went forth in the land, among the people, standing upon the hills and the high places, and cried with a loud voice, testifying against their works; and all men were offended because of him.

38 And they came forth to hear him, upon the high places, saying unto the tent-keepers: Tarry ye here and keep the tents, while we go yonder to behold the seer, for he prophesieth, and there is a strange thing in the land; a wild man hath come among us.

39 And it came to pass when they heard him, no man laid hands on him; for fear came on all them that heard him; for he walked with God.

According to verse 31, how did Enoch feel about himself and his ability to do what the Lord had commanded him? Despite Enoch's self-doubt, what promises did the Lord offer if he would go forth and open his mouth? Consider any doubts you may have about your own abilities. How can the Lord help you overcome these doubts and accomplish good things, even if they are difficult?

ENOCH TEACHES OF THE FALL THAT CAME BY ADAM AND THE SALVATION THAT COMES ONLY THROUGH JESUS CHRIST

Adam and Eve's posterity had reached six generations. Many of their descendants were wicked. Enoch, a righteous descendant of Adam's son Seth, was called by God to preach repentance. Enoch felt he was too young, not a good speaker, and that the people hated him. But God commanded him to preach, and Enoch obeyed. Many people journeyed to hear Enoch's powerful preaching and were amazed, for "he walked with God" (Moses 6:39).

MOSES 6:43–56

And Enoch continued his speech, saying: The Lord which spake with me, the same is the God of heaven, and he is my God, and your God, and ye are my brethren, and why counsel ye yourselves, and deny the God of heaven?

44 The heavens he made; the earth is his footstool; and the foundation thereof is his. Behold, he laid it, an host of men hath he brought in upon the face thereof.

45 And death hath come upon our fathers; nevertheless we know them, and cannot deny, and even the first of all we know, even Adam.

46 For a book of remembrance we have written among us, according to the pattern given by the finger of God; and it is given in our own language.

47 And as Enoch spake forth the words of God, the people trembled, and could not stand in his presence.

48 And he said unto them: Because that Adam fell, we are; and by his fall came death; and we are made partakers of misery and woe.

49 Behold Satan hath come among the children of men, and tempteth them to worship him; and men have become carnal, sensual, and devilish, and are shut out from the presence of God.

50 But God hath made known unto our fathers that all men must repent.

51 And he called upon our father Adam by his own voice, saying: I am God; I made the world, and men before they were in the flesh.

52 And he also said unto him: If thou wilt turn unto me, and hearken unto my voice, and believe, and repent of all thy transgressions, and be baptized, even in water, in the name of mine Only Begotten Son, who is full of grace and truth, which is Jesus Christ, the only name which shall be given under heaven, whereby salvation shall come unto the children of men, ye shall receive the gift of the Holy Ghost, asking all things in his name, and whatsoever ye shall ask, it shall be given you.

53 And our father Adam spake unto the Lord, and said: Why is it that men must repent and be baptized in water? And the Lord said unto Adam: Behold I have forgiven thee thy transgression in the Garden of Eden.

54 Hence came the saying abroad among the people, that the Son of God hath atoned for original guilt, wherein the sins of the parents cannot be answered upon the heads of the children, for they are whole from the foundation of the world.

55 And the Lord spake unto Adam, saying: Inasmuch as thy children are conceived in sin, even so when they begin to grow up, sin conceiveth in their hearts, and they taste the bitter, that they may know to prize the good.

56 And it is given unto them to know good from evil; wherefore they are agents unto themselves, and I have given unto you another law and commandment.

What are some of the important truths Enoch taught the people? How can you apply these truths to your own life? Enoch taught that men know good from evil and are "agents unto themselves." What does that phrase mean? What are some good choices you have made this week?

ENOCH TEACHES THAT NO UNCLEAN THING CAN DWELL IN THE KINGDOM OF GOD AND THAT ALL MUST BE BAPTIZED

After six generations, much of Adam and Eve's posterity lived in wickedness and bloodshed. God commanded Enoch to call the people to repentance. After powerfully teaching of the Fall that came by Adam and Eve and the salvation that comes only through Jesus Christ, Enoch's preaching continued as he quoted words that God had spoken to Adam.

MOSES 6:57–68

Wherefore teach it unto your children, that all men, everywhere, must repent, or they can in nowise inherit the kingdom of God, for no unclean thing can dwell there, or dwell in his presence; for, in the language of Adam, Man of Holiness is his name, and the name of his Only Begotten is the Son of Man, even Jesus Christ, a righteous Judge, who shall come in the meridian of time.

58 Therefore I give unto you a commandment, to teach these things freely unto your children, saying:

59 That by reason of transgression cometh the fall, which fall bringeth death, and inasmuch as ye were born into the world by water, and blood, and the spirit, which I have made, and so became of dust a living soul, even so ye must be born again into the kingdom of heaven, of water, and of the Spirit, and be cleansed by blood, even the blood of mine Only Begotten; that ye might be sanctified from all sin, and enjoy the words of eternal life in this world, and eternal life in the world to come, even immortal glory;

60 For by the water ye keep the commandment; by the Spirit ye are justified, and by the blood ye are sanctified;

61 Therefore it is given to abide in you; the record of heaven; the Comforter; the peaceable things of immortal glory; the truth of all things; that which quickeneth all things, which maketh alive all things; that which knoweth all things, and hath all power according to wisdom, mercy, truth, justice, and judgment.

62 And now, behold, I say unto you: This is the plan of salvation unto all men, through the blood of mine Only Begotten, who shall come in the meridian of time.

63 And behold, all things have their likeness, and all things are created and made to bear record of me, both things which are temporal, and things which are spiritual; things which are in the heavens above, and things which are on the earth, and things which are in the earth, and things which are under the earth, both above and beneath: all things bear record of me.

64 And it came to pass, when the Lord had spoken with Adam, our father, that Adam cried unto the Lord, and he was caught away by the Spirit of the Lord, and was carried down into the water, and was laid under the water, and was brought forth out of the water.

65 And thus he was baptized, and the Spirit of God descended upon him, and thus he was born of the Spirit, and became quickened in the inner man.

66 And he heard a voice out of heaven, saying: Thou art baptized with fire, and with the Holy Ghost. This is the record of the Father, and the Son, from henceforth and forever;

67 And thou art after the order of him who was without beginning of days or end of years, from all eternity to all eternity.

68 Behold, thou art one in me, a son of God; and thus may all become my sons. Amen.

According to verses 57 through 59, what were Adam and Eve commanded to teach their children? How would you explain the plan of salvation to someone who has never heard of it? What role does Jesus Christ have in our Heavenly Father's plan?

ENOCH EXHIBITS MIGHTY FAITH, CONTINUALLY PREACHES RIGHTEOUSNESS, AND ESTABLISHES THE CITY OF ZION

The prophet Enoch obeyed God and preached among the wicked with great power, thus fulfilling God's will that the plan of redemption be taught to all people. His work as a prophet then continued.

MOSES 7:13, 17–21

*A*nd so great was the faith of Enoch that he led the people of God, and their enemies came to battle against them; and he spake the word of the Lord, and the earth trembled, and the mountains fled, even according to his command; and the rivers of water were turned out of their course; and the roar of the lions was heard out of the wilderness; and all nations feared greatly, so powerful was the word of Enoch, and so great was the power of the language which God had given him.

17 The fear of the Lord was upon all nations, so great was the glory of the Lord, which was upon his people. And the Lord blessed the land, and they were blessed upon the mountains, and upon the high places, and did flourish.

18 And the Lord called his people Zion, because they were of one heart and one mind, and dwelt in righteousness; and there was no poor among them.

19 And Enoch continued his preaching in righteousness unto the people of God. And it came to pass in his days, that he built a city that was called the City of Holiness, even Zion.

20 And it came to pass that Enoch talked with the Lord; and he said unto the Lord: Surely Zion shall dwell in safety forever. But the Lord said unto Enoch: Zion have I blessed, but the residue of the people have I cursed.

21 And it came to pass that the Lord showed unto Enoch all the inhabitants of the earth; and he beheld, and lo, Zion, in process of time, was taken up into heaven. And the Lord said unto Enoch: Behold mine abode forever.

Although Enoch considered himself unlearned and weak, what mighty works was he able to accomplish with God's help? According to verse 18, what makes a "Zion" people? What can you do to help build Zion today?

ENOCH SEES GOD WEEP OVER THE WICKEDNESS OF HIS CHILDREN

Enoch was shown a mighty vision of the inhabitants of the earth, and saw that the Lord would eventually take the city of Zion into heaven. As the vision continued, he also saw there would be great wickedness on the earth, causing God to weep.

MOSES 7:23–37

And after that Zion was taken up into heaven, Enoch beheld, and lo, all the nations of the earth were before him;

24 And there came generation upon generation; and Enoch was high and lifted up, even in the bosom of the Father, and of the Son of Man; and behold, the power of Satan was upon all the face of the earth.

25 And he saw angels descending out of heaven; and he heard a loud voice saying: Wo, wo be unto the inhabitants of the earth.

26 And he beheld Satan; and he had a great chain in his hand, and it veiled the whole face of the earth with darkness; and he looked up and laughed, and his angels rejoiced.

27 And Enoch beheld angels descending out of heaven, bearing testimony of the Father and Son; and the Holy Ghost fell on many, and they were caught up by the powers of heaven into Zion.

28 And it came to pass that the God of heaven looked upon the residue of the people, and he wept; and Enoch bore record of it, saying: How is it that the heavens weep, and shed forth their tears as the rain upon the mountains?

29 And Enoch said unto the Lord: How is it that thou canst weep, seeing thou art holy, and from all eternity to all eternity?

30 And were it possible that man could number the particles of the earth, yea, millions of earths like this, it would not be a beginning to the number of thy creations; and thy curtains are stretched out still; and yet thou art there, and thy bosom is there; and also thou art just; thou art merciful and kind forever;

31 And thou hast taken Zion to thine own bosom, from all thy creations, from all eternity to all eternity; and naught but peace, justice, and truth is the habitation of thy throne; and mercy shall go before thy face and have no end; how is it thou canst weep?

32 The Lord said unto Enoch: Behold these thy brethren; they are the workmanship of mine own hands, and I gave unto them their knowledge, in the day I created them; and in the Garden of Eden, gave I unto man his agency;

33 And unto thy brethren have I said, and also given commandment, that they should love one another, and that they should choose me, their Father; but behold, they are without affection, and they hate their own blood;

34 And the fire of mine indignation is kindled against them; and in my hot displeasure will I send in the floods upon them, for my fierce anger is kindled against them.

35 Behold, I am God; Man of Holiness is my name; Man of Counsel is my name; and Endless and Eternal is my name, also.

36 Wherefore, I can stretch forth mine hands and hold all the creations which I have made; and mine eye can pierce them also, and among all the workmanship of mine hands there has not been so great wickedness as among thy brethren.

37 But behold, their sins shall be upon the heads of their fathers; Satan shall be their father, and misery shall be their doom; and the whole heavens shall weep over them, even all the workmanship of mine hands; wherefore should not the heavens weep, seeing these shall suffer?

In Enoch's vision, what caused God to weep? What would be one consequence of the people's wickedness (see verse 34)? Consider verse 33. How can we "choose" Heavenly Father?

ENOCH SEES THE PRESERVATION OF HIS POSTERITY AND THE COMING OF JESUS CHRIST IN THE MERIDIAN OF TIME

Enoch was shown a vision in which God wept at the vast wickedness found on earth. Viewing the wicked, God said, "Satan shall be their father, and misery shall be their doom" (Moses 7:37). God's words then continued as He referred to the righteous prophet Noah, who would come three generations after Enoch.

MOSES 7:38–47

But behold, these which thine eyes are upon shall perish in the floods; and behold, I will shut them up; a prison have I prepared for them.

39 And that which I have chosen hath pled before my face. Wherefore, he suffereth for their sins; inasmuch as they will repent in the day that my Chosen shall return unto me, and until that day they shall be in torment;

40 Wherefore, for this shall the heavens weep, yea, and all the workmanship of mine hands.

41 And it came to pass that the Lord spake unto Enoch, and told Enoch all the doings of the children of men; wherefore Enoch knew, and looked upon their wickedness, and their misery, and wept and stretched forth his arms, and his heart swelled wide as eternity; and his bowels yearned; and all eternity shook.

42 And Enoch also saw Noah, and his family; that the posterity of all the sons of Noah should be saved with a temporal salvation;

43 Wherefore Enoch saw that Noah built an ark; and that the Lord smiled upon it, and held it in his own hand; but upon the residue of the wicked the floods came and swallowed them up.

44 And as Enoch saw this, he had bitterness of soul, and wept over his brethren, and said unto the heavens: I will refuse to be comforted; but the Lord said unto Enoch: Lift up your heart, and be glad; and look.

45 And it came to pass that Enoch looked; and from Noah, he beheld all the families of the earth; and he cried unto the Lord, saying: When shall the day of the Lord come? When shall the blood of the Righteous be shed, that all they that mourn may be sanctified and have eternal life?

46 And the Lord said: It shall be in the meridian of time, in the days of wickedness and vengeance.

47 And behold, Enoch saw the day of the coming of the Son of Man, even in the flesh; and his soul rejoiced, saying: The Righteous is lifted up, and the Lamb is slain from the foundation of the world; and through faith I am in the bosom of the Father, and behold, Zion is with me.

Although Enoch was saddened by the wickedness he saw upon the earth, what caused him to rejoice? How can an understanding of Jesus Christ and His Atonement bring you happiness in times of trouble?

ENOCH SEES JESUS CHRIST LIFTED UP ON THE CROSS AND HIS ASCENSION TO GOD THE FATHER

God had shown Enoch that the wicked would be destroyed in a flood while Noah and his family would be spared. Enoch wept bitterly over the wickedness on earth and refused to be comforted. He was then shown the time of Jesus Christ's mortal ministry, and Enoch rejoiced. Enoch's pleading with the Lord then continued.

MOSES 7:50–60

And it came to pass that Enoch continued his cry unto the Lord, saying: I ask thee, O Lord, in the name of thine Only Begotten, even Jesus Christ, that thou wilt have mercy upon Noah and his seed, that the earth might never more be covered by the floods.

51 And the Lord could not withhold; and he covenanted with Enoch, and sware unto him with an oath, that he would stay the floods; that he would call upon the children of Noah;

52 And he sent forth an unalterable decree, that a remnant of his seed should always be found among all nations, while the earth should stand;

53 And the Lord said: Blessed is he through whose seed Messiah shall come; for he saith—I am Messiah, the King of Zion, the Rock of Heaven, which is broad as eternity; whoso cometh in at the gate and climbeth up by me shall never fall; wherefore, blessed are they of whom I have spoken, for they shall come forth with songs of everlasting joy.

54 And it came to pass that Enoch cried unto the Lord, saying: When the Son of Man cometh in the flesh, shall the earth rest? I pray thee, show me these things.

55 And the Lord said unto Enoch: Look, and he looked and beheld the Son of Man lifted up on the cross, after the manner of men;

56 And he heard a loud voice; and the heavens were veiled; and all the creations of God mourned; and the earth groaned; and the rocks were rent; and the saints arose, and were crowned at the right hand of the Son of Man, with crowns of glory;

57 And as many of the spirits as were in prison came forth, and stood on the right hand of God; and the remainder were reserved in chains of darkness until the judgment of the great day.

58 And again Enoch wept and cried unto the Lord, saying: When shall the earth rest?

59 And Enoch beheld the Son of Man ascend up unto the Father; and he called unto the Lord, saying: Wilt thou not come again upon the earth? Forasmuch as thou art God, and I know thee, and thou hast sworn unto me, and commanded me that I should ask in the name of thine Only Begotten; thou hast made me, and given unto me a right to thy throne, and not of myself, but through thine own grace; wherefore, I ask thee if thou wilt not come again on the earth.

60 And the Lord said unto Enoch: As I live, even so will I come in the last days, in the days of wickedness and vengeance, to fulfil the oath which I have made unto you concerning the children of Noah;

What did Enoch request of God, and what was God's reply (see verses 50–52)? Several titles of Jesus Christ are given in verse 53. What do those titles mean to you? Consider researching the meaning and significance of those titles in the Bible Dictionary and Topical Guide.

ENOCH SEES THE SECOND COMING OF JESUS CHRIST AND HIS MILLENNIAL REIGN

In a mighty vision, Enoch was shown the vast wickedness on earth and the destroying flood that would come in the days of Noah. These revelations caused Enoch to weep, but he then rejoiced when he saw the day of Christ's mortal ministry and atoning sacrifice. God promised Enoch that after the time of Noah, He would never again flood the earth, and He told Enoch that Jesus Christ would return to earth in the last days. God's words to Enoch then continued.

MOSES 7:61–69

And the day shall come that the earth shall rest, but before that day the heavens shall be darkened, and a veil of darkness shall cover the earth; and the heavens shall shake, and also the earth; and great tribulations shall be among the children of men, but my people will I preserve;

62 And righteousness will I send down out of heaven; and truth will I send forth out of the earth, to bear testimony of mine Only Begotten; his resurrection from the dead; yea, and also the resurrection of all men; and righteousness and truth will I cause to sweep the earth as with a flood, to gather out mine elect from the four quarters of the earth, unto a place which I shall prepare, an Holy City, that my people may gird up their loins, and be looking forth for the time of my coming; for there shall be my tabernacle, and it shall be called Zion, a New Jerusalem.

63 And the Lord said unto Enoch: Then shalt thou and all thy city meet them there, and we will receive them into our bosom, and they shall see us; and we will fall upon their necks, and they shall fall upon our necks, and we will kiss each other;

64 And there shall be mine abode, and it shall be Zion, which shall come forth out of all the creations which I have made; and for the space of a thousand years the earth shall rest.

65 And it came to pass that Enoch saw the day of the coming of the Son of Man, in the last days, to dwell on the earth in righteousness for the space of a thousand years;

66 But before that day he saw great tribulations among the wicked; and he also saw the sea, that it was troubled, and men's hearts failing them, looking forth with fear for the judgments of the Almighty God, which should come upon the wicked.

67 And the Lord showed Enoch all things, even unto the end of the world; and he saw the day of the righteous, the hour of their redemption, and received a fulness of joy;

68 And all the days of Zion, in the days of Enoch, were three hundred and sixty-five years.

69 And Enoch and all his people walked with God, and he dwelt in the midst of Zion; and it came to pass that Zion was not, for God received it up into his own bosom; and from thence went forth the saying, Zion is Fled.

According to verse 61, what will be the state of the world prior to Christ's return? Consider verse 62. What truths did God promise to send forth in the last days? How can you see this prophecy being fulfilled today?

GOD COMMANDS NOAH TO BUILD AN ARK
TO SURVIVE THE CLEANSING FLOOD

Much of Adam and Eve's posterity had been mired in gross wickedness for several generations. Meanwhile, Enoch led the righteous and established the city of Zion, which was then taken into heaven. In fulfillment of God's promise, Enoch's son Methuselah was not taken into heaven, allowing Enoch's posterity to remain on earth, through which Noah would be born as Enoch's great-grandson. Thus, about a thousand years after Adam and Eve were cast out of the Garden of Eden, Noah was born in the tenth generation.

GENESIS 6:5–22; JOSEPH SMITH TRANSLATION, GENESIS 8:13, 15, 23–24

*A*nd God saw that the wickedness of man was great in the earth, and that every imagination of the thoughts of his heart was only evil continually.

6 And it repented *Noah, and his heart was pained,* that *the Lord* had made man on the earth, and it grieved him at his heart. [JST, Genesis 8:13]

7 And the Lord said, I will destroy man whom I have created from the face of the earth; both man, and beast, and the creeping thing, and the fowls of the air; for it repenteth *Noah* that I have *created* them. [*JST, Genesis 8:15*]

8 But Noah found grace in the eyes of the Lord.

9 These are the generations of Noah: Noah was a just man and perfect in his generations, and Noah walked with God.

10 And Noah begat three sons, Shem, Ham, and Japheth.

11 The earth also was corrupt before God, and the earth was filled with violence.

12 And God looked upon the earth, and, behold, it was corrupt; for all flesh had corrupted his way upon the earth.

13 And God said unto Noah, The end of all flesh is come before me; for the earth is filled with violence through them; and, behold, I will destroy them with the earth.

14 Make thee an ark of gopher wood; rooms shalt thou make in the ark, and shalt pitch it within and without with pitch.

15 And this is the fashion which thou shalt make it of: The length of the ark shall be three hundred cubits, the breadth of it fifty cubits, and the height of it thirty cubits.

16 A window shalt thou make to the ark, and in a cubit shalt thou finish it above; and the door of the ark shalt thou set in the side thereof; with lower, second, and third stories shalt thou make it.

17 And, behold, I, even I, do bring a flood of waters upon the earth, to destroy all flesh, wherein is the breath of life, from under heaven; and every thing that is in the earth shall die.

18 But with thee will I establish my covenant, *even as I have sworn unto thy father, Enoch, that of thy posterity shall come all nations.* And thou shalt come into the ark, thou, and thy sons, and thy wife, and thy sons' wives with thee. [*JST, Genesis 8:23–24*]

19 And of every living thing of all flesh, two of every sort shalt thou bring into the ark, to keep them alive with thee; they shall be male and female.

20 Of fowls after their kind, and of cattle after their kind, of every creeping thing of the earth after his kind, two of every sort shall come unto thee, to keep them alive.

21 And take thou unto thee of all food that is eaten, and thou shalt gather it to thee; and it shall be for food for thee, and for them.

22 Thus did Noah; according to all that God commanded him, so did he.

What was Noah commanded to bring with him on the ark? Verse 22 notes that Noah did "all that God commanded him." What are some commandments from God that you have obeyed? Consider what commandments you can strive to obey more fully.

NOAH AND HIS FAMILY ENTER THE ARK AS GOD SENDS A FLOOD THAT DESTROYS ALL LIVING THINGS LEFT ON EARTH

In the time of Noah, violence and corruption continued throughout most of Adam and Eve's posterity. God told Noah He would destroy the wicked from the earth by a great flood and gave Noah precise measurements for building a massive ark for his family and animals of every kind. Noah obeyed God's commandments.

GENESIS 7:11–24

In the six hundredth year of Noah's life, in the second month, the seventeenth day of the month, the same day were all the fountains of the great deep broken up, and the windows of heaven were opened.

12 And the rain was upon the earth forty days and forty nights.

13 In the selfsame day entered Noah, and Shem, and Ham, and Japheth, the sons of Noah, and Noah's wife, and the three wives of his sons with them, into the ark;

14 They, and every beast after his kind, and all the cattle after their kind, and every creeping thing that creepeth upon the earth after his kind, and every fowl after his kind, every bird of every sort.

15 And they went in unto Noah into the ark, two and two of all flesh, wherein is the breath of life.

16 And they that went in, went in male and female of all flesh, as God had commanded him: and the Lord shut him in.

17 And the flood was forty days upon the earth; and the waters increased, and bare up the ark, and it was lift up above the earth.

18 And the waters prevailed, and were increased greatly upon the earth; and the ark went upon the face of the waters.

19 And the waters prevailed exceedingly upon the earth; and all the high hills, that were under the whole heaven, were covered.

20 Fifteen cubits upward did the waters prevail; and the mountains were covered.

21 And all flesh died that moved upon the earth, both of fowl, and of cattle, and of beast, and of every creeping thing that creepeth upon the earth, and every man:

22 All in whose nostrils was the breath of life, of all that was in the dry land, died.

23 And every living substance was destroyed which was upon the face of the ground, both man, and cattle, and the creeping things, and the fowl of the heaven; and they were destroyed from the earth: and Noah only remained alive, and they that were with him in the ark.

24 And the waters prevailed upon the earth an hundred and fifty days.

What blessings did Noah and his family receive for obeying the Lord's command to build an ark? What commandments has the Lord given us in our day? What blessings are we promised for obeying those commandments, and how have you seen those blessings in your life?

THE FLOOD CEASES, AND NOAH AND HIS FAMILY EXIT THE ARK AND OFFER SACRIFICE TO GOD

Noah, his family, and animals of every kind had been kept safely in the ark as God sent a flood that destroyed living things from the earth. The Flood lasted for 150 days.

GENESIS 8:1–3, 6, 8–13, 15–16, 18, 20–22; JOSEPH SMITH TRANSLATION, GENESIS 9:4–6

And God remembered Noah, and every living thing, and all the cattle that was with him in the ark: and God made a wind to pass over the earth, and the waters assuaged;

2 The fountains also of the deep and the windows of heaven were stopped, and the rain from heaven was restrained;

3 And the waters returned from off the earth continually: and after the end of the hundred and fifty days the waters were abated.

6 And it came to pass at the end of forty days, that Noah opened the window of the ark which he had made:

8 Also he sent forth a dove from him, to see if the waters were abated from off the face of the ground;

9 But the dove found no rest for the sole of her foot, and she returned unto him into the ark, for the waters were on the face of the whole earth: then he put forth his hand, and took her, and pulled her in unto him into the ark.

10 And he stayed yet other seven days; and again he sent forth the dove out of the ark;

11 And the dove came in to him in the evening; and, lo, in her mouth was an olive leaf plucked off: so Noah knew that the waters were abated from off the earth.

12 And he stayed yet other seven days; and sent forth the dove; which returned not again unto him any more.

13 And it came to pass in the six hundredth and first year, in the first month, the first day of the month, the waters were dried up from off the earth: and Noah removed the covering of the ark, and looked, and, behold, the face of the ground was dry.

15 And God spake unto Noah, saying,

16 Go forth of the ark, thou, and thy wife, and thy sons, and thy sons' wives with thee.

18 And Noah went forth, and his sons, and his wife, and his sons' wives with him:

20 And Noah builded an altar unto the Lord, and took of every clean beast, and of every clean fowl, and offered burnt offerings on the altar; *and gave thanks unto the Lord, and rejoiced in his heart.*

21 *And the Lord spake unto Noah, and he blessed him.* And *Noah* smelled a sweet savor, and *he* said in his heart;

22 *I will call on the name of the Lord, that he* will not again curse the ground any more for man's sake, for the imagination of man's heart is evil from his youth; *and that he* will *not* again smite any more every thing living, as *he* hath done, while the earth remaineth; [*JST, Genesis 9:4–6*]

How did Noah learn that the waters were receding from the earth? After Noah and his family left the ark, what did he do to thank the Lord? What blessing did Noah ask of the Lord? How has the Lord helped you through great challenges, and how can you show gratitude for His help?

ABRAHAM SEEKS RIGHTEOUSNESS, KNOWLEDGE, AND THE BLESSINGS OF THE PRIESTHOOD

At the conclusion of the Flood, God promised Noah He would never again flood the earth. God commanded Noah and his posterity to multiply, and the earth began again to fill with people who settled different regions. In one region, approximately 100–200 years after the Flood, some people began constructing a tall building now referred to as the Tower of Babel. The people hoped the tower would reach up to heaven, but God disapproved of their actions and punished them by confounding their language. Instead of everyone speaking one language, many languages were now spoken, and the people struggled to understand each other. With differing languages and a growing population, the people were further divided as time went on. Nine generations after Noah (about 350 years after the Flood), Abraham was born and eventually recorded his own history. Note that the Old Testament indicates that Abraham's name was originally Abram. When God covenanted with him later in his life, He changed Abram's named to Abraham.

ABRAHAM 1:1–4

In the land of the Chaldeans, at the residence of my fathers, I, Abraham, saw that it was needful for me to obtain another place of residence;

2 And, finding there was greater happiness and peace and rest for me, I sought for the blessings of the fathers, and the right whereunto I should be ordained to administer the same; having been myself a follower of righteousness, desiring also to be one who possessed great knowledge, and to be a greater follower of righteousness, and to possess a greater knowledge, and to be a father of many nations, a prince of peace, and desiring to receive instructions, and to keep the commandments of God, I became a rightful heir, a High Priest, holding the right belonging to the fathers.

3 It was conferred upon me from the fathers; it came down from the fathers, from the beginning of time, yea, even from the beginning, or before the foundation of the earth, down to the present time, even the right of the firstborn, or the first man, who is Adam, or first father, through the fathers unto me.

4 I sought for mine appointment unto the Priesthood according to the appointment of God unto the fathers concerning the seed.

According to verse 2, what did Abraham seek? What are some ways people seek happiness today? Where did Abraham turn to find greater happiness?

JEHOVAH SAVES ABRAHAM FROM BEING SACRIFICED BY WICKED PRIESTS

Abraham desired knowledge, righteousness, and the blessings of the priesthood, but those around him had fallen into wicked traditions. The record of his life continued as told in his own words.

ABRAHAM 1:5–8, 11–12, 15–19

My fathers, having turned from their righteousness, and from the holy commandments which the Lord their God had given unto them, unto the worshiping of the gods of the heathen, utterly refused to hearken to my voice;

6 For their hearts were set to do evil, and were wholly turned to the god of Elkenah, and the god of Libnah, and the god of Mahmackrah, and the god of Korash, and the god of Pharaoh, king of Egypt;

7 Therefore they turned their hearts to the sacrifice of the heathen in offering up their children unto these dumb idols, and hearkened not unto my voice, but endeavored to take away my life by the hand of the priest of Elkenah. The priest of Elkenah was also the priest of Pharaoh.

8 Now, at this time it was the custom of the priest of Pharaoh, the king of Egypt, to offer up upon the altar which was built in the land of Chaldea, for the offering unto these strange gods, men, women, and children.

11 Now, this priest had offered upon this altar three virgins at one time, who were the daughters of Onitah, one of the royal descent directly from the loins of Ham. These virgins were offered up because of their virtue; they would not bow down to worship gods of wood or of stone, therefore they were killed upon this altar, and it was done after the manner of the Egyptians.

12 And it came to pass that the priests laid violence upon me, that they might slay me also, as they did those virgins upon this altar; and that you may have a knowledge of this altar, I will refer you to the representation at the commencement of this record.

15 And as they lifted up their hands upon me, that they might offer me up and take away my life, behold, I lifted up my voice unto the Lord my God, and the Lord hearkened and heard, and he filled me with the vision of the Almighty, and the angel of his presence stood by me, and immediately unloosed my bands;

16 And his voice was unto me: Abraham, Abraham, behold, my name is Jehovah, and I have heard thee, and have come down to deliver thee, and to take thee away from thy father's house, and from all thy kinsfolk, into a strange land which thou knowest not of;

17 And this because they have turned their hearts away from me, to worship the god of Elkenah, and the god of Libnah, and the god of Mahmackrah, and the god of Korash, and the god of Pharaoh, king of Egypt; therefore I have come down to visit them, and to destroy him who hath lifted up his hand against thee, Abraham, my son, to take away thy life.

18 Behold, I will lead thee by my hand, and I will take thee, to put upon thee my name, even the Priesthood of thy father, and my power shall be over thee.

19 As it was with Noah so shall it be with thee; but through thy ministry my name shall be known in the earth forever, for I am thy God.

How did Abraham show trust in God when he was about to be killed by the wicked priests? Share an experience of how prayer has helped you when you have been afraid or in danger. How was Abraham delivered from the wicked priests who sought to take his life? What promises did Abraham receive from Jehovah?

GOD PROMISES TO BLESS THE ENTIRE WORLD THROUGH ABRAHAM

Abraham had sought for righteousness and the blessings of the priesthood, but wicked priests attempted to offer him as a human sacrifice to false gods. After Abraham cried out to God, Jehovah intervened, saved Abraham, and said, "I will lead thee by my hand, . . . for I am thy God" (Abraham 1:18–19). The wickedness of the priests resulted in the land being smitten with a famine, and God commanded Abraham to flee the land and the wicked influence of his father's house. Abraham obeyed and took family members with him, including his wife Sarai (whose name God later changed to Sarah—see Genesis 17:15) and his nephew Lot.

ABRAHAM 2:6–16 (SEE ALSO GENESIS 12:1–6)

But I, Abraham, and Lot, my brother's son, prayed unto the Lord, and the Lord appeared unto me, and said unto me: Arise, and take Lot with thee; for I have purposed to take thee away out of Haran, and to make of thee a minister to bear my name in a strange land which I will give unto thy seed after thee for an everlasting possession, when they hearken to my voice.

7 For I am the Lord thy God; I dwell in heaven; the earth is my footstool; I stretch my hand over the sea, and it obeys my voice; I cause the wind and the fire to be my chariot; I say to the mountains—Depart hence—and behold, they are taken away by a whirlwind, in an instant, suddenly.

8 My name is Jehovah, and I know the end from the beginning; therefore my hand shall be over thee.

9 And I will make of thee a great nation, and I will bless thee above measure, and make thy name great among all nations, and thou shalt be a blessing unto thy seed after thee, that in their hands they shall bear this ministry and Priesthood unto all nations;

10 And I will bless them through thy name; for as many as receive this Gospel shall be called after thy name, and shall be accounted thy seed, and shall rise up and bless thee, as their father;

11 And I will bless them that bless thee, and curse them that curse thee; and in thee (that is, in thy Priesthood) and in thy seed (that is, thy Priesthood), for I give unto thee a promise that this right shall continue in thee, and in thy seed after thee (that is to say, the literal seed, or the seed of the body) shall all the families of the earth be blessed, even with the blessings of the Gospel, which are the blessings of salvation, even of life eternal.

12 Now, after the Lord had withdrawn from speaking to me, and withdrawn his face from me, I said in my heart: Thy servant has sought thee earnestly; now I have found thee;

13 Thou didst send thine angel to deliver me from the gods of Elkenah, and I will do well to hearken unto thy voice, therefore let thy servant rise up and depart in peace.

14 So I, Abraham, departed as the Lord had said unto me, and Lot with me; and I, Abraham, was sixty and two years old when I departed out of Haran.

15 And I took Sarai, whom I took to wife when I was in Ur, in Chaldea, and Lot, my brother's son, and all our substance that we had gathered, and the souls that we had won in Haran, and came forth in the way to the land of Canaan, and dwelt in tents as we came on our way;

16 Therefore, eternity was our covering and our rock and our salvation, as we journeyed from Haran by the way of Jershon, to come to the land of Canaan.

What are some of the great promises Abraham received from the Lord? The Lord promised Abraham that through the priesthood covenants Abraham made with the Lord, all the families of the earth would be blessed. How does the priesthood bless families? How have you been blessed through the priesthood?

AN ANGEL APPEARS TO HAGAR, WHO GIVES BIRTH TO ABRAHAM'S SON ISHMAEL

After being rescued by Jehovah, Abraham fled the land that had been cursed with famine, eventually journeying as far south as Egypt with his wife Sarai, his nephew Lot, and other family members. Later they returned from Egypt and settled north in Hebron. Throughout his journeys, Abraham built altars and prayed to God. In Hebron, God spoke to Abraham and told him to look to the north, south, east, and west, "for all the land which thou seest, to thee will I give it, and to thy seed for ever. And I will make thy seed as the dust of the earth: so that if a man can number the dust of the earth, then shall thy seed also be numbered" (Genesis 13:15–16). This was a significant promise to Abraham because he and Sarai (Sarah) wanted to have children but had been unable to conceive. Abraham was also told that for four hundred years, his descendants would be "a stranger in a land that is not theirs" (Genesis 15:13), a reference to the children of Israel who would be in bondage to the Egyptians and later freed by Moses. Abraham and Sarai's journeys and challenges then continued. In these verses, a "handmaid" is a type of servant.

GENESIS 16:1–12, 15–16

Now Sarai Abram's wife bare him no children: and she had an handmaid, an Egyptian, whose name was Hagar.

2 And Sarai said unto Abram, Behold now, the Lord hath restrained me from bearing: I pray thee, go in unto my maid; it may be that I may obtain children by her. And Abram hearkened to the voice of Sarai.

3 And Sarai Abram's wife took Hagar her maid the Egyptian, after Abram had dwelt ten years in the land of Canaan, and gave her to her husband Abram to be his wife.

4 And he went in unto Hagar, and she conceived: and when she saw that she had conceived, her mistress was despised in her eyes.

5 And Sarai said unto Abram, My wrong be upon thee: I have given my maid into thy bosom; and when she saw that she had conceived, I was despised in her eyes: the Lord judge between me and thee.

6 But Abram said unto Sarai, Behold, thy maid is in thy hand; do to her as it pleaseth thee. And when Sarai dealt hardly with her, she fled from her face.

7 And the angel of the Lord found her by a fountain of water in the wilderness, by the fountain in the way to Shur.

8 And he said, Hagar, Sarai's maid, whence camest thou? and whither wilt thou go? And she said, I flee from the face of my mistress Sarai.

9 And the angel of the Lord said unto her, Return to thy mistress, and submit thyself under her hands.

10 And the angel of the Lord said unto her, I will multiply thy seed exceedingly, that it shall not be numbered for multitude.

11 And the angel of the Lord said unto her, Behold, thou art with child, and shalt bear a son, and shalt call his name Ishmael; because the Lord hath heard thy affliction.

12 And he will be a wild man; his hand will be against every man, and every man's hand against him; and he shall dwell in the presence of all his brethren.

15 And Hagar bare Abram a son: and Abram called his son's name, which Hagar bare, Ishmael.

16 And Abram was fourscore and six years old, when Hagar bare Ishmael to Abram.

What caused the contention between Sarai and Hagar? Who visited Hagar, and what instructions did that person give her? What blessing was Hagar promised to receive?

GOD ESTABLISHES A COVENANT WITH ABRAHAM, GIVES HIM A NEW NAME, AND INSTITUTES THE TOKEN OF CIRCUMCISION

Sarai was unable to conceive, and she offered her servant Hagar to Abraham, with whom she bore a son named Ishmael. Abraham's name was originally Abram. In these verses, God made a covenant with Abraham, gave him a new name, and commanded that he be circumcised. All of God's covenants have tokens associated with them to help give meaning and remembrance to the covenant itself. The Bible Dictionary defines the token of circumcision as "the token of the Abrahamic covenant during Old Testament dispensations. Those who received it thenceforth enjoyed the privileges and undertook the responsibilities of the covenant. It symbolized some aspects of separation or dedication (1) to God, to whom Israel belonged; (2) from the world, the uncircumcised with whom Israel might not mix; (3) from sin."

GENESIS 17:1–12, 23; JOSEPH SMITH TRANSLATION, GENESIS 17:3–12

And when Abram was ninety years old and nine, the Lord appeared to Abram, and said unto him, I am the Almighty God; walk before me, and be thou perfect.

2 And I will make my covenant between me and thee, and will multiply thee exceedingly.

3 And *it came to pass, that* Abram fell on his face, *and called upon the name of the Lord.*

4 And God talked with him, saying, *My people have gone astray from my precepts, and have not kept mine ordinances, which I gave unto their fathers;*

5 *And they have not observed mine anointing, and the burial, or baptism wherewith I commanded them;*

6 *But have turned from the commandment, and taken unto themselves the washing of children, and the blood of sprinkling;*

7 *And have said that the blood of the righteous Abel was shed for sins; and have not known wherein they are accountable before me.*

8 *But* as for *thee,* behold, *I will make* my covenant with thee, and thou shalt be a father of many nations.

9 *And this covenant I make, that thy children may be known among all nations.* Neither shall thy name any more be called Abram, but thy name shall be called Abraham; for, a father of many nations have I made thee.

10 And I will make thee exceedingly fruitful, and I will make nations of thee, and kings shall come of thee, *and of thy seed.*

11 And I will establish *a covenant of circumcision with thee, and it shall be* my covenant between me and thee, and thy seed after thee, in their generations; *that thou mayest know forever that children are not accountable before me until they are eight years old.*

12 *And thou shalt observe to keep all my covenants wherein I covenanted with thy fathers; and thou shalt keep the commandments which I have given thee with mine own mouth, and I will be a God unto thee and thy seed after thee.*

23 And Abraham took Ishmael his son, and all that were born in his house, and all that were bought with his money, every male among the men of Abraham's house; and circumcised the flesh of their foreskin in the selfsame day, as God had said unto him.

The covenant God made with Abraham is called the Abrahamic Covenant. What are some blessing and requirements of this covenant? In these verses, how did Abraham respond to God's commandments?

33

GOD COVENANTS WITH SARAH, CHANGES HER NAME, AND PROMISES SHE WILL GIVE BIRTH TO A CHILD

God had made a covenant with Abraham in which he was promised a large and royal posterity, and the covenant token of circumcision was instituted. In these verses, God then made a covenant with Sarah, whose name had originally been Sarai. Previously, Sarah had offered her handmaid Hagar to Abraham to ensure him a posterity. Through that union was born a son named Ishmael, but Sarah had had no children of her own.

Genesis 17:15–22; Joseph Smith Translation, Genesis 17:23–24

And God said unto Abraham, As for Sarai thy wife, thou shalt not call her name Sarai, but Sarah shall her name be.

16 And I will bless her, and give thee a son also of her: yea, I will bless her, and she shall be a mother of nations; kings of people shall be of her.

17 Then Abraham fell on his face and *rejoiced*, and said in his heart, *There* shall a child be born unto him that is an hundred years old, and Sarah that is ninety years old *shall bear*.

18 And Abraham said unto God, Oh that Ishmael might live *uprightly* before thee! [JST Genesis 17:23–24]

19 And God said, Sarah thy wife shall bear thee a son indeed; and thou shalt call his name Isaac: and I will establish my covenant with him for an everlasting covenant, and with his seed after him.

20 And as for Ishmael, I have heard thee: Behold, I have blessed him, and will make him fruitful, and will multiply him exceedingly; twelve princes shall he beget, and I will make him a great nation.

21 But my covenant will I establish with Isaac, which Sarah shall bear unto thee at this set time in the next year.

22 And he left off talking with him, and God went up from Abraham.

Genesis 18:11–14

11 Now Abraham and Sarah were old and well stricken in age; and it ceased to be with Sarah after the manner of women.

12 Therefore Sarah laughed within herself, saying, After I am waxed old shall I have pleasure, my lord being old also?

13 And the Lord said unto Abraham, Wherefore did Sarah laugh, saying, Shall I of a surety bear a child, which am old?

14 Is any thing too hard for the Lord? At the time appointed I will return unto thee, according to the time of life, and Sarah shall have a son.

How did Abraham and Sarah react when they heard they would have a son? In Genesis 18:14, what encouraging words did God say to them? What miraculous things has God done in your life?

SARAH GIVES BIRTH TO ISAAC; HAGAR AND HER SON ISHMAEL DEPART FROM ABRAHAM'S HOUSE

God had entered into a covenant with Abraham and Sarah. Sarah was promised she would give birth to a son, whom she was commanded to name Isaac. Abraham was visited by holy messengers who repeated the promise that Sarah would bear a child. Those same messengers then led Abraham's nephew Lot and his family out of the wicked city of Sodom, which was then consumed by fire from heaven. Lot's wife attempted to return to the city and was destroyed. Later, as Abraham and his family journeyed through the land, God's promise to Sarah was fulfilled.

Genesis 21:1–21

And the Lord visited Sarah as he had said, and the Lord did unto Sarah as he had spoken.

2 For Sarah conceived, and bare Abraham a son in his old age, at the set time of which God had spoken to him.

3 And Abraham called the name of his son that was born unto him, whom Sarah bare to him, Isaac.

4 And Abraham circumcised his son Isaac being eight days old, as God had commanded him.

5 And Abraham was an hundred years old, when his son Isaac was born unto him.

6 And Sarah said, God hath made me to laugh, so that all that hear will laugh with me.

7 And she said, Who would have said unto Abraham, that Sarah should have given children suck? for I have born him a son in his old age.

8 And the child grew, and was weaned: and Abraham made a great feast the same day that Isaac was weaned.

9 And Sarah saw the son of Hagar the Egyptian, which she had born unto Abraham, mocking.

10 Wherefore she said unto Abraham, Cast out this bondwoman and her son: for the son of this bondwoman shall not be heir with my son, even with Isaac.

11 And the thing was very grievous in Abraham's sight because of his son.

12 And God said unto Abraham, Let it not be grievous in thy sight because of the lad, and because of thy bondwoman; in all that Sarah hath said unto thee, hearken unto her voice; for in Isaac shall thy seed be called.

13 And also of the son of the bondwoman will I make a nation, because he is thy seed.

14 And Abraham rose up early in the morning, and took bread, and a bottle of water, and gave it unto Hagar, putting it on her shoulder, and the child, and sent her away: and she departed, and wandered in the wilderness of Beer-sheba.

15 And the water was spent in the bottle, and she cast the child under one of the shrubs.

16 And she went, and sat her down over against him a good way off, as it were a bowshot: for she said, Let me not see the death of the child. And she sat over against him, and lift up her voice, and wept.

17 And God heard the voice of the lad; and the angel of God called to Hagar out of heaven, and said unto her, What aileth thee, Hagar? fear not; for God hath heard the voice of the lad where he is.

18 Arise, lift up the lad, and hold him in thine hand; for I will make him a great nation.

19 And God opened her eyes, and she saw a well of water; and she went, and filled the bottle with water, and gave the lad drink.

20 And God was with the lad; and he grew, and dwelt in the wilderness, and became an archer.

21 And he dwelt in the wilderness of Paran: and his mother took him a wife out of the land of Egypt.

How did Sarah feel when Isaac was born? Consider sharing your own example of having to wait a long time to receive a promised blessing. What promises did the Lord give Hagar about her son Ishmael?

ABRAHAM IS COMMANDED TO OFFER
HIS SON ISAAC AS A SACRIFICE

Abraham and Sarah had been obedient to all of God's commandments and were promised they would have a large and royal posterity. But not until Abraham was one hundred and Sarah was ninety did they finally have a child of their own—a son they named Isaac, as commanded by God. In these verses, the term "burnt offering" is a reference to sacrifices in which an animal was slain and then placed upon an altar and burned. Abraham would be commanded by God to offer his firstborn son Isaac as a sacrifice. This painful requirement would serve as an enduring reminder of the offering of God's firstborn Son as a sacrifice for all.

GENESIS 22:1–19

And it came to pass after these things, that God did tempt Abraham, and said unto him, Abraham: and he said, Behold, *here* I *am.*

2 And he said, Take now thy son, thine only son Isaac, whom thou lovest, and get thee into the land of Moriah; and offer him there for a burnt offering upon one of the mountains which I will tell thee of.

3 And Abraham rose up early in the morning, and saddled his ass, and took two of his young men with him, and Isaac his son, and clave the wood for the burnt offering, and rose up, and went unto the place of which God had told him.

4 Then on the third day Abraham lifted up his eyes, and saw the place afar off.

5 And Abraham said unto his young men, Abide ye here with the ass; and I and the lad will go yonder and worship, and come again to you.

6 And Abraham took the wood of the burnt offering, and laid it upon Isaac his son; and he took the fire in his hand, and a knife; and they went both of them together.

7 And Isaac spake unto Abraham his father, and said, My father: and he said, Here am I, my son. And he said, Behold the fire and the wood: but where is the lamb for a burnt offering?

8 And Abraham said, My son, God will provide himself a lamb for a burnt offering: so they went both of them together.

9 And they came to the place which God had told him of; and Abraham built an altar there, and laid the wood in order, and bound Isaac his son, and laid him on the altar upon the wood.

10 And Abraham stretched forth his hand, and took the knife to slay his son.

11 And the angel of the Lord called unto him out of heaven, and said, Abraham, Abraham: and he said, Here am I.

12 And he said, Lay not thine hand upon the lad, neither do thou any thing unto him: for now I know that thou fearest God, seeing thou hast not withheld thy son, thine only son from me.

13 And Abraham lifted up his eyes, and looked, and behold behind him a ram caught in a thicket by his horns: and Abraham went and took the ram, and offered him up for a burnt offering in the stead of his son.

14 And Abraham called the name of that place Jehovah-jireh: as it is said to this day, In the mount of the Lord it shall be seen.

15 And the angel of the Lord called unto Abraham out of heaven the second time,

16 And said, By myself have I sworn, saith the Lord, for because thou hast done this thing, and hast not withheld thy son, thine only son:

17 That in blessing I will bless thee, and in multiplying I will multiply thy seed as the stars of the heaven, and as the sand which is upon the sea shore; and thy seed shall possess the gate of his enemies;

18 And in thy seed shall all the nations of the earth be blessed; because thou hast obeyed my voice.

19 So Abraham returned unto his young men, and they rose up and went together to Beer-sheba; and Abraham dwelt at Beer-sheba.

How did Abraham show God he was willing to obey all that He commanded? What is something you have sacrificed in order to obey God? Our Heavenly Father allowed His Only Begotten Son to be sacrificed for our sins. What do you think Abraham learned about Heavenly Father through the experience of being commanded to sacrifice Isaac?

ABRAHAM'S SERVANT IS DIVINELY GUIDED TO FIND REBEKAH, A WIFE FOR ISAAC

Thirty-seven years after giving birth to Isaac, Sarah died at age 127. God had covenanted with Abraham that he would greatly bless his posterity and told him that with those blessings came great and righteous expectations. Considering this, Abraham was concerned about the kind of woman Isaac would marry. Abraham commanded his most trusted servant to journey to the land of Abraham's youth and there find a worthy woman for Isaac to marry, promising the servant that he would be divinely guided.

GENESIS 24:10–27; JOSEPH SMITH TRANSLATION, GENESIS 24:16

And the servant took ten camels of the camels of his master, and departed; for all the goods of his master were in his hand: and he arose, and went to Mesopotamia, unto the city of Nahor.

11 And he made his camels to kneel down without the city by a well of water at the time of the evening, even the time that women go out to draw water.

12 And he said, O Lord God of my master Abraham, I pray thee, send me good speed this day, and shew kindness unto my master Abraham.

13 Behold, I stand here by the well of water; and the daughters of the men of the city come out to draw water:

14 And let it come to pass, that the damsel to whom I shall say, Let down thy pitcher, I pray thee, that I may drink; and she shall say, Drink, and I will give thy camels drink also: let the same be she that thou hast appointed for thy servant Isaac; and thereby shall I know that thou hast shewed kindness unto my master.

15 And it came to pass, before he had done speaking, that, behold, Rebekah came out, who was born to Bethuel, son of Milcah, the wife of Nahor, Abraham's brother, with her pitcher upon her shoulder.

16 And the damsel was very fair to look upon, a virgin, neither had any man known *the like unto* her: and she went down to the well, and filled her pitcher, and came up.

17 And the servant ran to meet her, and said, Let me, I pray thee, drink a little water of thy pitcher.

18 And she said, Drink, my lord: and she hasted, and let down her pitcher upon her hand, and gave him drink.

19 And when she had done giving him drink, she said, I will draw water for thy camels also, until they have done drinking.

20 And she hasted, and emptied her pitcher into the trough, and ran again unto the well to draw water, and drew for all his camels.

21 And the man wondering at her held his peace, to wit whether the Lord had made his journey prosperous or not.

22 And it came to pass, as the camels had done drinking, that the man took a golden earring of half a shekel weight, and two bracelets for her hands of ten shekels weight of gold;

23 And said, Whose daughter art thou? tell me, I pray thee: is there room in thy father's house for us to lodge in?

24 And she said unto him, I am the daughter of Bethuel the son of Milcah, which she bare unto Nahor.

25 She said moreover unto him, We have both straw and provender enough, and room to lodge in.

26 And the man bowed down his head, and worshipped the Lord.

27 And he said, Blessed be the Lord God of my master Abraham, who hath not left destitute my master of his mercy and his truth: I being in the way, the Lord led me to the house of my master's brethren.

What did Abraham's servant pray for as he searched for Isaac's future wife? What can you learn about prayer through the servant's example? What do verses 16–20 teach us about the kind of person Rebekah was?

REBEKAH CONSENTS TO BE ISAAC'S WIFE, THEN JOURNEYS TO MEET HIM

Abraham had commanded his most trusted servant to go to the land of Abraham's upbringing and find a worthy wife for his son Isaac. The servant pleaded with the Lord for guidance and journeyed to the city of Abraham's brother, Nahor. He was led to a well and there saw a beautiful woman named Rebekah, who offered water to him and his camels. The servant learned that Rebekah was a relative of Abraham, and he praised God for mercifully leading him to "the house of my master's brethren" (Genesis 24:27). The servant was invited into the house of Rebekah's family, where he explained to all—including Rebekah's brother Laban and father Bethuel—the divine guidance that had brought him there. The servant then asked if Rebekah would consent to be Isaac's wife.

GENESIS 24:49–67

And now if ye will deal kindly and truly with my master, tell me: and if not, tell me; that I may turn to the right hand, or to the left.

50 Then Laban and Bethuel answered and said, The thing proceedeth from the Lord: we cannot speak unto thee bad or good.

51 Behold, Rebekah is before thee, take her, and go, and let her be thy master's son's wife, as the Lord hath spoken.

52 And it came to pass, that, when Abraham's servant heard their words, he worshipped the Lord, bowing himself to the earth.

53 And the servant brought forth jewels of silver, and jewels of gold, and raiment, and gave them to Rebekah: he gave also to her brother and to her mother precious things.

54 And they did eat and drink, he and the men that were with him, and tarried all night; and they rose up in the morning, and he said, Send me away unto my master.

55 And her brother and her mother said, Let the damsel abide with us a few days, at the least ten; after that she shall go.

56 And he said unto them, Hinder me not, seeing the Lord hath prospered my way; send me away that I may go to my master.

57 And they said, We will call the damsel, and inquire at her mouth.

58 And they called Rebekah, and said unto her, Wilt thou go with this man? And she said, I will go.

59 And they sent away Rebekah their sister, and her nurse, and Abraham's servant, and his men.

60 And they blessed Rebekah, and said unto her, Thou art our sister, be thou the mother of thousands of millions, and let thy seed possess the gate of those which hate them.

61 And Rebekah arose, and her damsels, and they rode upon the camels, and followed the man: and the servant took Rebekah, and went his way.

62 And Isaac came from the way of the well Lahai-roi; for he dwelt in the south country.

63 And Isaac went out to meditate in the field at the eventide: and he lifted up his eyes, and saw, and, behold, the camels were coming.

64 And Rebekah lifted up her eyes, and when she saw Isaac, she lighted off the camel.

65 For she had said unto the servant, What man is this that walketh in the field to meet us? And the servant had said, It is my master: therefore she took a veil, and covered herself.

66 And the servant told Isaac all things that he had done.

67 And Isaac brought her into his mother Sarah's tent, and took Rebekah, and she became his wife; and he loved her: and Isaac was comforted after his mother's death.

Rebekah didn't hesitate to leave her family and go with Abraham's servant. When have you quickly followed a spiritual prompting, even if it was inconvenient? What blessings have you received from being willing to quickly follow a spiritual prompting?

ESAU SELLS HIS BIRTHRIGHT TO JACOB

Abraham's servant had been divinely guided to the land of Abraham's youth and there found Rebekah, who consented to journey to Canaan and marry Isaac. Later, Abraham died, and his sons Isaac and Ishmael buried him. Upon Abraham's death, Isaac—the firstborn son through Sarah—inherited all that Abraham had. This was in accordance with the Old Testament practice of the firstborn son receiving the "birthright." The Bible Dictionary states, "Under the patriarchal order, the right or inheritance of the firstborn is known as birthright. This generally included a land inheritance as well as the authority to preside." In these verses, the issue of the birthright is contested between Isaac's sons.

GENESIS 25:20–34

And Isaac was forty years old when he took Rebekah to wife, the daughter of Bethuel the Syrian of Padan-aram, the sister to Laban the Syrian.

21 And Isaac entreated the Lord for his wife, because she was barren: and the Lord was entreated of him, and Rebekah his wife conceived.

22 And the children struggled together within her; and she said, If it be so, why am I thus? And she went to inquire of the Lord.

23 And the Lord said unto her, Two nations are in thy womb, and two manner of people shall be separated from thy bowels; and the one people shall be stronger than the other people; and the elder shall serve the younger.

24 And when her days to be delivered were fulfilled, behold, there were twins in her womb.

25 And the first came out red, all over like an hairy garment; and they called his name Esau.

26 And after that came his brother out, and his hand took hold on Esau's heel; and his name was called Jacob: and Isaac was threescore years old when she bare them.

27 And the boys grew: and Esau was a cunning hunter, a man of the field; and Jacob was a plain man, dwelling in tents.

28 And Isaac loved Esau, because he did eat of his venison: but Rebekah loved Jacob.

29 And Jacob sod pottage: and Esau came from the field, and he was faint:

30 And Esau said to Jacob, Feed me, I pray thee, with that same red pottage; for I am faint: therefore was his name called Edom.

31 And Jacob said, Sell me this day thy birthright.

32 And Esau said, Behold, I am at the point to die: and what profit shall this birthright do to me?

33 And Jacob said, Swear to me this day; and he sware unto him: and he sold his birthright unto Jacob.

34 Then Jacob gave Esau bread and pottage of lentiles; and he did eat and drink, and rose up, and went his way: thus Esau despised his birthright.

Esau sold his birthright to Jacob for a bowl of "pottage" or stew. Based on what you read in verses 29–34, why do you think Esau made that choice? In what ways do people trade something of great value for something of far lesser value? What are some things that should be most precious to us? How can we show we value them?

JACOB IS SHOWN A VISION OF GOD STANDING ATOP A LADDER STRETCHING BETWEEN EARTH AND HEAVEN

Esau had sold his birthright to his brother Jacob. Later, when Isaac was old and blind, he desired to bless Esau (his eldest son), but Rebekah worked with Jacob to ensure that Isaac unknowingly laid his hands on Jacob's head. In the blessing, Jacob was promised that he would rule over many people and nations. Esau was angry with Jacob and planned to kill him, but Rebekah warned Jacob to flee from Canaan. Around the same time, Isaac gave Jacob a command similar to the one that had been given by Abraham to Isaac: to not marry a woman from the land of Canaan, but instead from the land of Abraham's people. Jacob obeyed and journeyed toward the land of Laban, his mother's brother. Meanwhile, Esau married women from the land of Canaan, which grieved his parents. During Jacob's journey to the land of Laban, he was shown a remarkable vision.

GENESIS 28:10–22

And Jacob went out from Beer-sheba, and went toward Haran.

11 And he lighted upon a certain place, and tarried there all night, because the sun was set; and he took of the stones of that place, and put them for his pillows, and lay down in that place to sleep.

12 And he dreamed, and behold a ladder set up on the earth, and the top of it reached to heaven: and behold the angels of God ascending and descending on it.

13 And, behold, the Lord stood above it, and said, I am the Lord God of Abraham thy father, and the God of Isaac: the land whereon thou liest, to thee will I give it, and to thy seed;

14 And thy seed shall be as the dust of the earth, and thou shalt spread abroad to the west, and to the east, and to the north, and to the south: and in thee and in thy seed shall all the families of the earth be blessed.

15 And, behold, I am with thee, and will keep thee in all places whither thou goest, and will bring thee again into this land; for I will not leave thee, until I have done that which I have spoken to thee of.

16 And Jacob awaked out of his sleep, and he said, Surely the Lord is in this place; and I knew it not.

17 And he was afraid, and said, How dreadful is this place! this is none other but the house of God, and this is the gate of heaven.

18 And Jacob rose up early in the morning, and took the stone that he had put for his pillows, and set it up for a pillar, and poured oil upon the top of it.

19 And he called the name of that place Beth-el: but the name of that city was called Luz at the first.

20 And Jacob vowed a vow, saying, If God will be with me, and will keep me in this way that I go, and will give me bread to eat, and raiment to put on,

21 So that I come again to my father's house in peace; then shall the Lord be my God:

22 And this stone, which I have set for a pillar, shall be God's house: and of all that thou shalt give me I will surely give the tenth unto thee.

What promises did the Lord give to Jacob concerning his children? What promises did the Lord give Jacob concerning land? What did Jacob vow to do in return? What covenants have you made with God, and what promises has He given you through those covenants?

JACOB PLEADS FOR GOD'S HELP AS HE PREPARES
TO MEET HIS ESTRANGED BROTHER ESAU

Jacob had been commanded by his father Isaac to leave Canaan and find a wife among the people of Laban, his uncle. During his journey, God promised Jacob a great posterity. After Jacob entered the land inhabited by Laban, he met and fell in love with Laban's daughter Rachel. Jacob agreed to work for Laban for seven years in order to marry Rachel, but at the end of seven years Laban insisted that Jacob first marry Rachel's older sister Leah and then work another seven years for Rachel. Jacob agreed to this. Jacob would go on to father the twelve sons who would become the heads of the twelve tribes of Israel: Reuben, Simeon, Levi, Judah, Issachar, and Zebulun (through Leah); Gad and Asher (through Zilpah, Leah's handmaid); Dan and Naphtali (through Bilhah, Rachel's handmaid); and Joseph and Benjamin (through Rachel). After about fourteen years, Jacob was commanded by God to return with his own growing family to the land of Canaan. During his journey, Jacob learned that his brother Esau was journeying out to meet him. Fearing that Esau still desired to kill him, Jacob pleaded with God for help.

GENESIS 32:9–12

And Jacob said, O God of my father Abraham, and God of my father Isaac, the Lord which saidst unto me, Return unto thy country, and to thy kindred, and I will deal well with thee:

10 I am not worthy of the least of all the mercies, and of all the truth, which thou hast shewed unto thy servant; for with my staff I passed over this Jordan; and now I am become two bands.

11 Deliver me, I pray thee, from the hand of my brother, from the hand of Esau: for I fear him, lest he will come and smite me, and the mother with the children.

12 And thou saidst, I will surely do thee good, and make thy seed as the sand of the sea, which cannot be numbered for multitude.

Why was Jacob worried about meeting his brother Esau? To whom did Jacob turn when he was afraid? Consider the words Jacob uses in his prayer in Genesis 32. How does Jacob address God? What can you do to pray mightily like Jacob? When has prayer been a help to you when you have been worried or scared?

JACOB WRESTLES WITH AN ANGEL AND HIS NAME IS CHANGED TO ISRAEL

Having been commanded by God, Jacob began returning to the land of Canaan with his wives, their hand-maids, and their children. After he learned that his estranged brother Esau was journeying out to meet him and he pleaded with God for protection, he made a plan and took action.

GENESIS 32:13–30

And he lodged there that same night; and took of that which came to his hand a present for Esau his brother;

14 Two hundred she goats, and twenty he goats, two hundred ewes, and twenty rams,

15 Thirty milch camels with their colts, forty kine, and ten bulls, twenty she asses, and ten foals.

16 And he delivered them into the hand of his servants, every drove by themselves; and said unto his servants, Pass over before me, and put a space betwixt drove and drove.

17 And he commanded the foremost, saying, When Esau my brother meeteth thee, and asketh thee, saying, Whose art thou? And whither goest thou? And whose are these before thee?

18 Then thou shalt say, They be thy servant Jacob's; it is a present sent unto my lord Esau: and, behold, also he is behind us.

19 And so commanded he the second, and the third, and all that followed the droves, saying, On this manner shall ye speak unto Esau, when ye find him.

20 And say ye moreover, Behold, thy servant Jacob is behind us. For he said, I will appease him with the present that goeth before me, and afterward I will see his face; peradventure he will accept of me.

21 So went the present over before him: and himself lodged that night in the company.

22 And he rose up that night, and took his two wives, and his two womenservants, and his eleven sons, and passed over the ford Jabbok.

23 And he took them, and sent them over the brook, and sent over that he had.

24 And Jacob was left alone; and there wrestled a man with him until the breaking of the day.

25 And when he saw that he prevailed not against him, he touched the hollow of his thigh; and the hollow of Jacob's thigh was out of joint, as he wrestled with him.

26 And he said, Let me go, for the day breaketh. And he said, I will not let thee go, except thou bless me.

27 And he said unto him, What is thy name? And he said, Jacob.

28 And he said, Thy name shall be called no more Jacob, but Israel: for as a prince hast thou power with God and with men, and hast prevailed.

29 And Jacob asked him, and said, Tell me, I pray thee, thy name. And he said, Wherefore is it that thou dost ask after my name? And he blessed him there.

30 And Jacob called the name of the place Peniel: for I have seen God face to face, and my life is preserved.

Note that the Old Testament book of Hosea contains a reference to Jacob's "wrestle" (see Hosea 12:4). There, the "man" is identified as an "angel."

After praying for help, what actions did Jacob take to prepare to meet his brother? After doing all he could do, Jacob "wrestled," or struggled to receive a blessing from an angel. What name did the angel give Jacob as a blessing? Consider sharing an experience of when you've had to struggle to seek for guidance or blessings.

AFTER MANY YEARS APART, JACOB AND ESAU ARE RECONCILED

About fourteen years earlier, Jacob—with help from his mother—received a blessing from his father Isaac that had been intended for Esau. Esau was enraged and wanted to kill Jacob, prompting Jacob to flee from Canaan. While in the land of his mother's brother, Jacob married Leah and Rachel and began a large family of his own. He was then commanded by God to return to Canaan. During that journey Jacob learned that Esau was journeying out to meet him. This greatly worried Jacob. He prayed to God for help, then prepared a gift of many camels, cows, and sheep for his estranged brother.

GENESIS 33:1–16

And Jacob lifted up his eyes, and looked, and, behold, Esau came, and with him four hundred men. And he divided the children unto Leah, and unto Rachel, and unto the two handmaids.

2 And he put the handmaids and their children foremost, and Leah and her children after, and Rachel and Joseph hindermost.

3 And he passed over before them, and bowed himself to the ground seven times, until he came near to his brother.

4 And Esau ran to meet him, and embraced him, and fell on his neck, and kissed him: and they wept.

5 And he lifted up his eyes, and saw the women and the children; and said, Who are those with thee? And he said, The children which God hath graciously given thy servant.

6 Then the handmaidens came near, they and their children, and they bowed themselves.

7 And Leah also with her children came near, and bowed themselves: and after came Joseph near and Rachel, and they bowed themselves.

8 And he said, What meanest thou by all this drove which I met? And he said, These are to find grace in the sight of my lord.

9 And Esau said, I have enough, my brother; keep that thou hast unto thyself.

10 And Jacob said, Nay, I pray thee, if now I have found grace in thy sight, then receive my present at my hand: for therefore I have seen thy face, as though I had seen the face of God, and thou wast pleased with me.

11 Take, I pray thee, my blessing that is brought to thee; because God hath dealt graciously with me, and because I have enough. And he urged him, and he took it.

12 And he said, Let us take our journey, and let us go, and I will go before thee.

13 And he said unto him, My lord knoweth that the children are tender, and the flocks and herds with young are with me: and if men should overdrive them one day, all the flock will die.

14 Let my lord, I pray thee, pass over before his servant: and I will lead on softly, according as the cattle that goeth before me and the children be able to endure, until I come unto my lord unto Seir.

15 And Esau said, Let me now leave with thee some of the folk that are with me. And he said, What needeth it? let me find grace in the sight of my lord.

16 So Esau returned that day on his way unto Seir.

What was the reunion like between Esau and Jacob? What does the story of Jacob and Esau teach us about forgiveness? Consider your own relationships. Is there someone you can forgive to restore a friendship? Do you need to seek forgiveness from someone?

JOSEPH IS SHOWN A DREAM IN WHICH HIS FAMILY WILL BOW DOWN TO HIM

Jacob—also known as Israel—fathered twelve sons, and they were known as the house of Israel. Joseph, the second youngest son of Jacob, had many spiritual gifts that would greatly bless his family. But he first endured a series of significant trials.

GENESIS 37:1–11

And Jacob dwelt in the land wherein his father was a stranger, in the land of Canaan.

2 These are the generations of Jacob. Joseph, being seventeen years old, was feeding the flock with his brethren; and the lad was with the sons of Bilhah, and with the sons of Zilpah, his father's wives: and Joseph brought unto his father their evil report.

3 Now Israel loved Joseph more than all his children, because he was the son of his old age: and he made him a coat of many colours.

4 And when his brethren saw that their father loved him more than all his brethren, they hated him, and could not speak peaceably unto him.

5 And Joseph dreamed a dream, and he told it his brethren: and they hated him yet the more.

6 And he said unto them, Hear, I pray you, this dream which I have dreamed:

7 For, behold, we were binding sheaves in the field, and, lo, my sheaf arose, and also stood upright; and, behold, your sheaves stood round about, and made obeisance to my sheaf.

8 And his brethren said to him, Shalt thou indeed reign over us? or shalt thou indeed have dominion over us? And they hated him yet the more for his dreams, and for his words.

9 And he dreamed yet another dream, and told it his brethren, and said, Behold, I have dreamed a dream more; and, behold, the sun and the moon and the eleven stars made obeisance to me.

10 And he told it to his father, and to his brethren: and his father rebuked him, and said unto him, What is this dream that thou hast dreamed? Shall I and thy mother and thy brethren indeed come to bow down ourselves to thee to the earth?

11 And his brethren envied him; but his father observed the saying.

Why were Joseph's brothers angry with him? What problems can anger and contention cause in a family? What can you do to bring peace into your home?

JOSEPH'S BROTHERS SELL HIM AS A SLAVE AND CONVINCE THEIR FATHER HE WAS KILLED BY WILD BEASTS

Joseph was highly favored by his father Jacob, who made him a "coat of many colours" (Genesis 37:3). Joseph's ten older brothers were jealous of the affection shown to Joseph by their father. Their spiteful attitude toward their younger brother was further hardened when Joseph told his family of two dreams in which his family symbolically bowed themselves down to Joseph. Jacob was also perplexed by his son's dreams, but he closely considered what they might mean. Jacob then sent Joseph to check on his brothers, who were tending to their father's flocks. As Joseph approached, his brothers made a plan to kill him.

GENESIS 37:18–36

And when they saw him afar off, even before he came near unto them, they conspired against him to slay him.

19 And they said one to another, Behold, this dreamer cometh.

20 Come now therefore, and let us slay him, and cast him into some pit, and we will say, Some evil beast hath devoured him: and we shall see what will become of his dreams.

21 And Reuben heard it, and he delivered him out of their hands; and said, Let us not kill him.

22 And Reuben said unto them, Shed no blood, but cast him into this pit that is in the wilderness, and lay no hand upon him; that he might rid him out of their hands, to deliver him to his father again.

23 And it came to pass, when Joseph was come unto his brethren, that they stript Joseph out of his coat, his coat of many colours that was on him;

24 And they took him, and cast him into a pit: and the pit was empty, there was no water in it.

25 And they sat down to eat bread: and they lifted up their eyes and looked, and, behold, a company of Ishmeelites came from Gilead with their camels bearing spicery and balm and myrrh, going to carry it down to Egypt.

26 And Judah said unto his brethren, What profit is it if we slay our brother, and conceal his blood?

27 Come, and let us sell him to the Ishmeelites, and let not our hand be upon him; for he is our brother and our flesh. And his brethren were content.

28 Then there passed by Midianites merchantmen; and they drew and lifted up Joseph out of the pit, and sold Joseph to the Ishmeelites for twenty pieces of silver: and they brought Joseph into Egypt.

29 And Reuben returned unto the pit; and, behold, Joseph was not in the pit; and he rent his clothes.

30 And he returned unto his brethren, and said, The child is not; and I, whither shall I go?

31 And they took Joseph's coat, and killed a kid of the goats, and dipped the coat in the blood;

32 And they sent the coat of many colours, and they brought it to their father; and said, This have we found: know now whether it be thy son's coat or no.

33 And he knew it, and said, It is my son's coat; an evil beast hath devoured him; Joseph is without doubt rent in pieces.

34 And Jacob rent his clothes, and put sackcloth upon his loins, and mourned for his son many days.

35 And all his sons and all his daughters rose up to comfort him; but he refused to be comforted; and he said, For I will go down into the grave unto my son mourning. Thus his father wept for him.

36 And the Midianites sold him into Egypt unto Potiphar, an officer of Pharaoh's, and captain of the guard.

What did Joseph's brothers do to him? How did they cover up their actions? What effect did their actions have on their father, Jacob? Consider how your actions affect others. How can you affect others for good and not for bad?

WHILE A SLAVE IN EGYPT, JOSEPH IS PROSPERED BY THE LORD

Jacob's young son Joseph had been shown dreams in which his family bowed themselves down to him. Angry at this, and jealous of the favor Joseph was shown by their father, his brothers secretly sold him as a slave to merchants passing through the land and convinced their father that he had been killed by a wild beast. Jacob mourned the death of his son and remained unaware that he was actually alive and had been brought to Egypt, where he was sold to a high-ranking officer who served under Pharaoh, who was the king of Egypt.

GENESIS 39:1–6

And Joseph was brought down to Egypt; and Potiphar, an officer of Pharaoh, captain of the guard, an Egyptian, bought him of the hands of the Ishmaelites, which had brought him down thither.

2 And the Lord was with Joseph, and he was a prosperous man; and he was in the house of his master the Egyptian.

3 And his master saw that the Lord was with him, and that the Lord made all that he did to prosper in his hand.

4 And Joseph found grace in his sight, and he served him: and he made him overseer over his house, and all that he had he put into his hand.

5 And it came to pass from the time that he had made him overseer in his house, and over all that he had, that the Lord blessed the Egyptian's house for Joseph's sake; and the blessing of the Lord was upon all that he had in the house, and in the field.

6 And he left all that he had in Joseph's hand; and he knew not ought he had, save the bread which he did eat. And Joseph was a goodly person, and well favoured.

Although Joseph had been sold as a slave, what enabled him to rise above that great challenge? What did the people who knew Joseph think of him? Consider verse 2. What actions can you take to ensure that the Lord is "with" you? What effect can that have on those around you?

JOSEPH OVERCOMES THE TEMPTATIONS OF POTIPHAR'S WIFE BUT IS FALSELY ACCUSED AND THROWN IN PRISON

Joseph was working as a slave in Egypt for Potiphar, a captain under Pharaoh. While there, Joseph was prospered by the Lord and served faithfully under Potiphar. Potiphar's wife repeatedly tried to seduce Joseph, but Joseph consistently refused her temptations, saying, "How then can I do this great wickedness, and sin against God?" (Genesis 39:9). Even then, she continued to tempt Joseph.

GENESIS 39:7–23; JOSEPH SMITH TRANSLATION, GENESIS 39:8, 22

And it came to pass after these things, that his master's wife cast her eyes upon Joseph; and she said, Lie with me.

8 But he refused, and said unto his master's wife, Behold, my master *knoweth* not what is with me in the house, and he hath committed all that he hath to my hand;

9 There is none greater in this house than I; neither hath he kept back any thing from me but thee, because thou art his wife: how then can I do this great wickedness, and sin against God?

10 And it came to pass, as she spake to Joseph day by day, that he hearkened not unto her, to lie by her, or to be with her.

11 And it came to pass about this time, that Joseph went into the house to do his business; and there was none of the men of the house there within.

12 And she caught him by his garment, saying, Lie with me: and he left his garment in her hand, and fled, and got him out.

13 And it came to pass, when she saw that he had left his garment in her hand, and was fled forth,

14 That she called unto the men of her house, and spake unto them, saying, See, he hath brought in an Hebrew unto us to mock us; he came in unto me to lie with me, and I cried with a loud voice:

15 And it came to pass, when he heard that I lifted up my voice and cried, that he left his garment with me, and fled, and got him out.

16 And she laid up his garment by her, until his lord came home.

17 And she spake unto him according to these words, saying, The Hebrew servant, which thou hast brought unto us, came in unto me to mock me:

18 And it came to pass, as I lifted up my voice and cried, that he left his garment with me, and fled out.

19 And it came to pass, when his master heard the words of his wife, which she spake unto him, saying, After this manner did thy servant to me; that his wrath was kindled.

20 And Joseph's master took him, and put him into the prison, a place where the king's prisoners were bound: and he was there in the prison.

21 But the Lord was with Joseph, and shewed him mercy, and gave him favour in the sight of the keeper of the prison.

22 And the keeper of the prison committed to Joseph's hand all the prisoners that were in the prison; and whatsoever they did there, he was the *overseer* of it.

23 The keeper of the prison looked not to any thing that was under his hand; because the Lord was with him, and that which he did, the Lord made it to prosper.

What steps did Joseph take to resist the temptations of Potiphar's wife? What are some common temptations in today's world, and what steps can you take to overcome them?

WHILE IMPRISONED, JOSEPH INTERPRETS THE DREAMS OF PHARAOH'S BUTLER AND BAKER

While serving in Potiphar's house in Egypt, Joseph was repeatedly tempted by Potiphar's wife. But Joseph resisted, only to have her falsely accuse him. Joseph was thus cast into prison, but even then the Lord was with him and gave him "favour in the sight of the keeper of the prison" (Genesis 39:21), who trusted Joseph and gave him many responsibilities. While in prison, Joseph met Pharaoh's butler and baker and used his spiritual gifts to help them.

GENESIS 40:1–23

And it came to pass after these things, that the butler of the king of Egypt and his baker had offended their lord the king of Egypt.

2 And Pharaoh was wroth against two of his officers, against the chief of the butlers, and against the chief of the bakers.

3 And he put them in ward in the house of the captain of the guard, into the prison, the place where Joseph was bound.

4 And the captain of the guard charged Joseph with them, and he served them: and they continued a season in ward.

5 And they dreamed a dream both of them, each man his dream in one night, each man according to the interpretation of his dream, the butler and the baker of the king of Egypt, which were bound in the prison.

6 And Joseph came in unto them in the morning, and looked upon them, and, behold, they were sad.

7 And he asked Pharaoh's officers that were with him in the ward of his lord's house, saying, Wherefore look ye so sadly to day?

8 And they said unto him, We have dreamed a dream, and there is no interpreter of it. And Joseph said unto them, Do not interpretations belong to God? tell me them, I pray you.

9 And the chief butler told his dream to Joseph, and said to him, In my dream, behold, a vine was before me;

10 And in the vine were three branches: and it was as though it budded, and her blossoms shot forth; and the clusters thereof brought forth ripe grapes:

11 And Pharaoh's cup was in my hand: and I took the grapes, and pressed them into Pharaoh's cup, and I gave the cup into Pharaoh's hand.

12 And Joseph said unto him, This is the interpretation of it: The three branches are three days:

13 Yet within three days shall Pharaoh lift up thine head, and restore thee unto thy place: and thou shalt deliver Pharaoh's cup into his hand, after the former manner when thou wast his butler.

14 But think on me when it shall be well with thee, and shew kindness, I pray thee, unto me, and make mention of me unto Pharaoh, and bring me out of this house:

15 For indeed I was stolen away out of the land of the Hebrews: and here also have I done nothing that they should put me into the dungeon.

16 When the chief baker saw that the interpretation was good, he said unto Joseph, I also was in my dream, and, behold, I had three white baskets on my head:

17 And in the uppermost basket there was of all manner of bakemeats for Pharaoh; and the birds did eat them out of the basket upon my head.

18 And Joseph answered and said, This is the interpretation thereof: The three baskets are three days:

19 Yet within three days shall Pharaoh lift up thy head from off thee, and shall hang thee on a tree; and the birds shall eat thy flesh from off thee.

20 And it came to pass the third day, which was Pharaoh's birthday, that he made a feast unto all his servants: and he lifted up the head of the chief butler and of the chief baker among his servants.

21 And he restored the chief butler unto his butlership again; and he gave the cup into Pharaoh's hand:

22 But he hanged the chief baker: as Joseph had interpreted to them.

23 Yet did not the chief butler remember Joseph, but forgat him.

What did the butler and baker dream, and what interpretation did Joseph give them for their dreams? According to verse 8, how was Joseph able to interpret their dreams? How can you use your spiritual gifts to bless others?

JOSEPH IS CALLED FROM PRISON TO
INTERPRET PHARAOH'S DREAMS

Joseph had correctly interpreted the dreams of two fellow prisoners: Pharaoh's butler (who was soon restored to his position in Pharaoh's house) and Pharaoh's baker (who was soon executed at Pharaoh's command). Joseph had pleaded with the butler to make mention of his name to Pharaoh so that he too would be released. But upon his release, the butler forgot about Joseph, only to remember him two years later. In the following verses, "kine" is another word for cow.

GENESIS 41:1–16

And it came to pass at the end of two full years, that Pharaoh dreamed: and, behold, he stood by the river.

2 And, behold, there came up out of the river seven well favoured kine and fatfleshed; and they fed in a meadow.

3 And, behold, seven other kine came up after them out of the river, ill favoured and leanfleshed; and stood by the other kine upon the brink of the river.

4 And the ill favoured and leanfleshed kine did eat up the seven well favoured and fat kine. So Pharaoh awoke.

5 And he slept and dreamed the second time: and, behold, seven ears of corn came up upon one stalk, rank and good.

6 And, behold, seven thin ears and blasted with the east wind sprung up after them.

7 And the seven thin ears devoured the seven rank and full ears. And Pharaoh awoke, and, behold, it was a dream.

8 And it came to pass in the morning that his spirit was troubled; and he sent and called for all the magicians of Egypt, and all the wise men thereof: and Pharaoh told them his dream; but there was none that could interpret them unto Pharaoh.

9 Then spake the chief butler unto Pharaoh, saying, I do remember my faults this day:

10 Pharaoh was wroth with his servants, and put me in ward in the captain of the guard's house, both me and the chief baker:

11 And we dreamed a dream in one night, I and he; we dreamed each man according to the interpretation of his dream.

12 And there was there with us a young man, an Hebrew, servant to the captain of the guard; and we told him, and he interpreted to us our dreams; to each man according to his dream he did interpret.

13 And it came to pass, as he interpreted to us, so it was; me he restored unto mine office, and him he hanged.

14 Then Pharaoh sent and called Joseph, and they brought him hastily out of the dungeon: and he shaved himself, and changed his raiment, and came in unto Pharaoh.

15 And Pharaoh said unto Joseph, I have dreamed a dream, and there is none that can interpret it: and I have heard say of thee, that thou canst understand a dream to interpret it.

16 And Joseph answered Pharaoh, saying, It is not in me: God shall give Pharaoh an answer of peace.

What occurred in Pharaoh's dreams? Who attempted unsuccessfully to interpret them? Who did Joseph say would give Pharaoh an answer (see verse 16)? Joseph had the spiritual gift to interpret dreams, but he acknowledged God as the source of that power. What spiritual gifts do you have, and how can you recognize God as the source of those gifts?

IN INTERPRETING PHARAOH'S DREAMS, JOSEPH PROPHESIES OF SEVEN YEARS OF PLENTY FOLLOWED BY SEVEN YEARS OF FAMINE

Pharaoh, king of Egypt, had two disturbing dreams, one in which he saw seven lean cows eat seven fat cows, and another in which seven withered ears of corn devoured seven plentiful ears of corn. Pharaoh sent for magicians and wise men to interpret the dreams, but they could not. Pharaoh's butler then remembered that Joseph had correctly interpreted his dream while in prison and told this to Pharaoh. Joseph was quickly pulled from prison and presented to Pharaoh, who described his dreams to Joseph in great detail. Joseph then responded.

GENESIS 41:25–36

And Joseph said unto Pharaoh, The dream of Pharaoh is one: God hath shewed Pharaoh what he is about to do.

26 The seven good kine are seven years; and the seven good ears are seven years: the dream is one.

27 And the seven thin and ill favoured kine that came up after them are seven years; and the seven empty ears blasted with the east wind shall be seven years of famine.

28 This is the thing which I have spoken unto Pharaoh: What God is about to do he sheweth unto Pharaoh.

29 Behold, there come seven years of great plenty throughout all the land of Egypt:

30 And there shall arise after them seven years of famine; and all the plenty shall be forgotten in the land of Egypt; and the famine shall consume the land;

31 And the plenty shall not be known in the land by reason of that famine following; for it shall be very grievous.

32 And for that the dream was doubled unto Pharaoh twice; it is because the thing is established by God, and God will shortly bring it to pass.

33 Now therefore let Pharaoh look out a man discreet and wise, and set him over the land of Egypt.

34 Let Pharaoh do this, and let him appoint officers over the land, and take up the fifth part of the land of Egypt in the seven plenteous years.

35 And let them gather all the food of those good years that come, and lay up corn under the hand of Pharaoh, and let them keep food in the cities.

36 And that food shall be for store to the land against the seven years of famine, which shall be in the land of Egypt; that the land perish not through the famine.

What was the meaning of Pharaoh's dreams? What action did Joseph tell Pharaoh to take? What warnings have modern-day prophets given us? How have they told us to prepare for the future? What steps can you take to follow their counsel?

PHARAOH APPOINTS JOSEPH THE STEWARD OF EGYPT'S PREPARATIONS FOR SEVEN YEARS OF FAMINE

Joseph had been called from prison to interpret Pharaoh's dream in which seven lean cows ate seven fat cows and seven withered ears of corn devoured seven plentiful ears of corn. In interpreting the dream, Joseph prophesied that Egypt would enjoy seven years of plenty followed by seven years of famine. He advised Pharaoh to appoint a discreet and wise man to oversee the careful storage of extra food during the seven years of plenty.

GENESIS 41:37–52

And the thing was good in the eyes of Pharaoh, and in the eyes of all his servants.

38 And Pharaoh said unto his servants, Can we find such a one as this is, a man in whom the Spirit of God is?

39 And Pharaoh said unto Joseph, Forasmuch as God hath shewed thee all this, there is none so discreet and wise as thou art:

40 Thou shalt be over my house, and according unto thy word shall all my people be ruled: only in the throne will I be greater than thou.

41 And Pharaoh said unto Joseph, See, I have set thee over all the land of Egypt.

42 And Pharaoh took off his ring from his hand, and put it upon Joseph's hand, and arrayed him in vestures of fine linen, and put a gold chain about his neck;

43 And he made him to ride in the second chariot which he had; and they cried before him, Bow the knee: and he made him ruler over all the land of Egypt.

44 And Pharaoh said unto Joseph, I am Pharaoh, and without thee shall no man lift up his hand or foot in all the land of Egypt.

45 And Pharaoh called Joseph's name Zaphnath-paaneah; and he gave him to wife Asenath the daughter of Poti-pherah priest of On. And Joseph went out over all the land of Egypt.

46 And Joseph was thirty years old when he stood before Pharaoh king of Egypt. And Joseph went out from the presence of Pharaoh, and went throughout all the land of Egypt.

47 And in the seven plenteous years the earth brought forth by handfuls.

48 And he gathered up all the food of the seven years, which were in the land of Egypt, and laid up the food in the cities: the food of the field, which was round about every city, laid he up in the same.

49 And Joseph gathered corn as the sand of the sea, very much, until he left numbering; for it was without number.

50 And unto Joseph were born two sons before the years of famine came, which Asenath the daughter of Poti-pherah priest of On bare unto him.

51 And Joseph called the name of the firstborn Manasseh: For God, said he, hath made me forget all my toil, and all my father's house.

52 And the name of the second called he Ephraim: For God hath caused me to be fruitful in the land of my affliction.

Why did Pharaoh put so much trust in Joseph (see verses 38–39)? How can you become trustworthy? Because of Joseph's counsel, all of Egypt was prepared for famine. What counsel have prophets given us to prepare for events in our time?

THE PROPHECIES OF JOSEPH'S YOUTH ARE FULFILLED AS HIS BROTHERS JOURNEY TO EGYPT AND BOW BEFORE HIM

Years after being thrown in a pit by his jealous brothers and sold as a slave into Egypt, Joseph found great success serving Pharaoh and overseeing Egypt's preparations for famine. He was now regarded as a man of great wisdom, second only to Pharaoh in power. In Canaan, Joseph's brothers remained unaware of his whereabouts, and his father Jacob was led to believe that his favored son had long been dead.

GENESIS 41:53–57

And the seven years of plenteousness, that was in the land of Egypt, were ended.

54 And the seven years of dearth began to come, according as Joseph had said: and the dearth was in all lands; but in all the land of Egypt there was bread.

55 And when all the land of Egypt was famished, the people cried to Pharaoh for bread: and Pharaoh said unto all the Egyptians, Go unto Joseph; what he saith to you, do.

56 And the famine was over all the face of the earth: And Joseph opened all the storehouses, and sold unto the Egyptians; and the famine waxed sore in the land of Egypt.

57 And all countries came into Egypt to Joseph for to buy corn; because that the famine was so sore in all lands.

GENESIS 42:1–20

1 Now when Jacob saw that there was corn in Egypt, Jacob said unto his sons, Why do ye look one upon another?

2 And he said, Behold, I have heard that there is corn in Egypt: get you down thither, and buy for us from thence; that we may live, and not die.

3 And Joseph's ten brethren went down to buy corn in Egypt.

4 But Benjamin, Joseph's brother, Jacob sent not with his brethren; for he said, Lest peradventure mischief befall him.

5 And the sons of Israel came to buy corn among those that came: for the famine was in the land of Canaan.

6 And Joseph was the governor over the land, and he it was that sold to all the people of the land: and Joseph's brethren came, and bowed down themselves before him with their faces to the earth.

7 And Joseph saw his brethren, and he knew them, but made himself strange unto them, and spake roughly unto them; and he said unto them, Whence come ye? And they said, From the land of Canaan to buy food.

8 And Joseph knew his brethren, but they knew not him.

9 And Joseph remembered the dreams which he dreamed of them, and said unto them, Ye are spies; to see the nakedness of the land ye are come.

10 And they said unto him, Nay, my lord, but to buy food are thy servants come.

11 We are all one man's sons; we are true men, thy servants are no spies.

12 And he said unto them, Nay, but to see the nakedness of the land ye are come.

13 And they said, Thy servants are twelve brethren, the sons of one man in the land of Canaan; and, behold, the youngest is this day with our father, and one is not.

14 And Joseph said unto them, That is it that I spake unto you, saying, Ye are spies:

15 Hereby ye shall be proved: By the life of Pharaoh ye shall not go forth hence, except your youngest brother come hither.

16 Send one of you, and let him fetch your brother, and ye shall be kept in prison, that your words may be proved, whether there be any truth in you: or else by the life of Pharaoh surely ye are spies.

17 And he put them all together into ward three days.

18 And Joseph said unto them the third day, This do, and live; for I fear God:

19 If ye be true men, let one of your brethren be bound in the house of your prison: go ye, carry corn for the famine of your houses:

20 But bring your youngest brother unto me; so shall your words be verified, and ye shall not die. And they did so.

What dreams did Joseph have as a youth, and how were they fulfilled in these verses (see Genesis 37:5–9)? What did Joseph command his brothers to do in order to prove they were not spies? Why do you think Joseph tested his brothers this way?

JACOB'S NINE OTHER SONS FEARFULLY RETURN TO EGYPT WITH BENJAMIN

The prophesied famine had arrived in Egypt and the surrounding lands. In Canaan, Jacob sent ten of his sons to Egypt to buy grain (keeping Benjamin in Canaan). There the brothers met Joseph and bowed down to him, in fulfilment of Joseph's boyhood prophecy. While Joseph recognized his brothers, they did not recognize him, and they told him they were from a family of twelve brothers, including one who had died and one who remained behind in Canaan. Joseph demanded that they return with the younger brother (Benjamin) and held Simeon in Egypt to guarantee their return. Before the brothers left Egypt, Joseph commanded his servants to secretly refill their bags with the money they had given in exchange for grain. Once they were back in Canaan, Jacob was distraught to hear that Simeon was held in Egypt and concerned that their family would be accused of thievery on account of the money they were shocked to find in their bags. Jacob's sons convinced their father to allow them to return to Egypt, this time with Benjamin, a double portion of the money they had originally paid, and many lavish gifts.

GENESIS 43:15–34

And the men took that present, and they took double money in their hand, and Benjamin; and rose up, and went down to Egypt, and stood before Joseph.

16 And when Joseph saw Benjamin with them, he said to the ruler of his house, Bring these men home, and slay, and make ready; for these men shall dine with me at noon.

17 And the man did as Joseph bade; and the man brought the men into Joseph's house.

18 And the men were afraid, because they were brought into Joseph's house; and they said, Because of the money that was returned in our sacks at the first time are we brought in; that he may seek occasion against us, and fall upon us, and take us for bondmen, and our asses.

19 And they came near to the steward of Joseph's house, and they communed with him at the door of the house,

20 And said, O sir, we came indeed down at the first time to buy food:

21 And it came to pass, when we came to the inn, that we opened our sacks, and, behold, every man's money was in the mouth of his sack, our money in full weight: and we have brought it again in our hand.

22 And other money have we brought down in our hands to buy food: we cannot tell who put our money in our sacks.

23 And he said, Peace be to you, fear not: your God, and the God of your father, hath given you treasure in your sacks: I had your money. And he brought Simeon out unto them.

24 And the man brought the men into Joseph's house, and gave them water, and they washed their feet; and he gave their asses provender.

25 And they made ready the present against Joseph came at noon: for they heard that they should eat bread there.

26 And when Joseph came home, they brought him the present which was in their hand into the house, and bowed themselves to him to the earth.

27 And he asked them of their welfare, and said, Is your father well, the old man of whom ye spake? Is he yet alive?

28 And they answered, Thy servant our father is in good health, he is yet alive. And they bowed down their heads, and made obeisance.

29 And he lifted up his eyes, and saw his brother Benjamin, his mother's son, and said, Is this your younger brother, of whom ye spake unto me? And he said, God be gracious unto thee, my son.

30 And Joseph made haste; for his bowels did yearn upon his brother: and he sought where to weep; and he entered into his chamber, and wept there.

31 And he washed his face, and went out, and refrained himself, and said, Set on bread.

32 And they set on for him by himself, and for them by themselves, and for the Egyptians, which did eat with him, by themselves: because the Egyptians might not eat bread with the Hebrews; for that is an abomination unto the Egyptians.

33 And they sat before him, the firstborn according to his birthright, and the youngest according to his youth: and the men marvelled one at another.

34 And he took and sent messes unto them from before him: but Benjamin's mess was five times so much as any of theirs. And they drank, and were merry with him.

How did Joseph treat his brothers upon their return? What was Joseph's reaction to seeing his brother Benjamin? What possible reactions could Joseph have had when he saw his brothers who had sold him as a slave? What experiences had Joseph so far endured, and how might they have prepared him for the moment he met his brothers?

JOSEPH REVEALS HIS IDENTITY TO HIS BROTHERS AND THEY REJOICE

Joseph's brothers had returned to Egypt, this time with Benjamin. Upon seeing Benjamin, Joseph was overcome with emotion, but he continued to conceal his identity. Joseph allowed his eleven brothers to return to Canaan, but he commanded his servant to secretly place Joseph's silver cup in Benjamin's sack. Soon after the brothers had departed, the servant halted their journey and demanded to know if someone had stolen Joseph's cup. The brothers denied the accusation and promised that if the cup was found in one of their sacks, that man would serve the rest of his days as a servant in Egypt. The brothers were then stunned when the cup was found in Benjamin's sack. They all returned to Egypt, where Judah personally offered his own life in exchange for Benjamin's, in the hope that Benjamin would be allowed to return to his father. Pleading his case, Judah told Joseph that their father had already lost one son, and if he were to lose another he would go down "with sorrow to the grave" (Genesis 44:31).

Then Joseph could not refrain himself before all them that stood by him; and he cried, Cause every man to go out from me. And there stood no man with him, while Joseph made himself known unto his brethren.

2 And he wept aloud: and the Egyptians and the house of Pharaoh heard.

3 And Joseph said unto his brethren, I am Joseph; doth my father yet live? And his brethren could not answer him; for they were troubled at his presence.

4 And Joseph said unto his brethren, Come near to me, I pray you. And they came near. And he said, I am Joseph your brother, whom ye sold into Egypt.

5 Now therefore be not grieved, nor angry with yourselves, that ye sold me hither: for God did send me before you to preserve life.

6 For these two years hath the famine been in the land: and yet there are five years, in the which there shall neither be earing nor harvest.

7 And God sent me before you to preserve you a posterity in the earth, and to save your lives by a great deliverance.

8 So now it was not you that sent me hither, but God: and he hath made me a father to Pharaoh, and lord of all his house, and a ruler throughout all the land of Egypt.

9 Haste ye, and go up to my father, and say unto him, Thus saith thy son Joseph, God hath made me lord of all Egypt: come down unto me, tarry not:

10 And thou shalt dwell in the land of Goshen, and thou shalt be near unto me, thou, and thy children, and thy children's children, and thy flocks, and thy herds, and all that thou hast:

11 And there will I nourish thee; for yet there are five years of famine; lest thou, and thy household, and all that thou hast, come to poverty.

12 And, behold, your eyes see, and the eyes of my brother Benjamin, that it is my mouth that speaketh unto you.

13 And ye shall tell my father of all my glory in Egypt, and of all that ye have seen; and ye shall haste and bring down my father hither.

14 And he fell upon his brother Benjamin's neck, and wept; and Benjamin wept upon his neck.

15 Moreover he kissed all his brethren, and wept upon them: and after that his brethren talked with him.

16 And the fame thereof was heard in Pharaoh's house, saying, Joseph's brethren are come: and it pleased Pharaoh well, and his servants.

17 And Pharaoh said unto Joseph, Say unto thy brethren, This do ye; lade your beasts, and go, get you unto the land of Canaan;

18 And take your father and your households, and come unto me: and I will give you the good of the land of Egypt, and ye shall eat the fat of the land.

25 And they went up out of Egypt, and came into the land of Canaan unto Jacob their father,

26 And told him, saying, Joseph is yet alive, and he is governor over all the land of Egypt. And Jacob's heart fainted, for he believed them not.

27 And they told him all the words of Joseph, which he had said unto them: and when he saw the wagons which Joseph had sent to carry him, the spirit of Jacob their father revived:

28 And Israel said, It is enough; Joseph my son is yet alive: I will go and see him before I die.

What reassuring words did Joseph speak when he revealed himself to his brothers? In what ways did Joseph see God's hand in his life? How have you seen God's hand in your own life—even during trials?

65

JACOB ADOPTS EPHRAIM AND MANASSEH
FROM JOSEPH AND BLESSES THEM

In Egypt, Joseph had finally revealed his identity to his brothers and together they rejoiced. Joseph sent them back to Canaan with food, money, clothing, and animals. Jacob could not at first believe that his son Joseph was alive—and a powerful ruler in Egypt—but he soon was convinced. Jacob and his family of about seventy people then began the journey to Egypt, during which God appeared to Jacob and told him to fear not, "for I will there make of thee a great nation" (Genesis 46:3). Joseph journeyed out from Egypt and met his father in Goshen, where they had a tearful reunion, at which Jacob said, "Now let me die, since I have seen thy face, because thou art yet alive" (v. 30). Joseph presented his family to Pharaoh. Jacob blessed Pharaoh, and Pharaoh designated the bounteous land of Goshen as the place Jacob and his family could permanently settle. Meanwhile, the famine continued to rage and Joseph continued to oversee Egypt's survival through the ongoing crisis. Before Jacob died, he desired to bless Joseph's children.

GENESIS 48:1–6, 8–20

And it came to pass after these things, that one told Joseph, Behold, thy father is sick: and he took with him his two sons, Manasseh and Ephraim.

2 And one told Jacob, and said, Behold, thy son Joseph cometh unto thee: and Israel strengthened himself, and sat upon the bed.

3 And Jacob said unto Joseph, God Almighty appeared unto me at Luz in the land of Canaan, and blessed me,

4 And said unto me, Behold, I will make thee fruitful, and multiply thee, and I will make of thee a multitude of people; and will give this land to thy seed after thee for an everlasting possession.

5 And now thy two sons, Ephraim and Manasseh, which were born unto thee in the land of Egypt before I came unto thee into Egypt, are mine; as Reuben and Simeon, they shall be mine.

6 And thy issue, which thou begettest after them, shall be thine, and shall be called after the name of their brethren in their inheritance.

8 And Israel beheld Joseph's sons, and said, Who are these?

9 And Joseph said unto his father, They are my sons, whom God hath given me in this place. And he said, Bring them, I pray thee, unto me, and I will bless them.

10 Now the eyes of Israel were dim for age, so that he could not see. And he brought them near unto him; and he kissed them, and embraced them.

11 And Israel said unto Joseph, I had not thought to see thy face: and, lo, God hath shewed me also thy seed.

12 And Joseph brought them out from between his knees, and he bowed himself with his face to the earth.

13 And Joseph took them both, Ephraim in his right hand toward Israel's left hand, and Manasseh in his left hand toward Israel's right hand, and brought them near unto him.

14 And Israel stretched out his right hand, and laid it upon Ephraim's head, who was the younger, and his left hand upon Manasseh's head, guiding his hands wittingly; for Manasseh was the firstborn.

15 And he blessed Joseph, and said, God, before whom my fathers Abraham and Isaac did walk, the God which fed me all my life long unto this day,

16 The Angel which redeemed me from all evil, bless the lads; and let my name be named on them, and the name of my fathers Abraham and Isaac; and let them grow into a multitude in the midst of the earth.

17 And when Joseph saw that his father laid his right hand upon the head of Ephraim, it displeased him: and he held up his father's hand, to remove it from Ephraim's head unto Manasseh's head.

18 And Joseph said unto his father, Not so, my father: for this is the firstborn; put thy right hand upon his head.

19 And his father refused, and said, I know it, my son, I know it: he also shall become a people, and he also shall be great: but truly his younger brother shall be greater than he, and his seed shall become a multitude of nations.

20 And he blessed them that day, saying, In thee shall Israel bless, saying, God make thee as Ephraim and as Manasseh: and he set Ephraim before Manasseh.

What unexpected blessing did Jacob receive in his old age (see verse 11)? What blessing did Jacob give to his grandsons Ephraim and Manasseh? We are each members of the house of Israel, and we learn which specific tribe we belong to when we receive our patriarchal blessing. Do you know what tribe of Israel you are a part of? What blessings are you given because you belong to the house of Israel?

JOSEPH REPEATS THE FORGIVENESS HE HAS GIVEN HIS BRETHREN AND PROMISES THEM MERCY

Leaving Canaan during the famine, Jacob and his large family had journeyed to Egypt, where Pharaoh designated the nearby land of Goshen as their own. Jacob adopted Joseph's sons Ephraim and Manasseh and simultaneously gave them a blessing, during which he intentionally placed his right hand on Ephraim's head (the youngest) and his left hand on Manasseh's head (the eldest). Joseph attempted to correct his father, but Jacob declared that though Manasseh would be great, "his younger brother shall be greater than he, and his seed shall become a multitude of nations" (Genesis 48:19). Later, Jacob gathered all his sons (the literal children of Israel) and offered descriptions of their traits and spiritual gifts and prophesied of what would become of their individual posterities. Soon after this, Jacob died, was embalmed by the Egyptians according to Joseph's command, and was returned to Canaan for burial.

GENESIS 50:14–26

And Joseph returned into Egypt, he, and his brethren, and all that went up with him to bury his father, after he had buried his father.

15 And when Joseph's brethren saw that their father was dead, they said, Joseph will peradventure hate us, and will certainly requite us all the evil which we did unto him.

16 And they sent a messenger unto Joseph, saying, Thy father did command before he died, saying,

17 So shall ye say unto Joseph, Forgive, I pray thee now, the trespass of thy brethren, and their sin; for they did unto thee evil: and now, we pray thee, forgive the trespass of the servants of the God of thy father. And Joseph wept when they spake unto him.

18 And his brethren also went and fell down before his face; and they said, Behold, we be thy servants.

19 And Joseph said unto them, Fear not: for am I in the place of God?

20 But as for you, ye thought evil against me; but God meant it unto good, to bring to pass, as it is this day, to save much people alive.

21 Now therefore fear ye not: I will nourish you, and your little ones. And he comforted them, and spake kindly unto them.

22 And Joseph dwelt in Egypt, he, and his father's house: and Joseph lived an hundred and ten years.

23 And Joseph saw Ephraim's children of the third generation: the children also of Machir the son of Manasseh were brought up upon Joseph's knees.

24 And Joseph said unto his brethren, I die: and God will surely visit you, and bring you out of this land unto the land which he sware to Abraham, to Isaac, and to Jacob.

25 And Joseph took an oath of the children of Israel, saying, God will surely visit you, and ye shall carry up my bones from hence.

26 So Joseph died, being an hundred and ten years old: and they embalmed him, and he was put in a coffin in Egypt.

Why did Joseph's brothers think he would hate them? How did Joseph react to their concerns? Even though Joseph suffered greatly because of his brothers, Joseph said that "God meant it unto good" (see verse 20). What good things have come to you through challenges and suffering?

JOSEPH PROPHESIES OF TWO OF HIS EVENTUAL DESCENDANTS: MOSES AND JOSEPH SMITH

Joseph lived to be 110 years old, and prior to his death he told his children of a covenant God had made with him that his people would one day be delivered out of Egypt. He also revealed God's promise that two specific prophets would be Joseph's direct descendants. These two prophets—Moses and Joseph Smith—would bless Israel in different time periods by bringing Joseph's descendants to a knowledge of God's covenants.

JOSEPH SMITH TRANSLATION, GENESIS 50:24–33

And Joseph said unto his brethren, I die, and go unto my fathers; and I go down to my grave with joy. The God of my father Jacob be with you, to deliver you out of affliction in the days of your bondage; for the Lord hath visited me, and I have obtained a promise of the Lord, that out of the fruit of my loins, the Lord God will raise up a righteous branch out of my loins; and unto thee, whom my father Jacob hath named Israel, a prophet; (not the Messiah who is called Shilo;) and this prophet shall deliver my people out of Egypt in the days of thy bondage.

25 And it shall come to pass that they shall be scattered again; and a branch shall be broken off, and shall be carried into a far country; nevertheless they shall be remembered in the covenants of the Lord, when the Messiah cometh; for he shall be made manifest unto them in the latter days, in the Spirit of power; and shall bring them out of darkness into light; out of hidden darkness, and out of captivity unto freedom.

26 A seer shall the Lord my God raise up, who shall be a choice seer unto the fruit of my loins.

27 Thus saith the Lord God of my fathers unto me, A choice seer will I raise up out of the fruit of thy loins, and he shall be esteemed highly among the fruit of thy loins; and unto him will I give commandment that he shall do a work for the fruit of thy loins, his brethren.

28 And he shall bring them to the knowledge of the covenants which I have made with thy fathers; and he shall do whatsoever work I shall command him.

29 And I will make him great in mine eyes, for he shall do my work; and he shall be great like unto him whom I have said I would raise up unto you,

to deliver my people, O house of Israel, out of the land of Egypt; for a seer will I raise up to deliver my people out of the land of Egypt; and he shall be called Moses. And by this name he shall know that he is of thy house; for he shall be nursed by the king's daughter, and shall be called her son.

30 And again, a seer will I raise up out of the fruit of thy loins, and unto him will I give power to bring forth my word unto the seed of thy loins; and not to the bringing forth of my word only, saith the Lord, but to the convincing them of my word, which shall have already gone forth among them in the last days;

31 Wherefore the fruit of thy loins shall write, and the fruit of the loins of Judah shall write; and that which shall be written by the fruit of thy loins, and also that which shall be written by the fruit of the loins of Judah, shall grow together unto the confounding of false doctrines, and laying down of contentions, and establishing peace among the fruit of thy loins, and bringing them to a knowledge of their fathers in the latter days; and also to the knowledge of my covenants, saith the Lord.

32 And out of weakness shall he be made strong, in that day when my work shall go forth among all my people, which shall restore them, who are of the house of Israel, in the last days.

33 And that seer will I bless, and they that seek to destroy him shall be confounded; for this promise I give unto you; for I will remember you from generation to generation; and his name shall be called Joseph, and it shall be after the name of his father; and he shall be like unto you; for the thing which the Lord shall bring forth by his hand shall bring my people unto salvation.

What were the names of the two prophets who would be descendants of Joseph? According to these verses, what works would they accomplish? Consider verse 28. How is God bringing people today to a knowledge of the covenants He made with their ancestors?

MOSES IS HIDDEN AS A BABY, IS RAISED IN PHARAOH'S HOUSE, THEN FLEES TO MIDIAN

It was now about 2,700 years since the time of Adam, and about 1,300 years before the birth of Jesus Christ. Joseph had saved Egypt—and his father's family—from the devastating famine. Pharaoh had given the nearby land of Goshen to Jacob and his posterity, who were known as the children of Israel or, beginning at this point in the biblical record, the Hebrews. In time, Joseph and all those of his generation died, after which "there arose up a new king over Egypt, which knew not Joseph" (Exodus 1:8). The new Pharaoh recognized that the Hebrews were growing larger in number and strength than the Egyptians and worried that they would one day overpower them. Pharaoh thus brought the Hebrews into slavery and commanded the midwives to kill all newborn Hebrew males—though the midwives secretly defied Pharaoh. The Hebrews lived under these harsh conditions for over four hundred years, at which time God raised up a prophet from among them to free them from bondage.

EXODUS 2:1–25

And there went a man of the house of Levi, and took to wife a daughter of Levi.

2 And the woman conceived, and bare a son: and when she saw him that he was a goodly child, she hid him three months.

3 And when she could not longer hide him, she took for him an ark of bulrushes, and daubed it with slime and with pitch, and put the child therein; and she laid it in the flags by the river's brink.

4 And his sister stood afar off, to wit what would be done to him.

5 And the daughter of Pharaoh came down to wash herself at the river; and her maidens walked along by the river's side; and when she saw the ark among the flags, she sent her maid to fetch it.

6 And when she had opened it, she saw the child: and, behold, the babe wept. And she had compassion on him, and said, This is one of the Hebrews' children.

7 Then said his sister to Pharaoh's daughter, Shall I go and call to thee a nurse of the Hebrew women, that she may nurse the child for thee?

8 And Pharaoh's daughter said to her, Go. And the maid went and called the child's mother.

9 And Pharaoh's daughter said unto her, Take this child away, and nurse it for me, and I will give thee thy wages. And the woman took the child, and nursed it.

10 And the child grew, and she brought him unto Pharaoh's daughter, and he became her son. And she called his name Moses: and she said, Because I drew him out of the water.

11 And it came to pass in those days, when Moses was grown, that he went out unto his brethren, and looked on their burdens: and he spied an Egyptian smiting an Hebrew, one of his brethren.

12 And he looked this way and that way, and when he saw that there was no man, he slew the Egyptian, and hid him in the sand.

13 And when he went out the second day, behold, two men of the Hebrews strove together: and he said to him that did the wrong, Wherefore smitest thou thy fellow?

14 And he said, Who made thee a prince and a judge over us? intendest thou to kill me, as thou killedst the Egyptian? And Moses feared, and said, Surely this thing is known.

15 Now when Pharaoh heard this thing, he sought to slay Moses. But Moses fled from the face of Pharaoh, and dwelt in the land of Midian: and he sat down by a well.

16 Now the priest of Midian had seven daughters: and they came and drew water, and filled the troughs to water their father's flock.

17 And the shepherds came and drove them away: but Moses stood up and helped them, and watered their flock.

18 And when they came to Reuel their father, he said, How is it that ye are come so soon to day?

19 And they said, An Egyptian delivered us out of the hand of the shepherds, and also drew water enough for us, and watered the flock.

20 And he said unto his daughters, And where is he? why is it that ye have left the man? call him, that he may eat bread.

21 And Moses was content to dwell with the man: and he gave Moses Zipporah his daughter.

22 And she bare him a son, and he called his name Gershom: for he said, I have been a stranger in a strange land.

23 And it came to pass in process of time, that the king of Egypt died: and the children of Israel sighed by reason of the bondage, and they cried, and their cry came up unto God by reason of the bondage.

24 And God heard their groaning, and God remembered his covenant with Abraham, with Isaac, and with Jacob.

25 And God looked upon the children of Israel, and God had respect unto them.

What efforts did Moses's family take to save him as a baby? Why did Moses suddenly flee from Egypt? (see verses 11–15). Consider verses 23–24. When have you cried unto God in prayer? Consider sharing an experience when you felt that God heard your prayer and remembered you.

MOSES WITNESSES A BURNING BUSH AND RECEIVES GOD'S CALL TO DELIVER THE HEBREWS FROM BONDAGE

The children of Israel had been in bondage to the Egyptians for over four hundred years. Moses, a Hebrew, was hidden as a baby to be kept safe and was then raised in Pharaoh's house. When he was grown, Moses witnessed an Egyptian taskmaster beating a Hebrew slave. Moses intervened and killed the Egyptian, then fled to Midian, where he married Zipporah, who gave birth to a son named Gershom.

EXODUS 3:1–15, 19–22

Now Moses kept the flock of Jethro his father in law, the priest of Midian: and he led the flock to the backside of the desert, and came to the mountain of God, even to Horeb.

2 And the angel of the Lord appeared unto him in a flame of fire out of the midst of a bush: and he looked, and, behold, the bush burned with fire, and the bush was not consumed.

3 And Moses said, I will now turn aside, and see this great sight, why the bush is not burnt.

4 And when the Lord saw that he turned aside to see, God called unto him out of the midst of the

bush, and said, Moses, Moses. And he said, Here am I.

5 And he said, Draw not nigh hither: put off thy shoes from off thy feet, for the place whereon thou standest is holy ground.

6 Moreover he said, I am the God of thy father, the God of Abraham, the God of Isaac, and the God of Jacob. And Moses hid his face; for he was afraid to look upon God.

7 And the Lord said, I have surely seen the affliction of my people which are in Egypt, and have heard their cry by reason of their taskmasters; for I know their sorrows;

8 And I am come down to deliver them out of the hand of the Egyptians, and to bring them up out of that land unto a good land and a large, unto a land flowing with milk and honey; unto the place of the Canaanites, and the Hittites, and the Amorites, and the Perizzites, and the Hivites, and the Jebusites.

9 Now therefore, behold, the cry of the children of Israel is come unto me: and I have also seen the oppression wherewith the Egyptians oppress them.

10 Come now therefore, and I will send thee unto Pharaoh, that thou mayest bring forth my people the children of Israel out of Egypt.

11 And Moses said unto God, Who am I, that I should go unto Pharaoh, and that I should bring forth the children of Israel out of Egypt?

12 And he said, Certainly I will be with thee; and this shall be a token unto thee, that I have sent thee: When thou hast brought forth the people out of Egypt, ye shall serve God upon this mountain.

13 And Moses said unto God, Behold, when I come unto the children of Israel, and shall say unto them, The God of your fathers hath sent me unto you; and they shall say to me, What is his name? what shall I say unto them?

14 And God said unto Moses, I AM THAT I AM: and he said, Thus shalt thou say unto the children of Israel, I AM hath sent me unto you.

15 And God said moreover unto Moses, Thus shalt thou say unto the children of Israel, The Lord God of your fathers, the God of Abraham, the God of Isaac, and the God of Jacob, hath sent me unto you: this is my name for ever, and this is my memorial unto all generations.

19 And I am sure that the king of Egypt will not let you go, no, not by a mighty hand.

20 And I will stretch out my hand, and smite Egypt with all my wonders which I will do in the midst thereof: and after that he will let you go.

21 And I will give this people favour in the sight of the Egyptians: and it shall come to pass, that, when ye go, ye shall not go empty:

22 But every woman shall borrow of her neighbour, and of her that sojourneth in her house, jewels of silver, and jewels of gold, and raiment: and ye shall put them upon your sons, and upon your daughters; and ye shall spoil the Egyptians.

What titles did God use to describe Himself when He spoke to Moses? What do those titles teach you about His character? In these verses, what message did God command Moses to deliver to the people (see verses 17–22)? In verse 7, God told Moses that He knew the sorrows of His people. How does God know your sorrows? How does knowing that make you feel?

GOD GRANTS MOSES THE ABILITY TO PERFORM MIRACULOUS SIGNS AND CALLS AARON AS HIS SPOKESMAN

Moses had fled from Egypt and lived in Midian, where he began a family. God told Moses that He had seen the afflictions of the children of Israel who were in bondage to the Egyptians and that He would send Moses to Pharaoh and demand the people be freed. Moses protested the calling, saying, "Who am I, that I should . . . bring forth the children of Israel out of Egypt?" (Exodus 3:11). God commanded Moses to tell the people he was sent by God Himself and assured Moses that his words would be fulfilled.

EXODUS 4:1–17, 27–31

And Moses answered and said, But, behold, they will not believe me, nor hearken unto my voice: for they will say, The Lord hath not appeared unto thee.

2 And the Lord said unto him, What is that in thine hand? And he said, A rod.

3 And he said, Cast it on the ground. And he cast it on the ground, and it became a serpent; and Moses fled from before it.

4 And the Lord said unto Moses, Put forth thine hand, and take it by the tail. And he put forth his hand, and caught it, and it became a rod in his hand:

5 That they may believe that the Lord God of their fathers, the God of Abraham, the God of Isaac, and the God of Jacob, hath appeared unto thee.

6 And the Lord said furthermore unto him, Put now thine hand into thy bosom. And he put his hand into his bosom: and when he took it out, behold, his hand was leprous as snow.

7 And he said, Put thine hand into thy bosom again. And he put his hand into his bosom again; and plucked it out of his bosom, and, behold, it was turned again as his other flesh.

8 And it shall come to pass, if they will not believe thee, neither hearken to the voice of the first sign, that they will believe the voice of the latter sign.

9 And it shall come to pass, if they will not believe also these two signs, neither hearken unto thy voice, that thou shalt take of the water of the river, and pour it upon the dry land: and the water which thou takest out of the river shall become blood upon the dry land.

10 And Moses said unto the Lord, O my Lord, I am not eloquent, neither heretofore, nor since thou hast spoken unto thy servant: but I am slow of speech, and of a slow tongue.

11 And the Lord said unto him, Who hath made man's mouth? or who maketh the dumb, or deaf, or the seeing, or the blind? have not I the Lord?

12 Now therefore go, and I will be with thy mouth, and teach thee what thou shalt say.

13 And he said, O my Lord, send, I pray thee, by the hand of him whom thou wilt send.

14 And the anger of the Lord was kindled against Moses, and he said, Is not Aaron the Levite thy brother? I know that he can speak well. And also, behold, he cometh forth to meet thee: and when he seeth thee, he will be glad in his heart.

15 And thou shalt speak unto him, and put words in his mouth: and I will be with thy mouth, and with his mouth, and will teach you what ye shall do.

16 And he shall be thy spokesman unto the people: and he shall be, even he shall be to thee instead of a mouth, and thou shalt be to him instead of God.

17 And thou shalt take this rod in thine hand, wherewith thou shalt do signs.

27 And the Lord said to Aaron, Go into the wilderness to meet Moses. And he went, and met him in the mount of God, and kissed him.

28 And Moses told Aaron all the words of the Lord who had sent him, and all the signs which he had commanded him.

29 And Moses and Aaron went and gathered together all the elders of the children of Israel:

30 And Aaron spake all the words which the Lord had spoken unto Moses, and did the signs in the sight of the people.

31 And the people believed: and when they heard that the Lord had visited the children of Israel, and that he had looked upon their affliction, then they bowed their heads and worshipped.

What three signs did God tell Moses to give the people, by which they would know he was called by God? According to verse 10, why was Moses worried about being a spokesman for God? Whom did the Lord send to help Moses? Consider some of your own weaknesses. How can the Lord help you overcome your weaknesses?

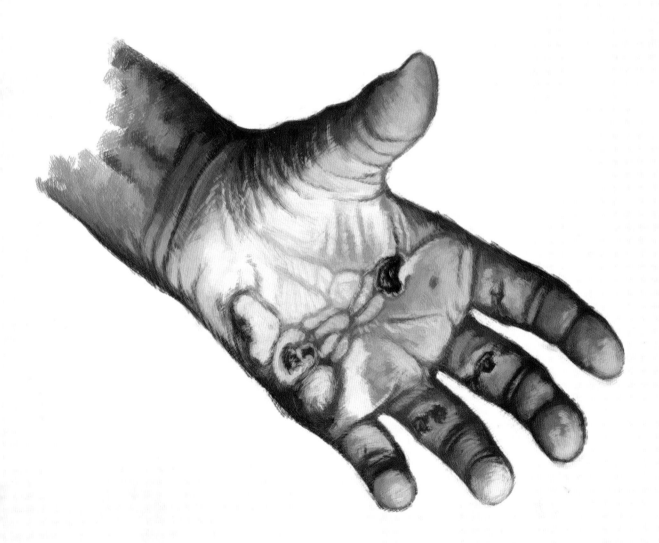

MOSES DEMANDS THAT PHARAOH FREE THE HEBREWS; PHARAOH MOCKS GOD AND INCREASES THE BURDENS PLACED UPON THE HEBREWS

God spoke to Moses and called him to appear before Pharaoh to demand that the Hebrews be freed from bondage. Moses initially protested his calling, but God granted him the ability to perform miraculous signs and called Aaron as his spokesman. Moses and Aaron then "gathered together all the elders of the children of Israel" (Exodus 4:29), showed them miraculous signs, and made known to them God's command that Israel be freed. In these verses, the word "tale" means a quota or a total, as in the total number of bricks (used for building) the Hebrews were required to produce.

EXODUS 5:1–23

And afterward Moses and Aaron went in, and told Pharaoh, Thus saith the Lord God of Israel, Let my people go, that they may hold a feast unto me in the wilderness.

2 And Pharaoh said, Who is the Lord, that I should obey his voice to let Israel go? I know not the Lord, neither will I let Israel go.

3 And they said, The God of the Hebrews hath met with us: let us go, we pray thee, three days' journey into the desert, and sacrifice unto the Lord our God; lest he fall upon us with pestilence, or with the sword.

4 And the king of Egypt said unto them, Wherefore do ye, Moses and Aaron, let the people from their works? get you unto your burdens.

5 And Pharaoh said, Behold, the people of the land now are many, and ye make them rest from their burdens.

6 And Pharaoh commanded the same day the taskmasters of the people, and their officers, saying,

7 Ye shall no more give the people straw to make brick, as heretofore: let them go and gather straw for themselves.

8 And the tale of the bricks, which they did make heretofore, ye shall lay upon them; ye shall not diminish ought thereof: for they be idle; therefore they cry, saying, Let us go and sacrifice to our God.

9 Let there more work be laid upon the men, that they may labour therein; and let them not regard vain words.

10 And the taskmasters of the people went out, and their officers, and they spake to the people, saying, Thus saith Pharaoh, I will not give you straw.

11 Go ye, get you straw where ye can find it: yet not ought of your work shall be diminished.

12 So the people were scattered abroad throughout all the land of Egypt to gather stubble instead of straw.

13 And the taskmasters hasted them, saying, Fulfil your works, your daily tasks, as when there was straw.

14 And the officers of the children of Israel, which Pharaoh's taskmasters had set over them, were beaten, and demanded, Wherefore have ye not fulfilled your task in making brick both yesterday and to day, as heretofore?

15 Then the officers of the children of Israel came and cried unto Pharaoh, saying, Wherefore dealest thou thus with thy servants?

16 There is no straw given unto thy servants, and they say to us, Make brick: and, behold, thy servants are beaten; but the fault is in thine own people.

17 But he said, Ye are idle, ye are idle: therefore ye say, Let us go and do sacrifice to the Lord.

18 Go therefore now, and work; for there shall no straw be given you, yet shall ye deliver the tale of bricks.

19 And the officers of the children of Israel did see that they were in evil case, after it was said, Ye shall not minish ought from your bricks of your daily task.

20 And they met Moses and Aaron, who stood in the way, as they came forth from Pharaoh:

21 And they said unto them, The Lord look upon you, and judge; because ye have made our savour to be abhorred in the eyes of Pharaoh, and in the eyes of his servants, to put a sword in their hand to slay us.

22 And Moses returned unto the Lord, and said, Lord, wherefore hast thou so evil entreated this people? why is it that thou hast sent me?

23 For since I came to Pharaoh to speak in thy name, he hath done evil to this people; neither hast thou delivered thy people at all.

What was Pharaoh's response to Moses's request that the children of Israel be freed? What did the Israelites say to Moses after their workloads were increased? Why might people who are trying to do the right thing sometimes experience suffering?

THE LORD POWERFULLY DECLARES HIS IDENTITY AND REAFFIRMS HIS COVENANT WITH ISRAEL

Moses and Aaron had appeared before Pharaoh and demanded that the Hebrews be freed from bondage so they could serve God. Pharaoh scoffed at the request, mocked God, and decreed that the Hebrews would have to find their own source of straw in the process of their brick-making duties—without any lowering of the number of bricks they were required to produce. For many generations, the Hebrews' burdens had been terribly oppressive. Now they became even worse. Some of the Hebrews protested to Moses and Aaron that their efforts to free them had only backfired. Moses took these same concerns to the Lord, saying, "For since I came to Pharaoh to speak in thy name, he hath done evil to this people; neither hast thou delivered thy people at all" (Exodus 5:23).

EXODUS 6:1–13; JOSEPH SMITH TRANSLATION, EXODUS 6:3

Then the Lord said unto Moses, Now shalt thou see what I will do to Pharaoh: for with a strong hand shall he let them go, and with a strong hand shall he drive them out of his land.

2 And God spake unto Moses, and said unto him, I am the Lord:

3 And I appeared unto Abraham, unto Isaac, and unto Jacob, *I am the Lord God Almighty; the Lord JEHOVAH. And was not my name known unto them?*

4 And I have also established my covenant with them, to give them the land of Canaan, the land of their pilgrimage, wherein they were strangers.

5 And I have also heard the groaning of the children of Israel, whom the Egyptians keep in bondage; and I have remembered my covenant.

6 Wherefore say unto the children of Israel, I am the Lord, and I will bring you out from under the burdens of the Egyptians, and I will rid you out of their bondage, and I will redeem you with a stretched out arm, and with great judgments:

7 And I will take you to me for a people, and I will be to you a God: and ye shall know that I am the Lord your God, which bringeth you out from under the burdens of the Egyptians.

8 And I will bring you in unto the land, concerning the which I did swear to give it to Abraham, to Isaac, and to Jacob; and I will give it you for an heritage: I am the Lord.

9 And Moses spake so unto the children of Israel: but they hearkened not unto Moses for anguish of spirit, and for cruel bondage.

10 And the Lord spake unto Moses, saying,

11 Go in, speak unto Pharaoh king of Egypt, that he let the children of Israel go out of his land.

12 And Moses spake before the Lord, saying, Behold, the children of Israel have not hearkened unto me; how then shall Pharaoh hear me, who am of uncircumcised lips?

13 And the Lord spake unto Moses and unto Aaron, and gave them a charge unto the children of Israel, and unto Pharaoh king of Egypt, to bring the children of Israel out of the land of Egypt.

What assurances did God tell Moses to give to the children of Israel? Consider verse 5, in which God declares, "I have remembered my covenant." What covenants has God made with you personally? How can you remember those covenants and better live them? Consider verse 7. What does it mean to be God's people?

MOSES SMITES THE WATERS OF EGYPT, TURNING THEM TO BLOOD

Moses and Aaron had obeyed God's commandment and demanded that Pharaoh free the Hebrews. But Pharaoh had scoffed at them, mocked God, and multiplied the burdens placed upon the Hebrews. Moses protested to God that things were only getting worse, after which God powerfully declared His divine identity, reaffirmed the covenant He had made with Israel, and again commanded Moses and Aaron to appear before Pharaoh and demand the Hebrews be freed.

Exodus 7:8–12, 14–17, 20–24

And the Lord spake unto Moses and unto Aaron, saying,

9 When Pharaoh shall speak unto you, saying, Shew a miracle for you: then thou shalt say unto Aaron, Take thy rod, and cast it before Pharaoh, and it shall become a serpent.

10 And Moses and Aaron went in unto Pharaoh, and they did so as the Lord had commanded: and Aaron cast down his rod before Pharaoh, and before his servants, and it became a serpent.

11 Then Pharaoh also called the wise men and the sorcerers: now the magicians of Egypt, they also did in like manner with their enchantments.

12 For they cast down every man his rod, and they became serpents: but Aaron's rod swallowed up their rods.

14 And the Lord said unto Moses, Pharaoh's heart is hardened, he refuseth to let the people go.

15 Get thee unto Pharaoh in the morning; lo, he goeth out unto the water; and thou shalt stand by the river's brink against he come; and the rod which was turned to a serpent shalt thou take in thine hand.

16 And thou shalt say unto him, The Lord God of the Hebrews hath sent me unto thee, saying, Let my people go, that they may serve me in the wilderness: and, behold, hitherto thou wouldest not hear.

17 Thus saith the Lord, In this thou shalt know that I am the Lord: behold, I will smite with the rod that is in mine hand upon the waters which are in the river, and they shall be turned to blood.

20 And Moses and Aaron did so, as the Lord commanded; and he lifted up the rod, and smote the waters that were in the river, in the sight of Pharaoh, and in the sight of his servants; and all the waters that were in the river were turned to blood.

21 And the fish that was in the river died; and the river stank, and the Egyptians could not drink of the water of the river; and there was blood throughout all the land of Egypt.

22 And the magicians of Egypt did so with their enchantments: and Pharaoh's heart was hardened, neither did he hearken unto them; as the Lord had said.

23 And Pharaoh turned and went into his house, neither did he set his heart to this also.

24 And all the Egyptians digged round about the river for water to drink; for they could not drink of the water of the river.

What miracles did Moses and Aaron perform before Pharaoh? Why would Pharaoh not allow the children of Israel to leave, even after he saw these miracles? What can you do to ensure you don't harden your heart against God?

MOSES SMITES EGYPT WITH ADDITIONAL PLAGUES; THE LORD INSTITUTES THE FEAST OF THE PASSOVER

Moses and Aaron had returned to Pharaoh and turned the water throughout the region to blood—a sign by which Pharaoh would know that they acted in the name of God. But Pharaoh's magicians were able to replicate the same sign, and Pharaoh refused to let the Hebrews go. At God's command, Moses and Aaron then smote Egypt with plagues of frogs, lice, and flies. Pharaoh's magicians could replicate the plague of frogs, but not that of lice and flies, prompting them to acknowledge to Pharaoh that this was the work of God. Through it all, Pharaoh repeated a cycle in which he promised to free the Hebrews, only to later refuse. Moses then cursed the Egyptian cattle to die, followed by boils upon the people, then hail and fire to rain down from heaven. In each case, the Hebrews were spared the effects of the plagues, but the Egyptians were greatly afflicted. Pharaoh's advisers begged him to free the Hebrews, as Egypt itself was slowly being destroyed. Finally, Moses called upon plagues of locusts and a thick darkness to cover the Egyptian lands. Pharaoh then refused to speak with Moses and cast him out of his presence.

Exodus 12:1–3, 5–8, 11–14

And the Lord spake unto Moses and Aaron in the land of Egypt, saying,

2 This month shall be unto you the beginning of months: it shall be the first month of the year to you.

3 Speak ye unto all the congregation of Israel, saying, In the tenth day of this month they shall take to them every man a lamb, according to the house of their fathers, a lamb for an house:

5 Your lamb shall be without blemish, a male of the first year: ye shall take it out from the sheep, or from the goats:

6 And ye shall keep it up until the fourteenth day of the same month: and the whole assembly of the congregation of Israel shall kill it in the evening.

7 And they shall take of the blood, and strike it on the two side posts and on the upper door post of the houses, wherein they shall eat it.

8 And they shall eat the flesh in that night, roast with fire, and unleavened bread; and with bitter herbs they shall eat it.

11 And thus shall ye eat it; with your loins girded, your shoes on your feet, and your staff in your hand; and ye shall eat it in haste: it is the Lord's passover.

12 For I will pass through the land of Egypt this night, and will smite all the firstborn in the land of Egypt, both man and beast; and against all the gods of Egypt I will execute judgment: I am the Lord.

13 And the blood shall be to you for a token upon the houses where ye are: and when I see the blood, I will pass over you, and the plague shall not be upon you to destroy you, when I smite the land of Egypt.

14 And this day shall be unto you for a memorial; and ye shall keep it a feast to the Lord throughout your generations; ye shall keep it a feast by an ordinance for ever.

Note: The Feast of the Passover would annually be observed by the children of Israel from that time forward, even to the time of Jesus Christ, who Himself attended the Feast of the Passover in Jerusalem.

What type of animal was to be sacrificed for the Feast of the Passover, and what were the people to do with the blood of this animal? How did this sacrifice point the children of Israel to the eventual sacrifice of Jesus Christ? What symbols do we have in the Church today to help us remember Jesus Christ?

THE DESTROYING ANGEL PASSES THROUGH
EGYPT, AND ISRAEL IS FREED

Moses had repeatedly demanded that Pharaoh free the Hebrews from bondage, but Pharaoh repeatedly refused. God sent plagues upon the Egyptians, destroying their water supplies, lands, crops, and cattle. God then gave detailed instructions to Moses for what would come to be known as the Feast of the Passover. While giving the instructions to Moses, God declared that on that night, He would "pass through" the land, smiting the firstborn of all men and beasts, but that he would "pass over" the houses marked with the blood of an unblemished lamb upon the doorframes. Moses then repeated these instructions to all Hebrews.

Exodus 12:21–42

Then Moses called for all the elders of Israel, and said unto them, Draw out and take you a lamb according to your families, and kill the passover.

22 And ye shall take a bunch of hyssop, and dip it in the blood that is in the basin, and strike the lintel and the two side posts with the blood that is in the basin; and none of you shall go out at the door of his house until the morning.

23 For the Lord will pass through to smite the Egyptians; and when he seeth the blood upon the lintel, and on the two side posts, the Lord will pass over the door, and will not suffer the destroyer to come in unto your houses to smite you.

24 And ye shall observe this thing for an ordinance to thee and to thy sons for ever.

25 And it shall come to pass, when ye be come to the land which the Lord will give you, according as he hath promised, that ye shall keep this service.

26 And it shall come to pass, when your children shall say unto you, What mean ye by this service?

27 That ye shall say, It is the sacrifice of the Lord's passover, who passed over the houses of the children of Israel in Egypt, when he smote the Egyptians, and delivered our houses. And the people bowed the head and worshipped.

28 And the children of Israel went away, and did as the Lord had commanded Moses and Aaron, so did they.

29 And it came to pass, that at midnight the Lord smote all the firstborn in the land of Egypt, from the firstborn of Pharaoh that sat on his throne unto the firstborn of the captive that was in the dungeon; and all the firstborn of cattle.

30 And Pharaoh rose up in the night, he, and all his servants, and all the Egyptians; and there was a great cry in Egypt; for there was not a house where there was not one dead.

31 And he called for Moses and Aaron by night, and said, Rise up, and get you forth from among my people, both ye and the children of Israel; and go, serve the Lord, as ye have said.

32 Also take your flocks and your herds, as ye have said, and be gone; and bless me also.

33 And the Egyptians were urgent upon the people, that they might send them out of the land in haste; for they said, We be all dead men.

34 And the people took their dough before it was leavened, their kneadingtroughs being bound up in their clothes upon their shoulders.

35 And the children of Israel did according to the word of Moses; and they borrowed of the Egyptians jewels of silver, and jewels of gold, and raiment:

36 And the Lord gave the people favour in the sight of the Egyptians, so that they lent unto them such things as they required. And they spoiled the Egyptians.

37 And the children of Israel journeyed from Rameses to Succoth, about six hundred thousand on foot that were men, beside children.

38 And a mixed multitude went up also with them; and flocks, and herds, even very much cattle.

39 And they baked unleavened cakes of the dough which they brought forth out of Egypt, for it was not leavened; because they were thrust out of Egypt, and could not tarry, neither had they prepared for themselves any victual.

40 Now the sojourning of the children of Israel, who dwelt in Egypt, was four hundred and thirty years.

41 And it came to pass at the end of the four hundred and thirty years, even the selfsame day it came to pass, that all the hosts of the Lord went out from the land of Egypt.

42 It is a night to be much observed unto the Lord for bringing them out from the land of Egypt: this is that night of the Lord to be observed of all the children of Israel in their generations.

What plague finally convinced Pharaoh to let the children of Israel go? The children of Israel were commanded to observe the Feast of the Passover in order to remember God's miracle in freeing them from Egypt. What blessings do we receive from remembering the miracles God has performed for us? What ordinances or traditions do you take part in that help you remember God and His miracles?

MOSES PARTS THE RED SEA AS THE CHILDREN OF ISRAEL ESCAPE THE PURSUING EGYPTIANS

After a series of devastating plagues that culminated in the death of the firstborn of all Egyptian houses, Pharaoh finally allowed the children of Israel to depart the land of Egypt. As they exited the land, "the Lord went before them by day in a pillar of a cloud, to lead them the way; and by night in a pillar of fire, to give them light" (Exodus 13:21). And "Moses took the bones of Joseph with him" (v. 19) in fulfillment of Joseph's prophecy that he would be laid to rest in Canaan. The children of Israel were a massive group—about 600,000 men alone (see Exodus 12:37). Moving such a large group even a short distance likely took great effort and time. As their journey commenced, Pharaoh and his servants became angry that their source of slave labor would be gone forever (see Map #1, B2 and B3).

Exodus 14:5–7, 10–31; Joseph Smith Translation, Exodus 14:17, 20

And it was told the king of Egypt that the people fled: and the heart of Pharaoh and of his servants was turned against the people, and they said, Why have we done this, that we have let Israel go from serving us?

6 And he made ready his chariot, and took his people with him:

7 And he took six hundred chosen chariots, and all the chariots of Egypt, and captains over every one of them.

10 And when Pharaoh drew nigh, the children of Israel lifted up their eyes, and, behold, the Egyptians marched after them; and they were sore afraid: and the children of Israel cried out unto the Lord.

11 And they said unto Moses, Because there were no graves in Egypt, hast thou taken us away to die in the wilderness? wherefore hast thou dealt thus with us, to carry us forth out of Egypt?

12 Is not this the word that we did tell thee in Egypt, saying, Let us alone, that we may serve the Egyptians? For it had been better for us to serve the Egyptians, than that we should die in the wilderness.

13 And Moses said unto the people, Fear ye not, stand still, and see the salvation of the Lord, which he will shew to you to day: for the Egyptians whom ye have seen to day, ye shall see them again no more for ever.

14 The Lord shall fight for you, and ye shall hold your peace.

15 And the Lord said unto Moses, Wherefore criest thou unto me? speak unto the children of Israel, that they go forward:

16 But lift thou up thy rod, and stretch out thine hand over the sea, and divide it: and the children of Israel shall go on dry ground through the midst of the sea.

17 *And I say unto thee the hearts of the Egyptians shall be hardened,* and they shall follow them: and I will get me honour upon Pharaoh, and upon all his host, upon his chariots, and upon his horsemen.

18 And the Egyptians shall know that I am the Lord, when I have gotten me honour upon Pharaoh, upon his chariots, and upon his horsemen.

19 And the angel of God, which went before the camp of Israel, removed and went behind them; and the pillar of the cloud went from before their face, and stood behind them:

20 And it came between the camp of the Egyptians and the camp of Israel; *and it was a cloud and darkness to the Egyptians, but it gave light by night to the Israelites:* so that the one came not near the other all the night.

21 And Moses stretched out his hand over the sea; and the Lord caused the sea to go back by a strong east wind all that night, and made the sea dry land, and the waters were divided.

22 And the children of Israel went into the midst of the sea upon the dry ground: and the waters

were a wall unto them on their right hand, and on their left.

23 And the Egyptians pursued, and went in after them to the midst of the sea, even all Pharaoh's horses, his chariots, and his horsemen.

24 And it came to pass, that in the morning watch the Lord looked unto the host of the Egyptians through the pillar of fire and of the cloud, and troubled the host of the Egyptians,

25 And took off their chariot wheels, that they drave them heavily: so that the Egyptians said, Let us flee from the face of Israel; for the Lord fighteth for them against the Egyptians.

26 And the Lord said unto Moses, Stretch out thine hand over the sea, that the waters may come again upon the Egyptians, upon their chariots, and upon their horsemen.

27 And Moses stretched forth his hand over the sea, and the sea returned to his strength when the morning appeared; and the Egyptians fled against it; and the Lord overthrew the Egyptians in the midst of the sea.

28 And the waters returned, and covered the chariots, and the horsemen, and all the host of Pharaoh that came into the sea after them; there remained not so much as one of them.

29 But the children of Israel walked upon dry land in the midst of the sea; and the waters were a wall unto them on their right hand, and on their left.

30 Thus the Lord saved Israel that day out of the hand of the Egyptians; and Israel saw the Egyptians dead upon the sea shore.

31 And Israel saw that great work which the Lord did upon the Egyptians: and the people feared the Lord, and believed the Lord, and his servant Moses.

According to verses 11 and 12, how did the Israelites react when they saw the Egyptians following them? How did Moses respond to them? What miracle allowed the children of Israel to escape as the Egyptians pursued them? Consider Moses's promise in verse 14 that "the Lord shall fight for you." Share an example of how the Lord has fought for you.

GOD PROVIDES FOOD FOR THE ISRAELITES
WITH MANNA FROM HEAVEN

Moses had parted the Red Sea, allowing the children of Israel to escape the pursuing Egyptians, whose captains and chariots were swallowed up in the sea. Abraham, Isaac, and Jacob's descendants were now finally and fully free from over four hundred years of slavery. The people sang praises to God and danced with joy. God covenanted with the Israelites that if they would obey His commandments, they would not suffer from the diseases that had plagued the Egyptians, declaring, "For I am the Lord that healeth thee" (Exodus 15:26). When God had first appeared to Moses, He promised to lead the people to "a land flowing with milk and honey" (Exodus 3:17). That journey had finally begun, but it would take many years, and new challenges quickly arose for the hundreds of thousands of men, women, and children who had need of food and water. In these verses, a "flesh pot" is a large pot of food, and "hoar frost" is thick, white frost that forms on the ground.

EXODUS 16:1–5, 12–14, 21–23, 30–31, 35

And they took their journey from Elim, and all the congregation of the children of Israel came unto the wilderness of Sin, which is between Elim and Sinai, on the fifteenth day of the second month after their departing out of the land of Egypt.

2 And the whole congregation of the children of Israel murmured against Moses and Aaron in the wilderness:

3 And the children of Israel said unto them, Would to God we had died by the hand of the Lord in the land of Egypt, when we sat by the flesh pots, and when we did eat bread to the full; for ye have brought us forth into this wilderness, to kill this whole assembly with hunger.

4 Then said the Lord unto Moses, Behold, I will rain bread from heaven for you; and the people shall go out and gather a certain rate every day, that I may prove them, whether they will walk in my law, or no.

5 And it shall come to pass, that on the sixth day they shall prepare that which they bring in; and it shall be twice as much as they gather daily.

12 I have heard the murmurings of the children of Israel: speak unto them, saying, At even ye shall eat flesh, and in the morning ye shall be filled with bread; and ye shall know that I am the Lord your God.

13 And it came to pass, that at even the quails came up, and covered the camp: and in the morning the dew lay round about the host.

14 And when the dew that lay was gone up, behold, upon the face of the wilderness there lay a small round thing, as small as the hoar frost on the ground.

21 And they gathered it every morning, every man according to his eating: and when the sun waxed hot, it melted.

22 And it came to pass, that on the sixth day they gathered twice as much bread, two omers for one man: and all the rulers of the congregation came and told Moses.

23 And he said unto them, This is that which the Lord hath said, To morrow is the rest of the holy sabbath unto the Lord: bake that which ye will bake to day, and seethe that ye will seethe; and that which remaineth over lay up for you to be kept until the morning.

30 So the people rested on the seventh day.

31 And the house of Israel called the name thereof Manna: and it was like coriander seed, white; and the taste of it was like wafers made with honey.

35 And the children of Israel did eat manna forty years, until they came to a land inhabited; they did eat manna, until they came unto the borders of the land of Canaan.

Why did the children of Israel complain to Moses after they had been freed from Egypt? In response, what two miracles did God perform for them? In what ways has God blessed you when you have been suffering? How have you seen God's power in your life?

JETHRO COUNSELS MOSES TO DELEGATE MANY OF HIS LEADERSHIP RESPONSIBILITIES

As the Israelites began their journey toward the promised land, they complained of hunger, so God provided them with quail and manna to eat. Later they were thirsty and complained bitterly to Moses, who feared the people were angry enough to kill him. At God's command, Moses struck a rock with his staff and water spilled from the rock for the people to drink. As their journey continued, the army of Amalek waged a battle against the Israelites, who sent forth men in defense. During the battle, Moses stood atop a hill. When his hands were raised, Israel prevailed. But as the battle continued, Moses became weary, and as he lowered his hands, Amalek began winning. Aaron and Hur then stood beside Moses and held up his hands for the duration of the battle until Israel was victorious. Later, Moses was met by his father-in-law, Jethro, who provided valuable instruction on how to handle the daily challenges that arose among the Israelites.

Exodus 18:13–26

And it came to pass on the morrow, that Moses sat to judge the people: and the people stood by Moses from the morning unto the evening.

14 And when Moses' father in law saw all that he did to the people, he said, What is this thing that thou doest to the people? why sittest thou thyself alone, and all the people stand by thee from morning unto even?

15 And Moses said unto his father in law, Because the people come unto me to inquire of God:

16 When they have a matter, they come unto me; and I judge between one and another, and I do make them know the statutes of God, and his laws.

17 And Moses' father in law said unto him, The thing that thou doest is not good.

18 Thou wilt surely wear away, both thou, and this people that is with thee: for this thing is too heavy for thee; thou art not able to perform it thyself alone.

19 Hearken now unto my voice, I will give thee counsel, and God shall be with thee: Be thou for the people to God-ward, that thou mayest bring the causes unto God:

20 And thou shalt teach them ordinances and laws, and shalt shew them the way wherein they must walk, and the work that they must do.

21 Moreover thou shalt provide out of all the people able men, such as fear God, men of truth, hating covetousness; and place such over them, to be rulers of thousands, and rulers of hundreds, rulers of fifties, and rulers of tens:

22 And let them judge the people at all seasons: and it shall be, that every great matter they shall bring unto thee, but every small matter they shall judge: so shall it be easier for thyself, and they shall bear the burden with thee.

23 If thou shalt do this thing, and God command thee so, then thou shalt be able to endure, and all this people shall also go to their place in peace.

24 So Moses hearkened to the voice of his father in law, and did all that he had said.

25 And Moses chose able men out of all Israel, and made them heads over the people, rulers of thousands, rulers of hundreds, rulers of fifties, and rulers of tens.

26 And they judged the people at all seasons: the hard causes they brought unto Moses, but every small matter they judged themselves.

What counsel did Jethro give to Moses? In what way is this same counsel followed by Church leaders today? How can we help our Church leaders with their many responsibilities?

THE ISRAELITES SANCTIFY THEMSELVES IN PREPARATION TO HEAR THE LORD

God had provided food and water for the Israelites as they journeyed, and, with the raising of Moses's hands, ensured they were victorious in battle. Moses's father-in-law wisely advised him to delegate many of his leadership responsibilities, which Moses did. The Israelites' journey then continued. In these verses, the term "sanctify" means to reverently prepare for a spiritual experience (see Map #1, C4).

EXODUS 19:1–25

In the third month, when the children of Israel were gone forth out of the land of Egypt, the same day came they into the wilderness of Sinai.

2 For they were departed from Rephidim, and were come to the desert of Sinai, and had pitched in the wilderness; and there Israel camped before the mount.

3 And Moses went up unto God, and the Lord called unto him out of the mountain, saying, Thus shalt thou say to the house of Jacob, and tell the children of Israel;

4 Ye have seen what I did unto the Egyptians, and how I bare you on eagles' wings, and brought you unto myself.

5 Now therefore, if ye will obey my voice indeed, and keep my covenant, then ye shall be a peculiar treasure unto me above all people: for all the earth is mine:

6 And ye shall be unto me a kingdom of priests, and an holy nation. These are the words which thou shalt speak unto the children of Israel.

7 And Moses came and called for the elders of the people, and laid before their faces all these words which the Lord commanded him.

8 And all the people answered together, and said, All that the Lord hath spoken we will do. And Moses returned the words of the people unto the Lord.

9 And the Lord said unto Moses, Lo, I come unto thee in a thick cloud, that the people may hear when I speak with thee, and believe thee for ever. And Moses told the words of the people unto the Lord.

10 And the Lord said unto Moses, Go unto the people, and sanctify them to day and to morrow, and let them wash their clothes,

11 And be ready against the third day: for the third day the Lord will come down in the sight of all the people upon mount Sinai.

12 And thou shalt set bounds unto the people round about, saying, Take heed to yourselves, that ye go not up into the mount, or touch the border of it: whosoever toucheth the mount shall be surely put to death:

13 There shall not an hand touch it, but he shall surely be stoned, or shot through; whether it be beast or man, it shall not live: when the trumpet soundeth long, they shall come up to the mount.

14 And Moses went down from the mount unto the people, and sanctified the people; and they washed their clothes.

15 And he said unto the people, Be ready against the third day: come not at your wives.

16 And it came to pass on the third day in the morning, that there were thunders and lightnings, and a thick cloud upon the mount, and the voice of the trumpet exceeding loud; so that all the people that was in the camp trembled.

17 And Moses brought forth the people out of the camp to meet with God; and they stood at the nether part of the mount.

18 And mount Sinai was altogether on a smoke, because the Lord descended upon it in fire: and the smoke thereof ascended as the smoke of a furnace, and the whole mount quaked greatly.

19 And when the voice of the trumpet sounded long, and waxed louder and louder, Moses spake, and God answered him by a voice.

20 And the Lord came down upon mount Sinai, on the top of the mount: and the Lord called Moses up to the top of the mount; and Moses went up.

21 And the Lord said unto Moses, Go down, charge the people, lest they break through unto the Lord to gaze, and many of them perish.

22 And let the priests also, which come near to the Lord, sanctify themselves, lest the Lord break forth upon them.

23 And Moses said unto the Lord, The people cannot come up to mount Sinai: for thou chargedst us, saying, Set bounds about the mount, and sanctify it.

24 And the Lord said unto him, Away, get thee down, and thou shalt come up, thou, and Aaron with thee: but let not the priests and the people break through to come up unto the Lord, lest he break forth upon them.

25 So Moses went down unto the people, and spake unto them.

In verses 5–6, God set forth a covenant with the children of Israel. As part of this covenant, what were the children of Israel required to do? What did God promise to do in return? Consider how the Israelites sanctified (or prepared) themselves to hear the voice of the Lord. Why is it important to properly prepare ourselves for spiritual experiences? How can you prepare yourself for spiritual experiences?

GOD DECLARES THE TEN COMMANDMENTS

God had spoken to Moses and promised that if the Israelites would obey His voice and keep His covenant that He would make the Israelites "a peculiar treasure" (Exodus 19:5). Moses reported this to the Israelites and "the people answered together, and said, All that the Lord hath spoken we will do" (Exodus 19:8). A period of sanctification then began and after three days the Lord's presence atop Mount Sinai was signified by billowing smoke, earthquakes, thunder, lightning, and the exceedingly loud sound of trumpets. Then, while the people remained below, Moses entered the top of the mount.

EXODUS 20:1–24

And God spake all these words, saying,

2 I am the Lord thy God, which have brought thee out of the land of Egypt, out of the house of bondage.

3 Thou shalt have no other gods before me.

4 Thou shalt not make unto thee any graven image, or any likeness of any thing that is in heaven above, or that is in the earth beneath, or that is in the water under the earth:

5 Thou shalt not bow down thyself to them, nor serve them: for I the Lord thy God am a jealous God, visiting the iniquity of the fathers upon the children unto the third and fourth generation of them that hate me;

6 And shewing mercy unto thousands of them that love me, and keep my commandments.

7 Thou shalt not take the name of the Lord thy God in vain; for the Lord will not hold him guiltless that taketh his name in vain.

8 Remember the sabbath day, to keep it holy.

9 Six days shalt thou labour, and do all thy work:

10 But the seventh day is the sabbath of the Lord thy God: in it thou shalt not do any work, thou, nor thy son, nor thy daughter, thy manservant, nor thy maidservant, nor thy cattle, nor thy stranger that is within thy gates:

11 For in six days the Lord made heaven and earth, the sea, and all that in them is, and rested the seventh day: wherefore the Lord blessed the sabbath day, and hallowed it.

12 Honour thy father and thy mother: that thy days may be long upon the land which the Lord thy God giveth thee.

13 Thou shalt not kill.

14 Thou shalt not commit adultery.

15 Thou shalt not steal.

16 Thou shalt not bear false witness against thy neighbour.

17 Thou shalt not covet thy neighbour's house, thou shalt not covet thy neighbour's wife, nor his manservant, nor his maidservant, nor his ox, nor his ass, nor any thing that is thy neighbour's.

18 And all the people saw the thunderings, and the lightnings, and the noise of the trumpet, and the mountain smoking: and when the people saw it, they removed, and stood afar off.

19 And they said unto Moses, Speak thou with us, and we will hear: but let not God speak with us, lest we die.

20 And Moses said unto the people, Fear not: for God is come to prove you, and that his fear may be before your faces, that ye sin not.

21 And the people stood afar off, and Moses drew near unto the thick darkness where God was.

22 And the Lord said unto Moses, Thus thou shalt say unto the children of Israel, Ye have seen that I have talked with you from heaven.

23 Ye shall not make with me gods of silver, neither shall ye make unto you gods of gold.

24 An altar of earth thou shalt make unto me, and shalt sacrifice thereon thy burnt offerings, and thy peace offerings, thy sheep, and thine oxen: in all places where I record my name I will come unto thee, and I will bless thee.

What are the Ten Commandments that God gave to the children of Israel? How do you live the Ten Commandments today? What evidence do you see of the blessings that come by living the Ten Commandments?

90

THE ISRAELITES COVENANT TO OBEY THE LAW OF MOSES; MANY ELDERS SEE GOD UPON MOUNT SINAI

Upon Mount Sinai, God had declared the Ten Commandments to all the children of Israel and said, "Thus thou shalt say unto the children of Israel, Ye have seen that I have talked with you from heaven" (Exodus 20:22). Later returning to the mount, Moses was given additional instructions from God for how the people were to treat each other and what to do when someone had been wronged. These instructions—or laws—were highly detailed and dealt with nearly every matter of human conduct, including marriage commitments, respect for parents, annual feasts, borrowing from one's neighbor, the treatment of strangers, the lending of money, theft, sexual sin, murder, and even what to do if an animal who was known to be unruly ended up injuring someone. These laws often required an exact punishment based on the offense, as described by "eye for eye, tooth for tooth, hand for hand, . . . stripe for stripe" (Exodus 21:24–25). In many cases, the punishment of death was inflicted upon someone who broke one of these laws. Over time, these laws became known as the law of Moses and would govern the children of Israel—including the people of the Book of Mormon—until the time of Jesus Christ.

EXODUS 24:3–11

And Moses came and told the people all the words of the Lord, and all the judgments: and all the people answered with one voice, and said, All the words which the Lord hath said will we do.

4 And Moses wrote all the words of the Lord, and rose up early in the morning, and builded an altar under the hill, and twelve pillars, according to the twelve tribes of Israel.

5 And he sent young men of the children of Israel, which offered burnt offerings, and sacrificed peace offerings of oxen unto the Lord.

6 And Moses took half of the blood, and put it in basins; and half of the blood he sprinkled on the altar.

7 And he took the book of the covenant, and read in the audience of the people: and they said, All that the Lord hath said will we do, and be obedient.

8 And Moses took the blood, and sprinkled it on the people, and said, Behold the blood of the covenant, which the Lord hath made with you concerning all these words.

9 Then went up Moses, and Aaron, Nadab, and Abihu, and seventy of the elders of Israel:

10 And they saw the God of Israel: and there was under his feet as it were a paved work of a sapphire stone, and as it were the body of heaven in his clearness.

11 And upon the nobles of the children of Israel he laid not his hand: also they saw God, and did eat and drink.

In these verses, what was the children of Israel's response to God's commandments? What promises have you made with God? What actions can you take to keep those promises? What blessings have you received from keeping your promises to God?

GOD COMMANDS MOSES TO BUILD A TABERNACLE WHERE HE "WILL MEET WITH THE CHILDREN OF ISRAEL"

God had commanded the Israelites to properly worship Him once they were freed from Egypt. Accordingly, God next commanded Moses to build a tabernacle—a type of portable temple the Israelites would use during their journey to perform sacred ordinances with reverence and exactness. God gave very specific instructions on how to build each part of the tabernacle, as well as the special clothing that Aaron and other priesthood holders from the tribe of Levi were to wear while conducting their duties within the tabernacle. God also gave detailed instructions for the ark of the covenant—a large wooden box ornately covered in gold and topped with statues of angels. The ark was the most sacred object in the tabernacle. Over time, it would be filled with special objects such as the tablets containing the Ten Commandments, a commemorative pot of manna, and Aaron's staff. The tabernacle consisted of a rectangular courtyard marked by high walls (with no roof), separating it from the outside world. Within the courtyard was a small, tent-like structure that had walls, a ceiling, and two separate areas, the most sacred of which—the Holy of Holies—held the ark of the covenant. Entering the tabernacle and progressing toward the Holy of Holies was symbolic of progressing closer to the presence of God. In some instances, God Himself would appear inside the Holy of Holies. As you read these verses, consider the types of materials God commanded to be used, who was asked to provide them, and the effect the tabernacle would have upon the people.

Exodus 25:1–9

And the Lord spake unto Moses, saying,

2 Speak unto the children of Israel, that they bring me an offering: of every man that giveth it willingly with his heart ye shall take my offering.

3 And this is the offering which ye shall take of them; gold, and silver, and brass,

4 And blue, and purple, and scarlet, and fine linen, and goats' hair,

5 And rams' skins dyed red, and badgers' skins, and shittim wood,

6 Oil for the light, spices for anointing oil, and for sweet incense,

7 Onyx stones, and stones to be set in the ephod, and in the breastplate.

8 And let them make me a sanctuary; that I may dwell among them.

9 According to all that I shew thee, after the pattern of the tabernacle, and the pattern of all the instruments thereof, even so shall ye make it.

Exodus 29:43–46

43 And there I will meet with the children of Israel, and the tabernacle shall be sanctified by my glory.

44 And I will sanctify the tabernacle of the congregation, and the altar: I will sanctify also both Aaron and his sons, to minister to me in the priest's office.

45 And I will dwell among the children of Israel, and will be their God.

46 And they shall know that I am the Lord their God, that brought them forth out of the land of Egypt, that I may dwell among them: I am the Lord their God.

What types of materials did God command the Israelites to use in the building of the tabernacle? What types of materials are used to build temples today? How can you contribute to the building of temples and temple work? What blessings do you receive from this?

IN MOSES'S ABSENCE, THE ISRAELITES WORSHIP A GOLDEN CALF, PROMPTING GOD'S FURY

Moses had returned to Mount Sinai for a period of "forty days and forty nights" (Exodus 24:1). There God had given him detailed instructions for the building of a tabernacle, the ark of the covenant, and special clothing for the priests to wear as they conducted sacrifices and ordinances. Meanwhile, during Moses's lengthy absence, the Israelites began to worship an idol.

EXODUS 32:1–14; JOSEPH SMITH TRANSLATION, EXODUS 32:12, 14

And when the people saw that Moses delayed to come down out of the mount, the people gathered themselves together unto Aaron, and said unto him, Up, make us gods, which shall go before us; for as for this Moses, the man that brought us up out of the land of Egypt, we wot not what is become of him.

2 And Aaron said unto them, Break off the golden earrings, which are in the ears of your wives, of your sons, and of your daughters, and bring them unto me.

3 And all the people brake off the golden earrings which were in their ears, and brought them unto Aaron.

4 And he received them at their hand, and fashioned it with a graving tool, after he had made it a molten calf: and they said, These be thy gods, O Israel, which brought thee up out of the land of Egypt.

5 And when Aaron saw it, he built an altar before it; and Aaron made proclamation, and said, To morrow is a feast to the Lord.

6 And they rose up early on the morrow, and offered burnt offerings, and brought peace offerings; and the people sat down to eat and to drink, and rose up to play.

7 And the Lord said unto Moses, Go, get thee down; for thy people, which thou broughtest out of the land of Egypt, have corrupted themselves:

8 They have turned aside quickly out of the way which I commanded them: they have made them a molten calf, and have worshipped it, and have sacrificed thereunto, and said, These be thy gods, O Israel, which have brought thee up out of the land of Egypt.

9 And the Lord said unto Moses, I have seen this people, and, behold, it is a stiffnecked people:

10 Now therefore let me alone, that my wrath may wax hot against them, and that I may consume them: and I will make of thee a great nation.

11 And Moses besought the Lord his God, and said, Lord, why doth thy wrath wax hot against thy people, which thou hast brought forth out of the land of Egypt with great power, and with a mighty hand?

12 Wherefore should the Egyptians speak, and say, For mischief did he bring them out, to slay them in the mountains, and to consume them from the face of the earth? Turn from thy fierce wrath, *Thy people will repent of this evil; therefore come thou not out against them.*

13 Remember Abraham, Isaac, and Israel, thy servants, to whom thou swarest by thine own self, and saidst unto them, I will multiply your seed as the stars of heaven, and all this land that I have spoken of will I give unto your seed, and they shall inherit it for ever.

14 And the Lord *said unto Moses, If they will repent* of the evil which *they have done, I will spare them, and turn away my fierce wrath; but, behold, thou shalt execute judgment upon all that will not repent of this evil this day. Therefore, see thou do this thing that I have commanded thee, or I will execute all that which I* had thought to do unto *my* people.

What did the children of Israel do that caused God to be angry with them? What did they need to do for God to spare their lives? What have modern-day prophets taught about repentance?

MOSES MELTS THE GOLDEN CALF, MAKES THE PEOPLE DRINK IT, AND COMMANDS THAT THE REBELLIOUS BE SLAIN

For "forty days and forty nights" upon Mount Sinai (Exodus 42:1), Moses had received what would come to be known as the law of Moses, as well as specific instructions for the building of a tabernacle. But during Moses's absence, the Israelites built a golden calf and worshipped it as the god who had brought them out of Egypt. God was exceedingly angry with the corruption of the people and told Moses He intended to destroy them. Moses pleaded on behalf of the people and God promised that the people could repent, but those who didn't would be destroyed. Moses then journeyed down from the mount, carrying with him two "tables"—or slabs of stone—upon which God had written the laws and instructions spoken to Moses. In verse 20, the word "strawed" means mixed or combined.

EXODUS 32:15–16, 19–35

And Moses turned, and went down from the mount, and the two tables of the testimony were in his hand: the tables were written on both their sides; on the one side and on the other were they written.

16 And the tables were the work of God, and the writing was the writing of God, graven upon the tables.

19 And it came to pass, as soon as he came nigh unto the camp, that he saw the calf, and the dancing: and Moses' anger waxed hot, and he cast the tables out of his hands, and brake them beneath the mount.

20 And he took the calf which they had made, and burnt it in the fire, and ground it to powder, and strawed it upon the water, and made the children of Israel drink of it.

21 And Moses said unto Aaron, What did this people unto thee, that thou hast brought so great a sin upon them?

22 And Aaron said, Let not the anger of my lord wax hot: thou knowest the people, that they are set on mischief.

23 For they said unto me, Make us gods, which shall go before us: for as for this Moses, the man that brought us up out of the land of Egypt, we wot not what is become of him.

24 And I said unto them, Whosoever hath any gold, let them break it off. So they gave it me: then I cast it into the fire, and there came out this calf.

25 And when Moses saw that the people were naked; (for Aaron had made them naked unto their shame among their enemies:)

26 Then Moses stood in the gate of the camp, and said, Who is on the Lord's side? let him come unto me. And all the sons of Levi gathered themselves together unto him.

27 And he said unto them, Thus saith the Lord God of Israel, Put every man his sword by his side, and go in and out from gate to gate throughout the camp, and slay every man his brother, and every man his companion, and every man his neighbour.

28 And the children of Levi did according to the word of Moses: and there fell of the people that day about three thousand men.

29 For Moses had said, Consecrate yourselves to day to the Lord, even every man upon his son, and upon his brother; that he may bestow upon you a blessing this day.

30 And it came to pass on the morrow, that Moses said unto the people, Ye have sinned a great sin: and now I will go up unto the Lord; peradventure I shall make an atonement for your sin.

31 And Moses returned unto the Lord, and said, Oh, this people have sinned a great sin, and have made them gods of gold.

32 Yet now, if thou wilt forgive their sin—; and if not, blot me, I pray thee, out of thy book which thou hast written.

33 And the Lord said unto Moses, Whosoever hath sinned against me, him will I blot out of my book.

34 Therefore now go, lead the people unto the place of which I have spoken unto thee: behold, mine Angel shall go before thee: nevertheless in the day when I visit I will visit their sin upon them.

35 And the Lord plagued the people, because they made the calf, which Aaron made.

What did the people do that made Moses angry? How did Moses respond? In verse 26, Moses asks the people, "Who is on the Lord's side?" What does it mean to be on the Lord's side? How can you show you're on the Lord's side today?

GOD SPEAKS TO MOSES FACE-TO-FACE, CHASTISES THE ISRAELITES FOR THEIR WICKEDNESS, AND WITHDRAWS HIS FULL PRESENCE

Returning from Mount Sinai, Moses found the Israelites worshipping a golden calf they had built. After Moses burned the idol, mixed the melted gold with water, and made the Israelites drink it, he called to the people, saying, "Who is on the Lord's side?" Those who rallied to Moses's side were then commanded to slay the rebellious, which they did. Moses told the people to consecrate themselves, then pleaded with God to forgive their sins. These verses contain God's reply. Note: The tabernacle referred to in verses 7–9 was not the tabernacle that would later be built according to God's precise instructions, but rather a forerunner to that tabernacle. Nonetheless, the tent-like structure referred to in these verses served as a type of temple where God and man communicated with each other.

EXODUS 33:1–23; JOSEPH SMITH TRANSLATION, EXODUS 33:20, 23

And the Lord said unto Moses, Depart, and go up hence, thou and the people which thou hast brought up out of the land of Egypt, unto the land which I sware unto Abraham, to Isaac, and to Jacob, saying, Unto thy seed will I give it:

2 And I will send an angel before thee; and I will drive out the Canaanite, the Amorite, and the Hittite, and the Perizzite, the Hivite, and the Jebusite:

3 Unto a land flowing with milk and honey: for I will not go up in the midst of thee; for thou art a stiffnecked people: lest I consume thee in the way.

4 And when the people heard these evil tidings, they mourned: and no man did put on him his ornaments.

5 For the Lord had said unto Moses, Say unto the children of Israel, Ye are a stiffnecked people: I will come up into the midst of thee in a moment, and consume thee: therefore now put off thy ornaments from thee, that I may know what to do unto thee.

6 And the children of Israel stripped themselves of their ornaments by the mount Horeb.

7 And Moses took the tabernacle, and pitched it without the camp, afar off from the camp, and called it the Tabernacle of the congregation. And it came to pass, that every one which sought the Lord went out unto the tabernacle of the congregation, which was without the camp.

8 And it came to pass, when Moses went out unto the tabernacle, that all the people rose up, and stood every man at his tent door, and looked after Moses, until he was gone into the tabernacle.

9 And it came to pass, as Moses entered into the tabernacle, the cloudy pillar descended, and stood at the door of the tabernacle, and the Lord talked with Moses.

10 And all the people saw the cloudy pillar stand at the tabernacle door: and all the people rose up and worshipped, every man in his tent door.

11 And the Lord spake unto Moses face to face, as a man speaketh unto his friend. And he turned again into the camp: but his servant Joshua, the son of Nun, a young man, departed not out of the tabernacle.

12 And Moses said unto the Lord, See, thou sayest unto me, Bring up this people: and thou hast not let me know whom thou wilt send with me. Yet thou hast said, I know thee by name, and thou hast also found grace in my sight.

13 Now therefore, I pray thee, if I have found grace in thy sight, shew me now thy way, that I may know thee, that I may find grace in thy sight: and consider that this nation is thy people.

14 And he said, My presence shall go with thee, and I will give thee rest.

15 And he said unto him, If thy presence go not with me, carry us not up hence.

16 For wherein shall it be known here that I and thy people have found grace in thy sight? is it not in that thou goest with us? so shall we be separated, I and thy people, from all the people that are upon the face of the earth.

17 And the Lord said unto Moses, I will do this thing also that thou hast spoken: for thou hast found grace in my sight, and I know thee by name.

18 And he said, I beseech thee, shew me thy glory.

19 And he said, I will make all my goodness pass before thee, and I will proclaim the name of the Lord before thee; and will be gracious to whom I will be gracious, and will shew mercy on whom I will shew mercy.

20 And he said *unto Moses*, Thou canst not see my face *at this time, lest mine anger be kindled against thee also, and I destroy thee, and thy people;* for there shall no man *among them* see me *at this time*, and live, *for they are exceeding sinful. And no sinful man hath at any time, neither shall there be any sinful man at any time, that shall see my face and live.*

21 And the Lord said, Behold, there is a place by me, and thou shalt stand upon a rock:

22 And it shall come to pass, while my glory passeth by, that I will put thee in a clift of the rock, and will cover thee with my hand while I pass by:

23 And I will take away mine hand, and thou shalt see my back parts: but my face shall not be seen, *as at other times; for I am angry with my people Israel.*

Although the Israelites had sinned, the Lord promised that if they would repent, He would still lead them to the promised land. What does this teach you about repentance? In verse 17, the Lord tells Moses that He knows him by his name. Share an experience of when you felt that the Lord knew you.

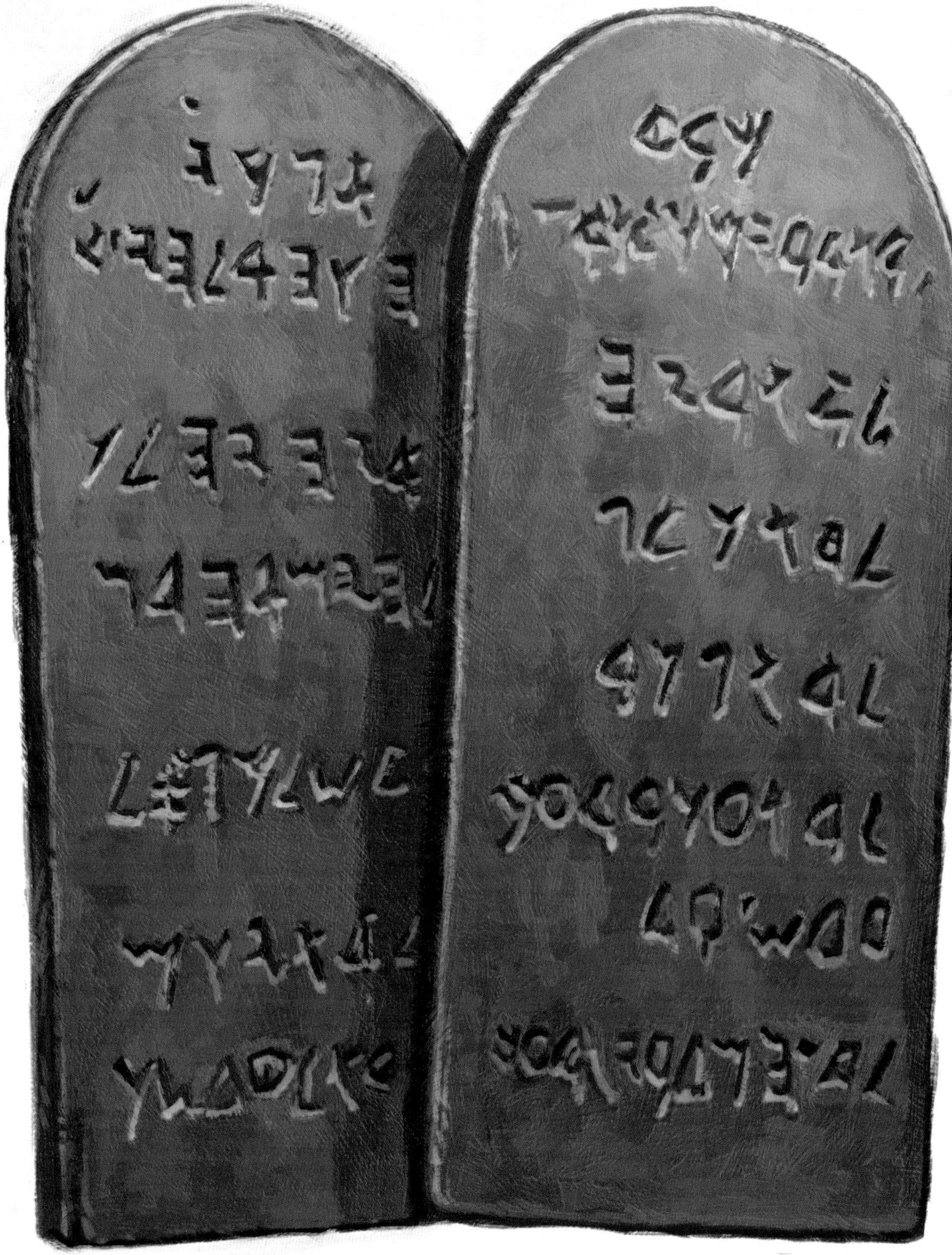

GOD MAKES A NEW COVENANT WITH ISRAEL, REMOVING THE MELCHIZEDEK PRIESTHOOD AND OFFERING THE AARONIC PRIESTHOOD

Moses had spoken with God face-to-face and pleaded for mercy on behalf of the wicked Israelites. Though God loved the children of Israel and would continue to lead them, their unwillingness to obey their initial covenant resulted in the need for a new covenant—one with lower requirements and fewer blessings. Latter-day revelation clarifies that the Melchizedek Priesthood and its corresponding ordinances were part of the first covenant (see Doctrine and Covenants 84:23–27). This priesthood was then taken from the people, and in its place was offered what became known as the Aaronic Priesthood, with its lesser ordinances and blessings. Previously, God had inscribed laws and covenants upon stone tablets that Moses broke in his fury upon witnessing the Israelites' wickedness.

EXODUS 34:1–2, 4–10; JOSEPH SMITH TRANSLATION, 34:1–2,7

And the Lord said unto Moses, Hew thee two *other* tables of stone, like unto the first, and I will write upon *them* also, the words *of the law, according as they were written at the first on the tables which thou brakest; but it shall not be according to the first, for I will take away the priesthood out of their midst; therefore my holy order, and the ordinances thereof, shall not go before them; for my presence shall not go up in their midst, lest I destroy them.*

2 But I will give unto them the law as at the first, but it shall be after the law of a carnal commandment; for I have sworn in my wrath, that they shall not enter into my presence, into my rest, in the days of their pilgrimage. Therefore do as I have commanded thee, and be ready in the morning, and come up in the morning unto mount Sinai, and present thyself there to me, in the top of the mount.

4 And he hewed two tables of stone like unto the first; and Moses rose up early in the morning, and went up unto mount Sinai, as the Lord had commanded him, and took in his hand the two tables of stone.

5 And the Lord descended in the cloud, and stood with him there, and proclaimed the name of the Lord.

6 And the Lord passed by before him, and proclaimed, The Lord, The Lord God, merciful and gracious, longsuffering, and abundant in goodness and truth,

7 Keeping mercy for thousands, forgiving iniquity and transgression and sin, and that will by no means clear *the rebellious*; visiting the iniquity of the fathers upon the children, and upon the children's children, unto the third and to the fourth generation.

8 And Moses made haste, and bowed his head toward the earth, and worshipped.

9 And he said, If now I have found grace in thy sight, O Lord, let my Lord, I pray thee, go among us; for it is a stiffnecked people; and pardon our iniquity and our sin, and take us for thine inheritance.

10 And he said, Behold, I make a covenant: before all thy people I will do marvels, such as have not been done in all the earth, nor in any nation: and all the people among which thou art shall see the work of the Lord: for it is a terrible thing that I will do with thee.

According to verses 1–2, what were the consequences Israel faced for breaking their covenants? Consider the descriptions of the Lord given in verses 6–7. How were these characteristics of the Lord shown to the children of Israel? How have they been shown to you?

THE ISRAELITES OBEDIENTLY CONSTRUCT THE TABERNACLE, AARON AND HIS SONS ARE WASHED AND ANOINTED, AND GOD'S PRESENCE DESCENDS UPON THE TABERNACLE

God had promised to forgive the repentant Israelites and offered a new covenant to them, albeit one with a lower law and fewer blessings. Moses prepared new stone tablets and returned to Mount Sinai, where he spoke with God and "wrote upon the tables the words of the covenant, the ten commandments" (Exodus 34:28). Moses returned with the tablets and informed the Israelites of their many obligations, including their duty to build the tabernacle. The Israelites responded with diligence. Wise men were called by God to oversee the construction of the tabernacle, the ark, and the ceremonial priesthood clothing, all according to God's precise instructions. The people donated so much material to the building of the tabernacle that Moses restrained them from donating more. "And Moses did look upon all the work, and, behold, they had done it as the Lord had commanded" (Exodus 39:43). God then instructed Moses to make final preparations for the tabernacle.

Exodus 40:12–18, 21, 24–29, 31–38

And thou shalt bring Aaron and his sons unto the door of the tabernacle of the congregation, and wash them with water.

13 And thou shalt put upon Aaron the holy garments, and anoint him, and sanctify him; that he may minister unto me in the priest's office.

14 And thou shalt bring his sons, and clothe them with coats:

15 And thou shalt anoint them, as thou didst anoint their father, that they may minister unto me in the priest's office: for their anointing shall surely be an everlasting priesthood throughout their generations.

16 Thus did Moses: according to all that the Lord commanded him, so did he.

17 And it came to pass in the first month in the second year, on the first day of the month, that the tabernacle was reared up.

18 And Moses reared up the tabernacle, and fastened his sockets, and set up the boards thereof, and put in the bars thereof, and reared up his pillars.

21 And he brought the ark into the tabernacle, and set up the veil of the covering, and covered the ark of the testimony; as the Lord commanded Moses.

24 And he put the candlestick in the tent of the congregation, over against the table, on the side of the tabernacle southward.

25 And he lighted the lamps before the Lord; as the Lord commanded Moses.

26 And he put the golden altar in the tent of the congregation before the veil:

27 And he burnt sweet incense thereon; as the Lord commanded Moses.

28 And he set up the hanging at the door of the tabernacle.

29 And he put the altar of burnt offering by the door of the tabernacle of the tent of the congregation, and offered upon it the burnt offering and the meat offering; as the Lord commanded Moses.

31 And Moses and Aaron and his sons washed their hands and their feet thereat:

32 When they went into the tent of the congregation, and when they came near unto the altar, they washed; as the Lord commanded Moses.

33 And he reared up the court round about the tabernacle and the altar, and set up the hanging of the court gate. So Moses finished the work.

34 Then a cloud covered the tent of the congregation, and the glory of the Lord filled the tabernacle.

35 And Moses was not able to enter into the tent of the congregation, because the cloud abode thereon, and the glory of the Lord filled the tabernacle.

36 And when the cloud was taken up from over the tabernacle, the children of Israel went onward in all their journeys:

37 But if the cloud were not taken up, then they journeyed not till the day that it was taken up.

38 For the cloud of the Lord was upon the tabernacle by day, and fire was on it by night, in the sight of all the house of Israel, throughout all their journeys.

Verse 16 states that Moses was obedient to "all that the Lord commanded him." How can you continually be obedient to all that God has commanded you? How did the Israelites prepare to make the tabernacle a place where the glory of God could dwell? What can we do to make our homes, church buildings, and temples holy places?

THE ISRAELITES ARE COMMANDED TO PERFORM ANIMAL SACRIFICES SO THAT AN "ATONEMENT" IS MADE FOR THEIR SINS

As commanded by God, the Israelites had constructed the tabernacle and received God's many laws. Obedience to those laws would qualify them for God's blessings. When they made mistakes, they could repent by confessing their sins, making restitution, and having a priest perform an animal sacrifice on their behalf. Male members of the tribe of Levi held the Aaronic Priesthood, and with this authority they could perform these animal sacrifices using animals that had no imperfections. These "perfect" animals and the shedding of their blood upon the altar of the tabernacle represented the sacrifice that would be made by Jesus Christ on behalf of all mankind. The following verses describe one type of animal sacrifice that God commanded the Israelites make once each year. The word "atonement" is used often in these verses, referring to the process of overcoming the consequences of sin. Also mentioned in these verses is a "bullock," which refers to male cattle.

LEVITICUS 16:3, 5–11, 16, 21–22, 30

Thus shall Aaron come into the holy place: with a young bullock for a sin offering, and a ram for a burnt offering.

5 And he shall take of the congregation of the children of Israel two kids of the goats for a sin offering, and one ram for a burnt offering.

6 And Aaron shall offer his bullock of the sin offering, which is for himself, and make an atonement for himself, and for his house.

7 And he shall take the two goats, and present them before the Lord at the door of the tabernacle of the congregation.

8 And Aaron shall cast lots upon the two goats; one lot for the Lord, and the other lot for the scapegoat.

9 And Aaron shall bring the goat upon which the Lord's lot fell, and offer him for a sin offering.

10 But the goat, on which the lot fell to be the scapegoat, shall be presented alive before the Lord, to make an atonement with him, and to let him go for a scapegoat into the wilderness.

11 And Aaron shall bring the bullock of the sin offering, which is for himself, and shall make an atonement for himself, and for his house, and shall kill the bullock of the sin offering which is for himself:

16 And he shall make an atonement for the holy place, because of the uncleanness of the children of Israel, and because of their transgressions in all their sins: and so shall he do for the tabernacle of the congregation, that remaineth among them in the midst of their uncleanness.

21 And Aaron shall lay both his hands upon the head of the live goat, and confess over him all the iniquities of the children of Israel, and all their transgressions in all their sins, putting them upon the head of the goat, and shall send him away by the hand of a fit man into the wilderness:

22 And the goat shall bear upon him all their iniquities unto a land not inhabited: and he shall let go the goat in the wilderness.

30 For on that day shall the priest make an atonement for you, to cleanse you, that ye may be clean from all your sins before the Lord.

According to verse 16, why was an atonement required? Consider the perfect lambs that were required for this animal sacrifice. How was Jesus Christ like those lambs? What did Jesus Christ's Atonement accomplish?

MOSES INSTRUCTS THE AILING ISRAELITES TO LOOK UPON THE BRASS SERPENT TO BE HEALED

As the Israelites continued their journey to the promised land, God emphasized many laws He had previously given and gave new ones, including a list of specific foods the Israelites were forbidden to eat (see Leviticus 11). The Israelites' goal was to reach the promised land—a region then referred to as the land of Canaan. Canaan was only about 430 miles (about 700 kilometers) away, but the Israelites often complained and resumed wicked practices, which greatly slowed their journey (see Map #1). It would eventually take forty years before the Israelites were prepared to enter the promised land. Along the way, many wicked Israelites were killed or stricken with plagues.

NUMBERS 21:4–9

And they journeyed from mount Hor by the way of the Red sea, to compass the land of Edom: and the soul of the people was much discouraged because of the way.

5 And the people spake against God, and against Moses, Wherefore have ye brought us up out of Egypt to die in the wilderness? for there is no bread, neither is there any water; and our soul loatheth this light bread.

6 And the Lord sent fiery serpents among the people, and they bit the people; and much people of Israel died.

7 Therefore the people came to Moses, and said, We have sinned, for we have spoken against the Lord, and against thee; pray unto the Lord, that he take away the serpents from us. And Moses prayed for the people.

8 And the Lord said unto Moses, Make thee a fiery serpent, and set it upon a pole: and it shall come to pass, that every one that is bitten, when he looketh upon it, shall live.

9 And Moses made a serpent of brass, and put it upon a pole, and it came to pass, that if a serpent had bitten any man, when he beheld the serpent of brass, he lived.

In about 600 B.C., the Book of Mormon prophet Nephi recounted many of the miracles performed by Moses. His description of the raising of the brass serpent, found in 1 Nephi 17:41, adds important context to this event: "And he did straiten them in the wilderness with his rod; for they hardened their hearts, even as ye have; and the Lord straitened them because of their iniquity. He sent fiery flying serpents among them; and after they were bitten he prepared a way that they might be healed; and the labor which they had to perform was to look; and because of the simpleness of the way, or the easiness of it, there were many who perished."

In these verses, why did the Israelites complain to God and Moses? What did the Israelites need to do to survive the serpents' bites? Why did some of them choose to not look at the brass serpent? Why do people often refuse to follow commandments given by today's prophets? What are some simple things today's prophets have commanded us to do?

MOSES INVITES THE ISRAELITES TO REMEMBER THE POWER AND MERCY AND GOODNESS OF GOD

The Israelites' journey from Egypt to Canaan took forty years, during which time God performed many mighty miracles to provide them safety, food, and comfort. As their journey neared an end, Moses spoke to the people at length about these miracles. He knew they would continue to face temptations and challenges, and he urged them to be obedient and remember the goodness of God. As you read, look for the many miracles and blessings Moses recounted.

DEUTERONOMY 4:30–40

When thou art in tribulation, and all these things are come upon thee, even in the latter days, if thou turn to the Lord thy God, and shalt be obedient unto his voice;

31 (For the Lord thy God is a merciful God;) he will not forsake thee, neither destroy thee, nor forget the covenant of thy fathers which he sware unto them.

32 For ask now of the days that are past, which were before thee, since the day that God created man upon the earth, and ask from the one side of heaven unto the other, whether there hath been any such thing as this great thing is, or hath been heard like it?

33 Did ever people hear the voice of God speaking out of the midst of the fire, as thou hast heard, and live?

34 Or hath God assayed to go and take him a nation from the midst of another nation, by temptations, by signs, and by wonders, and by war, and by a mighty hand, and by a stretched out arm, and by great terrors, according to all that the Lord your God did for you in Egypt before your eyes?

35 Unto thee it was shewed, that thou mightest know that the Lord he is God; there is none else beside him.

36 Out of heaven he made thee to hear his voice, that he might instruct thee: and upon earth he shewed thee his great fire; and thou heardest his words out of the midst of the fire.

37 And because he loved thy fathers, therefore he chose their seed after them, and brought thee out in his sight with his mighty power out of Egypt;

38 To drive out nations from before thee greater and mightier than thou art, to bring thee in, to give thee their land for an inheritance, as it is this day.

39 Know therefore this day, and consider it in thine heart, that the Lord he is God in heaven above, and upon the earth beneath: there is none else.

40 Thou shalt keep therefore his statutes, and his commandments, which I command thee this day, that it may go well with thee, and with thy children after thee, and that thou mayest prolong thy days upon the earth, which the Lord thy God giveth thee, for ever.

DEUTERONOMY 6:17–25

17 Ye shall diligently keep the commandments of the Lord your God, and his testimonies, and his statutes, which he hath commanded thee.

18 And thou shalt do that which is right and good in the sight of the Lord: that it may be well with thee, and that thou mayest go in and possess the good land which the Lord sware unto thy fathers,

19 To cast out all thine enemies from before thee, as the Lord hath spoken.

20 And when thy son asketh thee in time to come, saying, What mean the testimonies, and the statutes, and the judgments, which the Lord our God hath commanded you?

21 Then thou shalt say unto thy son, We were Pharaoh's bondmen in Egypt; and the Lord brought us out of Egypt with a mighty hand:

22 And the Lord shewed signs and wonders, great and sore, upon Egypt, upon Pharaoh, and upon all his household, before our eyes:

23 And he brought us out from thence, that he might bring us in, to give us the land which he sware unto our fathers.

24 And the Lord commanded us to do all these statutes, to fear the Lord our God, for our good always, that he might preserve us alive, as it is at this day.

25 And it shall be our righteousness, if we observe to do all these commandments before the Lord our God, as he hath commanded us.

What miracles and blessings did Moses recount to the children of Israel? Why was Moses so determined that the children of Israel remember all the Lord had done for them (see Deuteronomy 4:35)? In Deuteronomy 6:20–25, Moses asks the children of Israel to teach all these things to their children. Why is it important to share the knowledge we have of God with those who come after us? What can you do to remember and teach the goodness of God?

MOSES REMINDS THE ISRAELITES THAT THEY ARE A HOLY PEOPLE WHO WILL SERVE GOD WITH ALL THEIR HEART AND SOUL

As the Israelites' forty-year journey to the promised land neared an end, Moses reminded the people of the power, mercy, and goodness of God. His words then continued as he reminded the Israelites of their sacred obligations and covenants.

DEUTERONOMY 7:6–9

For thou art an holy people unto the Lord thy God: the Lord thy God hath chosen thee to be a special people unto himself, above all people that are upon the face of the earth.

7 The Lord did not set his love upon you, nor choose you, because ye were more in number than any people; for ye were the fewest of all people:

8 But because the Lord loved you, and because he would keep the oath which he had sworn unto your fathers, hath the Lord brought you out with a mighty hand, and redeemed you out of the house of bondmen, from the hand of Pharaoh king of Egypt.

9 Know therefore that the Lord thy God, he is God, the faithful God, which keepeth covenant and mercy with them that love him and keep his commandments to a thousand generations;

DEUTERONOMY 10:12–15, 17–22

12 And now, Israel, what doth the Lord thy God require of thee, but to fear the Lord thy God, to walk in all his ways, and to love him, and to serve the Lord thy God with all thy heart and with all thy soul,

13 To keep the commandments of the Lord, and his statutes, which I command thee this day for thy good?

14 Behold, the heaven and the heaven of heavens is the Lord's thy God, the earth also, with all that therein is.

15 Only the Lord had a delight in thy fathers to love them, and he chose their seed after them, even you above all people, as it is this day.

17 For the Lord your God is God of gods, and Lord of lords, a great God, a mighty, and a terrible, which regardeth not persons, nor taketh reward:

18 He doth execute the judgment of the fatherless and widow, and loveth the stranger, in giving him food and raiment.

19 Love ye therefore the stranger: for ye were strangers in the land of Egypt.

20 Thou shalt fear the Lord thy God; him shalt thou serve, and to him shalt thou cleave, and swear by his name.

21 He is thy praise, and he is thy God, that hath done for thee these great and terrible things, which thine eyes have seen.

22 Thy fathers went down into Egypt with threescore and ten persons; and now the Lord thy God hath made thee as the stars of heaven for multitude.

Consider Deuteronomy 7:6. What does it mean to be a "holy people"? According to Deuteronomy 10:12, what does the Lord require of us? What are some ways you show the Lord that you love Him? How can we fulfill the commandment given in Deuteronomy 10:19 to love "the stranger"?

GOD CALLS JOSHUA TO LEAD THE ISRAELITES AND COMMANDS HIM TO BE "STRONG AND OF A GOOD COURAGE"

The Israelites' forty-year journey to Canaan—the promised land—had finally come to an end (see Map #1). Just prior to their entering the land, God told Moses that he would be allowed to see it but would not enter it himself. Joshua was called by God to be the next prophet, and Moses was taken up into heaven without tasting of death (see Alma 45:19). Note that Moses would later appear on the Mount of Transfiguration to Jesus Christ and Peter, James, and John (see Matthew 17:3–4) and in the Kirtland Temple to bestow priesthood keys upon Joseph Smith (see Doctrine and Covenants 110:11). God then commanded Joshua to prepare to cross the river Jordan and take sole possession of the land of Canaan—a task that appeared to be very difficult, as the land was already possessed by people with strong fortifications. God spoke directly to Joshua and encouraged him to fulfill his duties.

JOSHUA 1:5–7, 9–11, 16–18

There shall not any man be able to stand before thee all the days of thy life: as I was with Moses, so I will be with thee: I will not fail thee, nor forsake thee.

6 Be strong and of a good courage: for unto this people shalt thou divide for an inheritance the land, which I sware unto their fathers to give them.

7 Only be thou strong and very courageous, that thou mayest observe to do according to all the law, which Moses my servant commanded thee: turn not from it to the right hand or to the left, that thou mayest prosper whithersoever thou goest.

9 Have not I commanded thee? Be strong and of a good courage; be not afraid, neither be thou dismayed: for the Lord thy God is with thee whithersoever thou goest.

10 Then Joshua commanded the officers of the people, saying,

11 Pass through the host, and command the people, saying, Prepare you victuals; for within three days ye shall pass over this Jordan, to go in to possess the land, which the Lord your God giveth you to possess it.

16 And they answered Joshua, saying, All that thou commandest us we will do, and whithersoever thou sendest us, we will go.

17 According as we hearkened unto Moses in all things, so will we hearken unto thee: only the Lord thy God be with thee, as he was with Moses.

18 Whosoever he be that doth rebel against thy commandment, and will not hearken unto thy words in all that thou commandest him, he shall be put to death: only be strong and of a good courage.

What commandments might require you to "be strong and of a good courage" today? Note the Israelites' willingness to follow Joshua. How can we follow today's living prophets? What is something our current prophet has recently asked us to do?

ACCORDING TO GOD'S COMMAND, THE RIVER JORDAN IS PARTED AND THE ISRAELITES MIRACULOUSLY ENTER THE PROMISED LAND

God had commanded Joshua to lead the Israelites and take sole possession of the land of Canaan. This land was already possessed by people with strong fortifications. God spoke to Joshua and commanded him to be strong and of good courage. Joshua obeyed and began preparing the people to cross the river Jordan—the final milestone of their forty-year journey.

JOSHUA 3:5–17

And Joshua said unto the people, Sanctify yourselves: for to morrow the Lord will do wonders among you.

6 And Joshua spake unto the priests, saying, Take up the ark of the covenant, and pass over before the people. And they took up the ark of the covenant, and went before the people.

7 And the Lord said unto Joshua, This day will I begin to magnify thee in the sight of all Israel, that they may know that, as I was with Moses, so I will be with thee.

8 And thou shalt command the priests that bear the ark of the covenant, saying, When ye are come to the brink of the water of Jordan, ye shall stand still in Jordan.

9 And Joshua said unto the children of Israel, Come hither, and hear the words of the Lord your God.

10 And Joshua said, Hereby ye shall know that the living God is among you, and that he will without fail drive out from before you the Canaanites, and the Hittites, and the Hivites, and the Perizzites, and the Girgashites, and the Amorites, and the Jebusites.

11 Behold, the ark of the covenant of the Lord of all the earth passeth over before you into Jordan.

12 Now therefore take you twelve men out of the tribes of Israel, out of every tribe a man.

13 And it shall come to pass, as soon as the soles of the feet of the priests that bear the ark of the Lord, the Lord of all the earth, shall rest in the waters of Jordan, that the waters of Jordan shall be cut off from the waters that come down from above; and they shall stand upon an heap.

14 And it came to pass, when the people removed from their tents, to pass over Jordan, and the priests bearing the ark of the covenant before the people;

15 And as they that bare the ark were come unto Jordan, and the feet of the priests that bare the ark were dipped in the brim of the water, (for Jordan overfloweth all his banks all the time of harvest,)

16 That the waters which came down from above stood and rose up upon an heap very far from the city Adam, that is beside Zaretan: and those that came down toward the sea of the plain, even the salt sea, failed, and were cut off: and the people passed over right against Jericho.

17 And the priests that bare the ark of the covenant of the Lord stood firm on dry ground in the midst of Jordan, and all the Israelites passed over on dry ground, until all the people were passed clean over Jordan.

Why do you think it is significant that the water didn't recede until *after* the priests first stepped into it? When have you had to move forward in faith? What blessings became evident after you showed your faith?

THE ISRAELITES SHOUT AND THE WALLS OF JERICHO FALL DOWN

God had commanded Joshua and the Israelites to prepare to enter the promised land. The people responded in faith, and God parted the Jordan River, allowing them to enter the promised land on dry ground. Once inside the land of Canaan, Joshua continued to lead the people in their assigned duty to take sole possession of the land. Joshua sent spies into the kingdom of Jericho (within the land of Canaan), where they were hidden from the king's men by a woman named Rahab. She confirmed to the spies that the people of Jericho feared the approaching Israelites. She asked that in return for concealing the spies, her family would be spared when the Israelites destroyed Jericho, which was enclosed by a wall.

JOSHUA 6:1–5, 12–17, 20–25, 27

Now Jericho was straitly shut up because of the children of Israel: none went out, and none came in.

2 And the Lord said unto Joshua, See, I have given into thine hand Jericho, and the king thereof, and the mighty men of valour.

3 And ye shall compass the city, all ye men of war, and go round about the city once. Thus shalt thou do six days.

4 And seven priests shall bear before the ark seven trumpets of rams' horns: and the seventh day ye shall compass the city seven times, and the priests shall blow with the trumpets.

5 And it shall come to pass, that when they make a long blast with the ram's horn, and when ye hear the sound of the trumpet, all the people shall shout with a great shout; and the wall of the city shall fall down flat, and the people shall ascend up every man straight before him.

12 And Joshua rose early in the morning, and the priests took up the ark of the Lord.

13 And seven priests bearing seven trumpets of rams' horns before the ark of the Lord went on continually, and blew with the trumpets: and the armed men went before them; but the rearward came after the ark of the Lord, the priests going on, and blowing with the trumpets.

14 And the second day they compassed the city once, and returned into the camp: so they did six days.

15 And it came to pass on the seventh day, that they rose early about the dawning of the day, and compassed the city after the same manner seven times: only on that day they compassed the city seven times.

16 And it came to pass at the seventh time, when the priests blew with the trumpets, Joshua said unto the people, Shout; for the Lord hath given you the city.

17 And the city shall be accursed, even it, and all that are therein, to the Lord: only Rahab the harlot shall live, she and all that are with her in the house, because she hid the messengers that we sent.

20 So the people shouted when the priests blew with the trumpets: and it came to pass, when the people heard the sound of the trumpet, and the people shouted with a great shout, that the wall fell down flat, so that the people went up into the city, every man straight before him, and they took the city.

21 And they utterly destroyed all that was in the city, both man and woman, young and old, and ox, and sheep, and ass, with the edge of the sword.

22 But Joshua had said unto the two men that had spied out the country, Go into the harlot's house, and bring out thence the woman, and all that she hath, as ye sware unto her.

23 And the young men that were spies went in, and brought out Rahab, and her father, and her mother, and her brethren, and all that she had;

and they brought out all her kindred, and left them without the camp of Israel.

24 And they burnt the city with fire, and all that was therein: only the silver, and the gold, and the vessels of brass and of iron, they put into the treasury of the house of the Lord.

25 And Joshua saved Rahab the harlot alive, and her father's household, and all that she had; and she dwelleth in Israel even unto this day; because she hid the messengers, which Joshua sent to spy out Jericho.

27 So the Lord was with Joshua; and his fame was noised throughout all the country.

How did the Israelites capture the city of Jericho? What happened to Rahab and her family after the Israelites conquered Jericho? What blessings have you received for helping the Lord's chosen leaders?

JOSHUA URGES THE ISRAELITES TO SHUN WICKED TRADITIONS AND EMBRACE THE GOD WHO HAS REPEATEDLY PRESERVED THEM

Joshua had led the Israelites across the river Jordan and into Canaan. As commanded by God, they circled the city of Jericho, blew their ram's horns, and shouted as a congregation. The city walls fell, the inhabitants were slaughtered, and the Israelites settled in the land. Over time, additional battles were fought in Canaan between the Israelites and other tribes of people. There were victories and defeats, and God again performed miracles that preserved the Israelites. Joshua divided the conquered land into twelve smaller regions, with the descendants of Jacob's twelve sons each becoming a tribe that inhabited its own region (see Map #2). Prior to his death, Joshua pleaded with the Israelites to forever turn away from the traditions of the Egyptians from whom they had fled and from the ungodly traditions of the non-Israelite cultures they would encounter in and around their new lands.

And it came to pass a long time after that the Lord had given rest unto Israel from all their enemies round about, that Joshua waxed old and stricken in age.

2 And Joshua called for all Israel, and for their elders, and for their heads, and for their judges, and for their officers, and said unto them, I am old and stricken in age:

3 And ye have seen all that the Lord your God hath done unto all these nations because of you; for the Lord your God is he that hath fought for you.

4 Behold, I have divided unto you by lot these nations that remain, to be an inheritance for your tribes, from Jordan, with all the nations that I have cut off, even unto the great sea westward.

5 And the Lord your God, he shall expel them from before you, and drive them from out of your sight; and ye shall possess their land, as the Lord your God hath promised unto you.

6 Be ye therefore very courageous to keep and to do all that is written in the book of the law of Moses, that ye turn not aside therefrom to the right hand or to the left;

7 That ye come not among these nations, these that remain among you; neither make mention of the name of their gods, nor cause to swear by them, neither serve them, nor bow yourselves unto them:

8 But cleave unto the Lord your God, as ye have done unto this day.

9 For the Lord hath driven out from before you great nations and strong: but as for you, no man hath been able to stand before you unto this day.

10 One man of you shall chase a thousand: for the Lord your God, he it is that fighteth for you, as he hath promised you.

11 Take good heed therefore unto yourselves, that ye love the Lord your God.

12 Else if ye do in any wise go back, and cleave unto the remnant of these nations, even these that remain among you, and shall make marriages with them, and go in unto them, and they to you:

13 Know for a certainty that the Lord your God will no more drive out any of these nations from before you; but they shall be snares and traps unto you, and scourges in your sides, and thorns in your eyes, until ye perish from off this good land which the Lord your God hath given you.

14 And, behold, this day I am going the way of all the earth: and ye know in all your hearts and in all your souls, that not one thing hath failed of all the good things which the Lord your God spake concerning you; all are come to pass unto you, and not one thing hath failed thereof.

15 Therefore it shall come to pass, that as all good things are come upon you, which the Lord your God promised you; so shall the Lord bring upon you all evil things, until he have destroyed you from off this good land which the Lord your God hath given you.

16 When ye have transgressed the covenant of the Lord your God, which he commanded you, and have gone and served other gods, and bowed yourselves to them; then shall the anger of the Lord be kindled against you, and ye shall perish quickly from off the good land which he hath given unto you.

Joshua pleaded with Israel to "cleave unto the Lord" and "love the Lord your God." What helps you cleave, or cling, to the Lord and His teachings? How do you show the Lord that you love Him? According to verses 15 and 16, what would happen to Israel if they served other gods?

DEBORAH THE PROPHETESS INSTRUCTS THE CAPTAIN OF THE ISRAELITE ARMY TO BATTLE THE CANAANITES ACCORDING TO GOD'S COMMAND

The Israelites had finally entered the promised land. About 700 years before, God had covenanted with Abraham, Isaac, and Jacob that He would greatly multiply their posterities and lead that posterity to a land that would be their own. At this point, the Israelites were divided into their respective tribes according to which of the twelve sons of Jacob they descended from. These "tribes" each inherited a specific region of land within Canaan (see Map #2). They shared the same covenant with God and were expected to live according to the many laws God had given to Moses and had repeated to Joshua, but the Israelites again began to drift from their covenants. Joshua then passed away, and a period of "judges" began that lasted for the next two hundred years. Instead of calling a single prophet to lead the people, "the Lord raised up judges" (Judges 2:16) from among the twelve tribes. These judges were similar to civil representatives or military leaders who tried to bring order and safety during this long period of turmoil, disobedience, and foreign oppression. One of these judges was a woman name Deborah, who was also a prophetess. During her time, Canaan oppressed Israel for twenty years. Jabin was king of Canaan, and Sisera was captain of the Canaanite army. Under these conditions, Deborah instructed Barak, the leader of the Israelite army, to follow God's command to overthrow the Canaanite army.

JUDGES 4:4–9, 14–16

And Deborah, a prophetess, the wife of Lapidoth, she judged Israel at that time. 5 And she dwelt under the palm tree of Deborah between Ramah and Beth-el in mount Ephraim: and the children of Israel came up to her for judgment.

6 And she sent and called Barak the son of Abinoam out of Kedesh-naphtali, and said unto him, Hath not the Lord God of Israel commanded, saying, Go and draw toward mount Tabor, and take with thee ten thousand men of the children of Naphtali and of the children of Zebulun?

7 And I will draw unto thee to the river Kishon Sisera, the captain of Jabin's army, with his chariots and his multitude; and I will deliver him into thine hand.

8 And Barak said unto her, If thou wilt go with me, then I will go: but if thou wilt not go with me, then I will not go.

9 And she said, I will surely go with thee: notwithstanding the journey that thou takest shall not be for thine honour; for the Lord shall sell Sisera into the hand of a woman. And Deborah arose, and went with Barak to Kedesh.

14 And Deborah said unto Barak, Up; for this is the day in which the Lord hath delivered Sisera into thine hand: is not the Lord gone out before thee? So Barak went down from mount Tabor, and ten thousand men after him.

15 And the Lord discomfited Sisera, and all his chariots, and all his host, with the edge of the sword before Barak; so that Sisera lighted down off his chariot, and fled away on his feet.

16 But Barak pursued after the chariots, and after the host, unto Harosheth of the Gentiles: and all the host of Sisera fell upon the edge of the sword; and there was not a man left.

What was Barak's response to Deborah's instructions? How were the Israelites blessed by obeying Deborah's instructions? What callings and responsibilities has God given to women in His Church today? How do these women bless the entire Church?

IN PREPARATION TO LEAD THE ISRAELITES IN BATTLE, GIDEON FIRST DESTROYS THE WICKED IDOLS OF HIS FATHER'S HOUSE

Deborah, a prophetess and judge in Israel, had instructed the captain of the Israelite army to obey God's commandment to give battle to the Canaanites. Together they obeyed and ensured Israel's victory over the Canaanites. Another noted judge during this period was a man named Gideon from the tribe of Manasseh. During his life, "the children of Israel did evil in the sight of the Lord: and the Lord delivered them into the hand of Midian seven years" (Judges 6:1). An angel then appeared to Gideon, who was called to lead the Israelites in a miraculous victory against the Midianites. In these verses, "Baal" is a reference to an idolatrous figure worshipped by the people.

JUDGES 6:12–16, 25–32

And the angel of the Lord appeared unto him, and said unto him, The Lord is with thee, thou mighty man of valour.

13 And Gideon said unto him, Oh my Lord, if the Lord be with us, why then is all this befallen us? and where be all his miracles which our fathers told us of, saying, Did not the Lord bring us up from Egypt? but now the Lord hath forsaken us, and delivered us into the hands of the Midianites.

14 And the Lord looked upon him, and said, Go in this thy might, and thou shalt save Israel from the hand of the Midianites: have not I sent thee?

15 And he said unto him, Oh my Lord, wherewith shall I save Israel? behold, my family is poor in Manasseh, and I am the least in my father's house.

16 And the Lord said unto him, Surely I will be with thee, and thou shalt smite the Midianites as one man.

25 And it came to pass the same night, that the Lord said unto him, Take thy father's young bullock, even the second bullock of seven years old, and throw down the altar of Baal that thy father hath, and cut down the grove that is by it:

26 And build an altar unto the Lord thy God upon the top of this rock, in the ordered place, and take the second bullock, and offer a burnt sacrifice with the wood of the grove which thou shalt cut down.

27 Then Gideon took ten men of his servants, and did as the Lord had said unto him: and so it was, because he feared his father's household, and the men of the city, that he could not do it by day, that he did it by night.

28 And when the men of the city arose early in the morning, behold, the altar of Baal was cast down, and the grove was cut down that was by it, and the second bullock was offered upon the altar that was built.

29 And they said one to another, Who hath done this thing? And when they inquired and asked, they said, Gideon the son of Joash hath done this thing.

30 Then the men of the city said unto Joash, Bring out thy son, that he may die: because he hath cast down the altar of Baal, and because he hath cut down the grove that was by it.

31 And Joash said unto all that stood against him, Will ye plead for Baal? will ye save him? he that will plead for him, let him be put to death whilst it is yet morning: if he be a god, let him plead for himself, because one hath cast down his altar.

32 Therefore on that day he called him Jerubbaal, saying, Let Baal plead against him, because he hath thrown down his altar.

What was Gideon's response when called by the angel? How was his response similar to other Old Testament prophets who had been called by God? In preparation for defeating the Israelites' wicked enemies, Gideon first rooted out wickedness in his own home. How can you follow that example?

GOD PROVES HIS MIGHT BY REDUCING GIDEON'S ARMY TO THREE HUNDRED MEN, WHO THEN MIRACULOUSLY DEFEAT THE MIDIANITES

As a result of their wickedness, the Israelites were delivered into bondage to the Midianites. Gideon was called by the Lord to lead the Israelites in overthrowing their oppressors. Gideon first rooted out wickedness within his father's house by destroying an altar to the idolatrous god of Baal. Some Israelites wanted Gideon killed for this, but Gideon's father interceded and said Gideon's actions were inspired by God, and Gideon became known also as Jerubbaal, or "he that striveth with Baal." Gideon then closely followed God's commands as the Israelites were miraculously freed from the Midianites. In these verses, the term "pitcher" is a reference to a pot or vessel that made a loud noise when broken. Gideon would use the sudden sight of torches and the sounds of trumpets and broken pitchers to startle the Midianites, who far outnumbered his three hundred men.

JUDGES 7:1–8, 16–23

Then Jerubbaal, who is Gideon, and all the people that were with him, rose up early, and pitched beside the well of Harod: so that the host of the Midianites were on the north side of them, by the hill of Moreh, in the valley.

2 And the Lord said unto Gideon, The people that are with thee are too many for me to give the Midianites into their hands, lest Israel vaunt themselves against me, saying, Mine own hand hath saved me.

3 Now therefore go to, proclaim in the ears of the people, saying, Whosoever is fearful and afraid, let him return and depart early from mount Gilead. And there returned of the people twenty and two thousand; and there remained ten thousand.

4 And the Lord said unto Gideon, The people are yet too many; bring them down unto the water, and I will try them for thee there: and it shall be, that of whom I say unto thee, This shall go with thee, the same shall go with thee; and of whomsoever I say unto thee, This shall not go with thee, the same shall not go.

5 So he brought down the people unto the water: and the Lord said unto Gideon, Every one that lappeth of the water with his tongue, as a dog lappeth, him shalt thou set by himself; likewise every one that boweth down upon his knees to drink.

6 And the number of them that lapped, putting their hand to their mouth, were three hundred men: but all the rest of the people bowed down upon their knees to drink water.

7 And the Lord said unto Gideon, By the three hundred men that lapped will I save you, and deliver the Midianites into thine hand: and let all the other people go every man unto his place.

8 So the people took victuals in their hand, and their trumpets: and he sent all the rest of Israel every man unto his tent, and retained those three hundred men: and the host of Midian was beneath him in the valley.

16 And he divided the three hundred men into three companies, and he put a trumpet in every man's hand, with empty pitchers, and lamps within the pitchers.

17 And he said unto them, Look on me, and do likewise: and, behold, when I come to the outside of the camp, it shall be that, as I do, so shall ye do.

18 When I blow with a trumpet, I and all that are with me, then blow ye the trumpets also on every side of all the camp, and say, The sword of the Lord, and of Gideon.

19 So Gideon, and the hundred men that were with him, came unto the outside of the camp in the beginning of the middle watch; and they had but newly set the watch: and they blew the trumpets, and brake the pitchers that were in their hands.

20 And the three companies blew the trumpets, and brake the pitchers, and held the lamps in their left hands, and the trumpets in their right hands to blow withal: and they cried, The sword of the Lord, and of Gideon.

21 And they stood every man in his place round about the camp: and all the host ran, and cried, and fled.

22 And the three hundred blew the trumpets, and the Lord set every man's sword against his fellow, even throughout all the host: and the host fled to Beth-shittah in Zererath, and to the border of Abel-meholah, unto Tabbath.

23 And the men of Israel gathered themselves together out of Naphtali, and out of Asher, and out of all Manasseh, and pursued after the Midianites.

After their surprise attack upon the Midianites, Gideon's forces were joined by additional Israelites. Together they pursued the confused and fleeing Midianites, who were destroyed, freeing the Israelites from their bondage that had lasted seven years.

The Lord promised to free the Israelites, but what instructions did they need to follow to gain their freedom? What can we learn from the Lord's ability to use three hundred men to defeat a large army? What are some limitations you have? How has the Lord helped you overcome those limitations as you have assisted in His work?

SAMSON TOPPLES A BUILDING, KILLING THOUSANDS OF PHILISTINES AND HIMSELF

The Israelites had become wicked and were delivered into the hands of the Midianites, who held them in bondage for seven years. God called Gideon to lead three hundred men in overthrowing the Midianites with a surprise attack. The Israelites were free once again, but they soon returned to idolatry and other forms of wickedness, prompting a forty-year period in which they were again brought into bondage—this time to a group called the Philistines. A woman from the tribe of Dan was visited by an angel who told her she would give birth to a son, upon whom "no razor shall come on his head: for the child shall be a Nazarite unto God from the womb: and he shall begin to deliver Israel out of the hand of the Philistines" (Judges 13:5). Nazarites were people who dedicated their lives to God and abstained from wine and cutting their hair (see Numbers 6). The woman gave birth to the child and named him Samson. He was gifted with unusual strength, "and the Spirit of the Lord began to move him at times" (Judges 13:25). He once killed a lion with his bare hands and later killed thirty Philistines. The Philistines responded by killing Samson's wife and father-in-law. In turn, Samson sought revenge and killed a thousand Philistines. Later, Samson fell in love with a Philistine woman named Delilah, who continually pleaded with Samson to reveal the source of his strength. Samson deceived Delilah three times as to the source of his strength before finally revealing to her the truth.

That he told her all his heart, and said unto her, There hath not come a razor upon mine head; for I have been a Nazarite unto God from my mother's womb: if I be shaven, then my strength will go from me, and I shall become weak, and be like any other man.

18 And when Delilah saw that he had told her all his heart, she sent and called for the lords of the Philistines, saying, Come up this once, for he hath shewed me all his heart. Then the lords of the Philistines came up unto her, and brought money in their hand.

19 And she made him sleep upon her knees; and she called for a man, and she caused him to shave off the seven locks of his head; and she began to afflict him, and his strength went from him.

20 And she said, The Philistines be upon thee, Samson. And he awoke out of his sleep, and said, I will go out as at other times before, and shake myself. And he wist not that the Lord was departed from him.

21 But the Philistines took him, and put out his eyes, and brought him down to Gaza, and bound him with fetters of brass; and he did grind in the prison house.

22 Howbeit the hair of his head began to grow again after he was shaven.

23 Then the lords of the Philistines gathered them together for to offer a great sacrifice unto Dagon their god, and to rejoice: for they said, Our god hath delivered Samson our enemy into our hand.

24 And when the people saw him, they praised their god: for they said, Our god hath delivered into our hands our enemy, and the destroyer of our country, which slew many of us.

25 And it came to pass, when their hearts were merry, that they said, Call for Samson, that he may make us sport. And they called for Samson out of the prison house; and he made them sport: and they set him between the pillars.

26 And Samson said unto the lad that held him by the hand, Suffer me that I may feel the pillars whereupon the house standeth, that I may lean upon them.

27 Now the house was full of men and women; and all the lords of the Philistines were there; and there were upon the roof about three thousand men and women, that beheld while Samson made sport.

28 And Samson called unto the Lord, and said, O Lord God, remember me, I pray thee, and strengthen me, I pray thee, only this once, O God, that I may be at once avenged of the Philistines for my two eyes.

29 And Samson took hold of the two middle pillars upon which the house stood, and on which it was borne up, of the one with his right hand, and of the other with his left.

30 And Samson said, Let me die with the Philistines. And he bowed himself with all his might; and the house fell upon the lords, and upon all the people that were therein. So the dead which he slew at his death were more than they which he slew in his life.

Where did Samson get his strength? What strengths has God given you? What choices did Samson make that caused him to lose his strength? What happened when Samson prayed to God to strengthen him once more? When have you called upon the Lord to strengthen you?

RUTH FOLLOWS HER MOTHER-IN-LAW, NAOMI, TO BETHLEHEM, DECLARING THAT SHE WILL BELIEVE IN THE GOD OF ISRAEL

As the era of judges in Israel continued, a famine arose in the land. An Israelite woman named Naomi journeyed with her husband and two sons to the land of Moab in search of food. There they lived for about ten years, during which time Naomi's husband died, both of her sons married, and both sons died as well. Naomi felt that God had abandoned her but desired to return to Canaan (to the city of Bethlehem) after hearing that God had provided food there for the people. Naomi expected that her non-Israelite daughters-in-law, Ruth and Orpah, would remain in Moab.

RUTH 1:7–9, 14–22

Wherefore she went forth out of the place where she was, and her two daughters in law with her; and they went on the way to return unto the land of Judah.

8 And Naomi said unto her two daughters in law, Go, return each to her mother's house: the Lord deal kindly with you, as ye have dealt with the dead, and with me.

9 The Lord grant you that ye may find rest, each of you in the house of her husband. Then she kissed them; and they lifted up their voice, and wept.

14 And they lifted up their voice, and wept again: and Orpah kissed her mother in law; but Ruth clave unto her.

15 And she said, Behold, thy sister in law is gone back unto her people, and unto her gods: return thou after thy sister in law.

16 And Ruth said, Entreat me not to leave thee, or to return from following after thee: for whither thou goest, I will go; and where thou lodgest, I will lodge: thy people shall be my people, and thy God my God:

17 Where thou diest, will I die, and there will I be buried: the Lord do so to me, and more also, if ought but death part thee and me.

18 When she saw that she was steadfastly minded to go with her, then she left speaking unto her.

19 So they two went until they came to Bethlehem. And it came to pass, when they were come to Beth-lehem, that all the city was moved about them, and they said, Is this Naomi?

20 And she said unto them, Call me not Naomi, call me Mara: for the Almighty hath dealt very bitterly with me.

21 I went out full, and the Lord hath brought me home again empty: why then call ye me Naomi, seeing the Lord hath testified against me, and the Almighty hath afflicted me?

22 So Naomi returned, and Ruth the Moabitess, her daughter in law, with her, which returned out of the country of Moab: and they came to Bethlehem in the beginning of barley harvest.

What was Ruth's reply when Naomi told her she could return to her people? Ruth's commitment to Naomi is a beautiful tribute to the love this mother and daughter-in-law shared. How do you express your love to your family? What could you do today to show others in your family that you love them?

RUTH WORKS IN THE HARVEST FIELDS; BOAZ IS IMPRESSED BY HER KINDNESS AND STRENGTH AND AGREES TO MARRY HER

Ruth the Moabite had followed her mother-in-law Naomi from Moab to the Israelite city of Bethlehem. In doing so, Ruth had declared to Naomi, "Whither thou goest, I will go; . . . thy people shall be my people, and thy God my God" (Ruth 1:16). Both women were widows during a time of famine, and Ruth would prove to be a kind, hardworking guardian of her mother-in-law. After farmers had harvested their grain and corn, it was customary to allow people to enter the fields and gather the small scatterings of grain that had been left behind—a job that required a great amount of work for a small amount of food. A man named Boaz owned one of these fields and would note Ruth's determination and kindness as she "gleaned," or gathered the bits of grain. After the events recounted in Ruth 2, Boaz would agree to marry Ruth, leading to the events recounted in Ruth 4.

RUTH 2:2–13, 17–20

And Ruth the Moabitess said unto Naomi, Let me now go to the field, and glean ears of corn after him in whose sight I shall find grace. And she said unto her, Go, my daughter.

3 And she went, and came, and gleaned in the field after the reapers: and her hap was to light on a part of the field belonging unto Boaz, who was of the kindred of Elimelech.

4 And, behold, Boaz came from Beth-lehem, and said unto the reapers, The Lord be with you. And they answered him, The Lord bless thee.

5 Then said Boaz unto his servant that was set over the reapers, Whose damsel is this?

6 And the servant that was set over the reapers answered and said, It is the Moabitish damsel that came back with Naomi out of the country of Moab:

7 And she said, I pray you, let me glean and gather after the reapers among the sheaves: so she came, and hath continued even from the morning until now, that she tarried a little in the house.

8 Then said Boaz unto Ruth, Hearest thou not, my daughter? Go not to glean in another field, neither go from hence, but abide here fast by my maidens:

9 Let thine eyes be on the field that they do reap, and go thou after them: have I not charged the young men that they shall not touch thee? and when thou art athirst, go unto the vessels, and drink of that which the young men have drawn.

10 Then she fell on her face, and bowed herself to the ground, and said unto him, Why have I found grace in thine eyes, that thou shouldest take knowledge of me, seeing I am a stranger?

11 And Boaz answered and said unto her, It hath fully been shewed me, all that thou hast done unto thy mother in law since the death of thine husband: and how thou hast left thy father and thy mother, and the land of thy nativity, and art come unto a people which thou knewest not heretofore.

12 The Lord recompense thy work, and a full reward be given thee of the Lord God of Israel, under whose wings thou art come to trust.

13 Then she said, Let me find favour in thy sight, my lord; for that thou hast comforted me, and for that thou hast spoken friendly unto thine handmaid, though I be not like unto one of thine handmaidens.

17 So she gleaned in the field until even, and beat out that she had gleaned: and it was about an ephah of barley.

18 And she took it up, and went into the city: and her mother in law saw what she had gleaned: and she brought forth, and gave to her that she had reserved after she was sufficed.

19 And her mother in law said unto her, Where hast thou gleaned to day? and where wroughtest thou? blessed be he that did take knowledge of thee. And she shewed her mother in law with whom she had wrought, and said, The man's name with whom I wrought to day is Boaz.

20 And Naomi said unto her daughter in law, Blessed be he of the Lord, who hath not left off

his kindness to the living and to the dead. And Naomi said unto her, The man is near of kin unto us, one of our next kinsmen.

RUTH 4:13–17

13 So Boaz took Ruth, and she was his wife: and when he went in unto her, the Lord gave her conception, and she bare a son.

14 And the women said unto Naomi, Blessed be the Lord, which hath not left thee this day without a kinsman, that his name may be famous in Israel.

15 And he shall be unto thee a restorer of thy life, and a nourisher of thine old age: for thy daughter in law, which loveth thee, which is better to thee than seven sons, hath born him.

16 And Naomi took the child, and laid it in her bosom, and became nurse unto it.

17 And the women her neighbours gave it a name, saying, There is a son born to Naomi; and they called his name Obed: he is the father of Jesse, the father of David.

Why was Boaz so impressed by Ruth (see Ruth 2:11–12)? What blessings did Ruth receive because she was loyal to the God of Israel? What eternal blessings do we receive for being loyal to our families and our God?

HANNAH PRESENTS HER SON SAMUEL TO SERVE AT THE TABERNACLE, HONORING HER PROMISE TO GOD

The period of the judges in Israel was drawing to an end. During the preceding two hundred years, the Israelites had repeated a cycle of wickedness, suffering, repentance, and obedience. A new era was on the horizon, in which prophets would once again be called by God to lead the twelve tribes of Israel. The first of these prophets was a man named Samuel. His mother was a woman named Hannah, one of two wives of Elkanah. Elkanah's other wife, Peninnah, had children, and she often mocked Hannah, who was unable to bear children. This was deeply painful to Hannah and continued for many years. At the time, the tabernacle was located in Shiloh, where annual feasts were observed. At one of these feasts, Hannah again felt tormented by her inability to bear children and pleaded with God to bless her.

1 Samuel 1:9–20, 24–28

So Hannah rose up after they had eaten in Shiloh, and after they had drunk. Now Eli the priest sat upon a seat by a post of the temple of the Lord.

10 And she was in bitterness of soul, and prayed unto the Lord, and wept sore.

11 And she vowed a vow, and said, O Lord of hosts, if thou wilt indeed look on the affliction of thine handmaid, and remember me, and not forget thine handmaid, but wilt give unto thine handmaid a man child, then I will give him unto the Lord all the days of his life, and there shall no razor come upon his head.

12 And it came to pass, as she continued praying before the Lord, that Eli marked her mouth.

13 Now Hannah, she spake in her heart; only her lips moved, but her voice was not heard: therefore Eli thought she had been drunken.

14 And Eli said unto her, How long wilt thou be drunken? put away thy wine from thee.

15 And Hannah answered and said, No, my lord, I am a woman of a sorrowful spirit: I have drunk neither wine nor strong drink, but have poured out my soul before the Lord.

16 Count not thine handmaid for a daughter of Belial: for out of the abundance of my complaint and grief have I spoken hitherto.

17 Then Eli answered and said, Go in peace: and the God of Israel grant thee thy petition that thou hast asked of him.

18 And she said, Let thine handmaid find grace in thy sight. So the woman went her way, and did eat, and her countenance was no more sad.

19 And they rose up in the morning early, and worshipped before the Lord, and returned, and came to their house to Ramah: and Elkanah knew Hannah his wife; and the Lord remembered her.

20 Wherefore it came to pass, when the time was come about after Hannah had conceived, that she bare a son, and called his name Samuel, saying, Because I have asked him of the Lord.

24 And when she had weaned him, she took him up with her, with three bullocks, and one ephah of flour, and a bottle of wine, and brought him unto the house of the Lord in Shiloh: and the child was young.

25 And they slew a bullock, and brought the child to Eli.

26 And she said, Oh my lord, as thy soul liveth, my lord, I am the woman that stood by thee here, praying unto the Lord.

27 For this child I prayed; and the Lord hath given me my petition which I asked of him:

28 Therefore also I have lent him to the Lord; as long as he liveth he shall be lent to the Lord. And he worshipped the Lord there.

What caused Hannah to be so sorrowful? To whom did she turn in her time of sadness? Who spoke to her in the temple and comforted her? Share an example of when you have prayed during a time of sorrow. What brought you comfort? How can you follow Eli's example today and bring comfort to someone who is sad?

SAMUEL RESPONDS TO THE VOICE OF GOD AND IS RECOGNIZED BY ALL OF ISRAEL AS A PROPHET

Hannah had pleaded with God for a son, promising that she would offer that son for a life of service to God. Samuel was then born and Hannah kept her promise. After Samuel was weaned, Hannah presented Samuel to Eli the priest at the tabernacle. Hannah praised God and was later blessed with additional children. Samuel began his duties at the tabernacle, earning the respect of both God and man. Meanwhile, Eli's own sons persisted in wickedness, prompting God to reject Eli's posterity as worthy heirs of priestly duties. In their place, God promised to "raise me up a faithful priest" (1 Samuel 2:35).

1 SAMUEL 3:1–21

And the child Samuel ministered unto the Lord before Eli. And the word of the Lord was precious in those days; there was no open vision.

2 And it came to pass at that time, when Eli was laid down in his place, and his eyes began to wax dim, that he could not see;

3 And ere the lamp of God went out in the temple of the Lord, where the ark of God was, and Samuel was laid down to sleep;

4 That the Lord called Samuel: and he answered, Here am I.

5 And he ran unto Eli, and said, Here am I; for thou calledst me. And he said, I called not; lie down again. And he went and lay down.

6 And the Lord called yet again, Samuel. And Samuel arose and went to Eli, and said, Here am I; for thou didst call me. And he answered, I called not, my son; lie down again.

7 Now Samuel did not yet know the Lord, neither was the word of the Lord yet revealed unto him.

8 And the Lord called Samuel again the third time. And he arose and went to Eli, and said, Here am I; for thou didst call me. And Eli perceived that the Lord had called the child.

9 Therefore Eli said unto Samuel, Go, lie down: and it shall be, if he call thee, that thou shalt say, Speak, Lord; for thy servant heareth. So Samuel went and lay down in his place.

10 And the Lord came, and stood, and called as at other times, Samuel, Samuel. Then Samuel answered, Speak; for thy servant heareth.

11 And the Lord said to Samuel, Behold, I will do a thing in Israel, at which both the ears of every one that heareth it shall tingle.

12 In that day I will perform against Eli all things which I have spoken concerning his house: when I begin, I will also make an end.

13 For I have told him that I will judge his house for ever for the iniquity which he knoweth; because his sons made themselves vile, and he restrained them not.

14 And therefore I have sworn unto the house of Eli, that the iniquity of Eli's house shall not be purged with sacrifice nor offering for ever.

15 And Samuel lay until the morning, and opened the doors of the house of the Lord. And Samuel feared to shew Eli the vision.

16 Then Eli called Samuel, and said, Samuel, my son. And he answered, Here am I.

17 And he said, What is the thing that the Lord hath said unto thee? I pray thee hide it not from me: God do so to thee, and more also, if thou hide any thing from me of all the things that he said unto thee.

18 And Samuel told him every whit, and hid nothing from him. And he said, It is the Lord: let him do what seemeth him good.

19 And Samuel grew, and the Lord was with him, and did let none of his words fall to the ground.

20 And all Israel from Dan even to Beer-sheba knew that Samuel was established to be a prophet of the Lord.

21 And the Lord appeared again in Shiloh: for the Lord revealed himself to Samuel in Shiloh by the word of the Lord.

When the Lord spoke to Samuel, who did Samuel mistakenly believe was speaking to him? Who helped Samuel recognize that he was hearing the Lord's voice? How can you recognize the presence of the Holy Ghost? Share an experience you recently had when you felt the influence of the Holy Ghost.

SAUL IS REMOVED AS KING OF ISRAEL AND TOLD BY SAMUEL, "TO OBEY IS BETTER THAN SACRIFICE"

As a young boy, Samuel had responded to the voice of God and was later recognized by all of Israel as a prophet. Israel was afflicted once again by the Philistines, and over the course of many years Samuel preached against wickedness and idolatry. The Israelites then began to desire a king to rule over all twelve tribes. This concerned Samuel, but he was persuaded by God to allow a king to rule over them—and God revealed that a man named Saul should be king. Saul boldly led the Israelites in many battles. Prior to a battle against the people of Amalek, Samuel gave strict instructions to Saul.

1 Samuel 15:3–5, 7–11, 13–26, 34–35; Joseph Smith Translation, 1 Samuel 15:11, 35

Now go and smite Amalek, and utterly destroy all that they have, and spare them not; but slay both man and woman, infant and suckling, ox and sheep, camel and ass.

4 And Saul gathered the people together, and numbered them in Telaim, two hundred thousand footmen, and ten thousand men of Judah.

5 And Saul came to a city of Amalek, and laid wait in the valley.

7 And Saul smote the Amalekites from Havilah until thou comest to Shur, that is over against Egypt.

8 And he took Agag the king of the Amalekites alive, and utterly destroyed all the people with the edge of the sword.

9 But Saul and the people spared Agag, and the best of the sheep, and of the oxen, and of the fatlings, and the lambs, and all that was good, and would not utterly destroy them: but every thing that was vile and refuse, that they destroyed utterly.

10 Then came the word of the Lord unto Samuel, saying,

11 *I have set up Saul to be a king, and he repenteth not that he hath sinned,* for he is turned back from following me, and hath not performed my commandments. And it grieved Samuel; and he cried unto the Lord all night.

13 And Samuel came to Saul: and Saul said unto him, Blessed be thou of the Lord: I have performed the commandment of the Lord.

14 And Samuel said, What meaneth then this bleating of the sheep in mine ears, and the lowing of the oxen which I hear?

15 And Saul said, They have brought them from the Amalekites: for the people spared the best of the sheep and of the oxen, to sacrifice unto the Lord thy God; and the rest we have utterly destroyed.

16 Then Samuel said unto Saul, Stay, and I will tell thee what the Lord hath said to me this night. And he said unto him, Say on.

17 And Samuel said, When thou wast little in thine own sight, wast thou not made the head of the tribes of Israel, and the Lord anointed thee king over Israel?

18 And the Lord sent thee on a journey, and said, Go and utterly destroy the sinners the Amalekites, and fight against them until they be consumed.

19 Wherefore then didst thou not obey the voice of the Lord, but didst fly upon the spoil, and didst evil in the sight of the Lord?

20 And Saul said unto Samuel, Yea, I have obeyed the voice of the Lord, and have gone the way which the Lord sent me, and have brought Agag the king of Amalek, and have utterly destroyed the Amalekites.

21 But the people took of the spoil, sheep and oxen, the chief of the things which should have been utterly destroyed, to sacrifice unto the Lord thy God in Gilgal.

22 And Samuel said, Hath the Lord as great delight in burnt offerings and sacrifices, as in obeying the voice of the Lord? Behold, to obey is better than sacrifice, and to hearken than the fat of rams.

23 For rebellion is as the sin of witchcraft, and stubbornness is as iniquity and idolatry. Because thou hast rejected the word of the Lord, he hath also rejected thee from being king.

24 And Saul said unto Samuel, I have sinned: for I have transgressed the commandment of the Lord, and thy words: because I feared the people, and obeyed their voice.

25 Now therefore, I pray thee, pardon my sin, and turn again with me, that I may worship the Lord.

26 And Samuel said unto Saul, I will not return with thee: for thou hast rejected the word of the Lord, and the Lord hath rejected thee from being king over Israel.

34 Then Samuel went to Ramah; and Saul went up to his house to Gibeah of Saul.

35 And Samuel came no more to see Saul until the day of his death: nevertheless Samuel mourned for Saul: and the Lord *rent the kingdom from Saul whom he had made king over Israel.*

What was Saul commanded to do once he had defeated the Amalekites? What did he do instead? How did he justify his actions of disobedience (see verse 21)? What did Samuel teach Saul in verse 22? How does that principle apply to us today?

GOD TEACHES SAMUEL THAT "THE LORD LOOKETH ON THE HEART" AND REVEALS THAT DAVID IS TO BE THE NEW KING OF ISRAEL

Samuel the prophet led the Israelites, but the people had also pleaded for a king to govern them. God granted their desire and appointed Saul as their king, but Saul failed to obey specific instructions given to him by Samuel. Samuel had chastised Saul and emphasized the importance of strict obedience, and Saul was removed as king.

1 Samuel 16:1–13

And the Lord said unto Samuel, How long wilt thou mourn for Saul, seeing I have rejected him from reigning over Israel? fill thine horn with oil, and go, I will send thee to Jesse the Beth-lehemite: for I have provided me a king among his sons.

2 And Samuel said, How can I go? if Saul hear it, he will kill me. And the Lord said, Take an heifer with thee, and say, I am come to sacrifice to the Lord.

3 And call Jesse to the sacrifice, and I will shew thee what thou shalt do: and thou shalt anoint unto me him whom I name unto thee.

4 And Samuel did that which the Lord spake, and came to Beth-lehem. And the elders of the town trembled at his coming, and said, Comest thou peaceably?

5 And he said, Peaceably: I am come to sacrifice unto the Lord: sanctify yourselves, and come with me to the sacrifice. And he sanctified Jesse and his sons, and called them to the sacrifice.

6 And it came to pass, when they were come, that he looked on Eliab, and said, Surely the Lord's anointed is before him.

7 But the Lord said unto Samuel, Look not on his countenance, or on the height of his stature; because I have refused him: for the Lord seeth not as man seeth; for man looketh on the outward appearance, but the Lord looketh on the heart.

8 Then Jesse called Abinadab, and made him pass before Samuel. And he said, Neither hath the Lord chosen this.

9 Then Jesse made Shammah to pass by. And he said, Neither hath the Lord chosen this.

10 Again, Jesse made seven of his sons to pass before Samuel. And Samuel said unto Jesse, The Lord hath not chosen these.

11 And Samuel said unto Jesse, Are here all thy children? And he said, There remaineth yet the youngest, and, behold, he keepeth the sheep. And Samuel said unto Jesse, Send and fetch him: for we will not sit down till he come hither.

12 And he sent, and brought him in. Now he was ruddy, and withal of a beautiful countenance, and goodly to look to. And the Lord said, Arise, anoint him: for this is he.

13 Then Samuel took the horn of oil, and anointed him in the midst of his brethren: and the Spirit of the Lord came upon David from that day forward. So Samuel rose up, and went to Ramah.

What did the Lord teach Samuel about judging people based on their outward appearance? What are some qualities we can't see in others if we judge them only by how they look? What are some positive "inner" qualities you have noticed in those around you?

YOUNG DAVID SLAYS THE MIGHTY GOLIATH

Saul had been removed as king of Israel, and God revealed to Samuel that David would eventually be the new king. For many years, the Philistines had waged war against the Israelites. Saul, though removed as king, continued to lead the Israelite army as another battle commenced, with the Philistines gathered on one side of a valley and the Israelites on the other. During this extended battle, David was assigned to care for his father's sheep while his older brothers participated in the battle. Later, David's father would ask him to take food to his brothers and report on the status of the battle.

1 Samuel 17:4–11, 20–23, 26, 31–37, 40–51

And there went out a champion out of the camp of the Philistines, named Goliath, of Gath, whose height was six cubits and a span.

5 And he had an helmet of brass upon his head, and he was armed with a coat of mail; and the weight of the coat was five thousand shekels of brass.

6 And he had greaves of brass upon his legs, and a target of brass between his shoulders.

7 And the staff of his spear was like a weaver's beam; and his spear's head weighed six hundred shekels of iron: and one bearing a shield went before him.

8 And he stood and cried unto the armies of Israel, and said unto them, Why are ye come out to set your battle in array? am not I a Philistine, and ye servants to Saul? choose you a man for you, and let him come down to me.

9 If he be able to fight with me, and to kill me, then will we be your servants: but if I prevail against him, and kill him, then shall ye be our servants, and serve us.

10 And the Philistine said, I defy the armies of Israel this day; give me a man, that we may fight together.

11 When Saul and all Israel heard those words of the Philistine, they were dismayed, and greatly afraid.

20 And David rose up early in the morning, and left the sheep with a keeper, and took, and went, as Jesse had commanded him; and he came to the trench, as the host was going forth to the fight, and shouted for the battle.

21 For Israel and the Philistines had put the battle in array, army against army.

22 And David left his carriage in the hand of the keeper of the carriage, and ran into the army, and came and saluted his brethren.

23 And as he talked with them, behold, there came up the champion, the Philistine of Gath, Goliath by name, out of the armies of the Philistines, and spake according to the same words: and David heard them.

26 And David spake to the men that stood by him, saying, What shall be done to the man that killeth this Philistine, and taketh away the reproach from Israel? for who is this uncircumcised Philistine, that he should defy the armies of the living God?

31 And when the words were heard which David spake, they rehearsed them before Saul: and he sent for him.

32 And David said to Saul, Let no man's heart fail because of him; thy servant will go and fight with this Philistine.

33 And Saul said to David, Thou art not able to go against this Philistine to fight with him: for thou art but a youth, and he a man of war from his youth.

34 And David said unto Saul, Thy servant kept his father's sheep, and there came a lion, and a bear, and took a lamb out of the flock:

35 And I went out after him, and smote him, and delivered it out of his mouth: and when he arose against me, I caught him by his beard, and smote him, and slew him.

36 Thy servant slew both the lion and the bear: and this uncircumcised Philistine shall be as one of them, seeing he hath defied the armies of the living God.

37 David said moreover, The Lord that delivered me out of the paw of the lion, and out of the paw of the bear, he will deliver me out of the hand of this Philistine. And Saul said unto David, Go, and the Lord be with thee.

40 And he took his staff in his hand, and chose him five smooth stones out of the brook, and put them in a shepherd's bag which he had, even in a scrip; and his sling was in his hand: and he drew near to the Philistine.

41 And the Philistine came on and drew near unto David; and the man that bare the shield went before him.

42 And when the Philistine looked about, and saw David, he disdained him: for he was but a youth, and ruddy, and of a fair countenance.

43 And the Philistine said unto David, Am I a dog, that thou comest to me with staves? And the Philistine cursed David by his gods.

44 And the Philistine said to David, Come to me, and I will give thy flesh unto the fowls of the air, and to the beasts of the field.

45 Then said David to the Philistine, Thou comest to me with a sword, and with a spear, and with a shield: but I come to thee in the name of the Lord of hosts, the God of the armies of Israel, whom thou hast defied.

46 This day will the Lord deliver thee into mine hand; and I will smite thee, and take thine head from thee; and I will give the carcases of the host of the Philistines this day unto the fowls of the air, and to the wild beasts of the earth; that all the earth may know that there is a God in Israel.

47 And all this assembly shall know that the Lord saveth not with sword and spear: for the battle is the Lord's, and he will give you into our hands.

48 And it came to pass, when the Philistine arose, and came and drew nigh to meet David, that David hasted, and ran toward the army to meet the Philistine.

49 And David put his hand in his bag, and took thence a stone, and slang it, and smote the Philistine in his forehead, that the stone sunk into his forehead; and he fell upon his face to the earth.

50 So David prevailed over the Philistine with a sling and with a stone, and smote the Philistine, and slew him; but there was no sword in the hand of David.

51 Therefore David ran, and stood upon the Philistine, and took his sword, and drew it out of the sheath thereof, and slew him, and cut off his head therewith. And when the Philistines saw their champion was dead, they fled.

In these verses, what physical descriptions were given of Goliath and of David? What gave David the courage to believe he could defeat Goliath (see verses 37 and 45)? What are some giant-like challenges you may face today, and how can the Lord help you overcome them?

DAVID GIVES WAY TO TEMPTATION, COMMITS ADULTERY WITH BATHSHEBA, AND ARRANGES THE DEATH OF HER HUSBAND

As a young man, David had heroically killed Goliath the giant, and Saul became jealous of the praise David received throughout Israel. For many years, Saul repeated a cycle of relying upon David's skill as a military leader, then plotting to kill David, then recognizing David's enduring goodness and asking forgiveness. Through it all, David was patient and refused to kill Saul, even when presented with opportunities for revenge. Saul was eventually killed in battle, as was his son Jonathan, with whom David had formed a deep friendship. After Saul's death, David—at age thirty—was recognized as king of all Israel and reigned for the next forty years. But despite his many heroic deeds, David would give in to temptation and cause great harm to himself and those around him. Joab, referred to in verse 14, was a captain in the Israelite army.

2 SAMUEL 11:1–17, 26–27

And it came to pass, after the year was expired, at the time when kings go forth to battle, that David sent Joab, and his servants with him, and all Israel; and they destroyed the children of Ammon, and besieged Rabbah. But David tarried still at Jerusalem.

2 And it came to pass in an eveningtide, that David arose from off his bed, and walked upon the roof of the king's house: and from the roof he saw a woman washing herself; and the woman was very beautiful to look upon.

3 And David sent and inquired after the woman. And one said, Is not this Bath-sheba, the daughter of Eliam, the wife of Uriah the Hittite?

4 And David sent messengers, and took her; and she came in unto him, and he lay with her; for she was purified from her uncleanness: and she returned unto her house.

5 And the woman conceived, and sent and told David, and said, I am with child.

6 And David sent to Joab, saying, Send me Uriah the Hittite. And Joab sent Uriah to David.

7 And when Uriah was come unto him, David demanded of him how Joab did, and how the people did, and how the war prospered.

8 And David said to Uriah, Go down to thy house, and wash thy feet. And Uriah departed out of the king's house, and there followed him a mess of meat from the king.

9 But Uriah slept at the door of the king's house with all the servants of his lord, and went not down to his house.

10 And when they had told David, saying, Uriah went not down unto his house, David said unto Uriah, Camest thou not from thy journey? why then didst thou not go down unto thine house?

11 And Uriah said unto David, The ark, and Israel, and Judah, abide in tents; and my lord Joab, and the servants of my lord, are encamped in the open fields; shall I then go into mine house, to eat and to drink, and to lie with my wife? as thou livest, and as thy soul liveth, I will not do this thing.

12 And David said to Uriah, Tarry here to day also, and to morrow I will let thee depart. So Uriah abode in Jerusalem that day, and the morrow.

13 And when David had called him, he did eat and drink before him; and he made him drunk: and at even he went out to lie on his bed with the servants of his lord, but went not down to his house.

14 And it came to pass in the morning, that David wrote a letter to Joab, and sent it by the hand of Uriah.

15 And he wrote in the letter, saying, Set ye Uriah in the forefront of the hottest battle, and retire ye from him, that he may be smitten, and die.

16 And it came to pass, when Joab observed the city, that he assigned Uriah unto a place where he knew that valiant men were.

17 And the men of the city went out, and fought with Joab: and there fell some of the people of the servants of David; and Uriah the Hittite died also.

26 And when the wife of Uriah heard that Uriah her husband was dead, she mourned for her husband.

27 And when the mourning was past, David sent and fetched her to his house, and she became his wife, and bare him a son. But the thing that David had done displeased the Lord.

What actions did King David take to cover up the fact that Bathsheba was pregnant with his child? How did the Lord feel about David's actions? What guidance have modern-day prophets given to help us avoid and overcome sexual temptation?

NATHAN CHASTISES DAVID FOR HIS SINFUL BEHAVIOR BY TELLING HIM THE PARABLE OF THE EWE LAMB

David, though mighty in battle and noble as a king, gave way to temptation and committed adultery with Bathsheba. He then tried to cover up his sin through a series of actions that resulted in the death of Bathsheba's husband. Bathsheba then became one of David's wives and gave birth to his son. But David would not escape the consequences of his actions. Several years prior, Samuel the prophet had died, and in his place, God had raised up Nathan as the spiritual leader of the Israelites. In these verses, a ewe is a female sheep.

2 Samuel 12:1–19; Joseph Smith Translation, 2 Samuel 12:13

And the Lord sent Nathan unto David. And he came unto him, and said unto him, There were two men in one city; the one rich, and the other poor.

2 The rich man had exceeding many flocks and herds:

3 But the poor man had nothing, save one little ewe lamb, which he had bought and nourished up: and it grew up together with him, and with his children; it did eat of his own meat, and drank of his own cup, and lay in his bosom, and was unto him as a daughter.

4 And there came a traveller unto the rich man, and he spared to take of his own flock and of his own herd, to dress for the wayfaring man that was come unto him; but took the poor man's lamb, and dressed it for the man that was come to him.

5 And David's anger was greatly kindled against the man; and he said to Nathan, As the Lord liveth, the man that hath done this thing shall surely die:

6 And he shall restore the lamb fourfold, because he did this thing, and because he had no pity.

7 And Nathan said to David, Thou art the man. Thus saith the Lord God of Israel, I anointed thee king over Israel, and I delivered thee out of the hand of Saul;

8 And I gave thee thy master's house, and thy master's wives into thy bosom, and gave thee the house of Israel and of Judah; and if that had been too little, I would moreover have given unto thee such and such things.

9 Wherefore hast thou despised the commandment of the Lord, to do evil in his sight? thou hast killed Uriah the Hittite with the sword, and hast taken his wife to be thy wife, and hast slain him with the sword of the children of Ammon.

10 Now therefore the sword shall never depart from thine house; because thou hast despised me, and hast taken the wife of Uriah the Hittite to be thy wife.

11 Thus saith the Lord, Behold, I will raise up evil against thee out of thine own house, and I will take thy wives before thine eyes, and give them unto thy neighbour, and he shall lie with thy wives in the sight of this sun.

12 For thou didst it secretly: but I will do this thing before all Israel, and before the sun.

13 And David said unto Nathan, I have sinned against the Lord. And Nathan said unto David, The Lord also hath *not* put away thy sin; *that* thou shalt not die.

14 Howbeit, because by this deed thou hast given great occasion to the enemies of the Lord to blaspheme, the child also that is born unto thee shall surely die.

15 And Nathan departed unto his house. And the Lord struck the child that Uriah's wife bare unto David, and it was very sick.

16 David therefore besought God for the child; and David fasted, and went in, and lay all night upon the earth.

17 And the elders of his house arose, and went to him, to raise him up from the earth: but he would not, neither did he eat bread with them.

18 And it came to pass on the seventh day, that the child died. And the servants of David feared to tell him that the child was dead: for they said, Behold, while the child was yet alive, we spake unto him, and he would not hearken unto our

voice: how will he then vex himself, if we tell him that the child is dead?

19 But when David saw that his servants whispered, David perceived that the child was dead: therefore David said unto his servants, Is the child dead? And they said, He is dead.

What message did Nathan deliver to King David? What consequences came upon David because of his sins? What effects do you see today when people choose to obey or disobey God's commandments? How can that strengthen your resolve to keep the commandments?

DAVID PRAISES THE LIFE-SAVING MERCY, MIGHT, AND SALVATION OF GOD

David had committed adultery and caused the death of Bathsheba's valiant husband. For this, David was chastised by the prophet Nathan and reaped the consequences of his sins. David's son born through Bathsheba was stricken and died, and God removed many of the blessings David would have otherwise received. It was a tragic fall for David, who for much of his life had been righteous and valiant and had been sustained and preserved by God in battle. Previous to David's fall from righteousness, he had recorded a poem that acknowledged the many times God had heard his prayers and saved him from destruction.

2 SAMUEL 22:1–7, 18–20, 26–37, 50–51

And David spake unto the Lord the words of this song in the day that the Lord had delivered him out of the hand of all his enemies, and out of the hand of Saul:

2 And he said, The Lord is my rock, and my fortress, and my deliverer;

3 The God of my rock; in him will I trust: he is my shield, and the horn of my salvation, my high tower, and my refuge, my saviour; thou savest me from violence.

4 I will call on the Lord, who is worthy to be praised: so shall I be saved from mine enemies.

5 When the waves of death compassed me, the floods of ungodly men made me afraid;

6 The sorrows of hell compassed me about; the snares of death prevented me;

7 In my distress I called upon the Lord, and cried to my God: and he did hear my voice out of his temple, and my cry did enter into his ears.

18 He delivered me from my strong enemy, and from them that hated me: for they were too strong for me.

19 They prevented me in the day of my calamity: but the Lord was my stay.

20 He brought me forth also into a large place: he delivered me, because he delighted in me.

26 With the merciful thou wilt shew thyself merciful, and with the upright man thou wilt shew thyself upright.

27 With the pure thou wilt shew thyself pure; and with the froward thou wilt shew thyself unsavoury.

28 And the afflicted people thou wilt save: but thine eyes are upon the haughty, that thou mayest bring them down.

29 For thou art my lamp, O Lord: and the Lord will lighten my darkness.

30 For by thee I have run through a troop: by my God have I leaped over a wall.

31 As for God, his way is perfect; the word of the Lord is tried: he is a buckler to all them that trust in him.

32 For who is God, save the Lord? and who is a rock, save our God?

33 God is my strength and power: and he maketh my way perfect.

34 He maketh my feet like hinds' feet: and setteth me upon my high places.

35 He teacheth my hands to war; so that a bow of steel is broken by mine arms.

36 Thou hast also given me the shield of thy salvation: and thy gentleness hath made me great.

37 Thou hast enlarged my steps under me; so that my feet did not slip.

50 Therefore I will give thanks unto thee, O Lord, among the heathen, and I will sing praises unto thy name.

51 He is the tower of salvation for his king: and sheweth mercy to his anointed, unto David, and to his seed for evermore.

What are some of the blessings David received for which he praised the Lord? Consider verse 29. In what way is the Lord a "lamp" to you, helping to "lighten" the darkness? How can you express gratitude for blessings you have received from God?

KING SOLOMON PLEASES GOD BY ASKING NOT FOR RICHES, BUT FOR WISDOM AND UNDERSTANDING

David and Bathsheba's first son had died on account of David's sinful behavior. Later, they had a son named Solomon. God loved Solomon, and in David's old age he designated Solomon as his heir to the throne. David then died, having reigned for forty years, the last thirty-three of which were in the city of Jerusalem (see Map #3, B4). He had lived a long and eventful life, and he knew firsthand the blessings that come from righteousness and the painful consequences of sin. Prior to his death, David advised Solomon to "keep the charge of the Lord thy God, to walk in his ways, to keep his statutes, and his commandments, and his judgments, and his testimonies, as it is written in the law of Moses" (1 Kings 2:3). It was now Solomon's time to prove his righteousness as he reigned in Jerusalem over the twelve tribes of Israel.

1 Kings 3:3–15

And Solomon loved the Lord, walking in the statutes of David his father: only he sacrificed and burnt incense in high places.

4 And the king went to Gibeon to sacrifice there; for that was the great high place: a thousand burnt offerings did Solomon offer upon that altar.

5 In Gibeon the Lord appeared to Solomon in a dream by night: and God said, Ask what I shall give thee.

6 And Solomon said, Thou hast shewed unto thy servant David my father great mercy, according as he walked before thee in truth, and in righteousness, and in uprightness of heart with thee; and thou hast kept for him this great kindness, that thou hast given him a son to sit on his throne, as it is this day.

7 And now, O Lord my God, thou hast made thy servant king instead of David my father: and I am but a little child: I know not how to go out or come in.

8 And thy servant is in the midst of thy people which thou hast chosen, a great people, that cannot be numbered nor counted for multitude.

9 Give therefore thy servant an understanding heart to judge thy people, that I may discern between good and bad: for who is able to judge this thy so great a people?

10 And the speech pleased the Lord, that Solomon had asked this thing.

11 And God said unto him, Because thou hast asked this thing, and hast not asked for thyself long life; neither hast asked riches for thyself, nor hast asked the life of thine enemies; but hast asked for thyself understanding to discern judgment;

12 Behold, I have done according to thy words: lo, I have given thee a wise and an understanding heart; so that there was none like thee before thee, neither after thee shall any arise like unto thee.

13 And I have also given thee that which thou hast not asked, both riches, and honour: so that there shall not be any among the kings like unto thee all thy days.

14 And if thou wilt walk in my ways, to keep my statutes and my commandments, as thy father David did walk, then I will lengthen thy days.

15 And Solomon awoke; and, behold, it was a dream. And he came to Jerusalem, and stood before the ark of the covenant of the Lord, and offered up burnt offerings, and offered peace offerings, and made a feast to all his servants.

What did Solomon ask the Lord for in verse 9? What did Solomon not ask for, thus pleasing the Lord? What are some gifts we can pray for that are better than worldly riches?

143

KING SOLOMON PROVES HIS WISDOM BY SUGGESTING A BABY BE CUT IN HALF, THUS CORRECTLY IDENTIFYING THE CHILD'S MOTHER

At the beginning of King Solomon's reign, he pleaded with God for wisdom and understanding, saying, "For who is able to judge this thy so great a people?" (1 Kings 3:9). This pleased God, and He promised Solomon not only wisdom, but also riches and honor. The need for wisdom soon presented itself as two bickering women approached the king, each claiming that the other had stolen her baby.

1 KINGS 3:16–28

Then came there two women, that were harlots, unto the king, and stood before him.

17 And the one woman said, O my lord, I and this woman dwell in one house; and I was delivered of a child with her in the house.

18 And it came to pass the third day after that I was delivered, that this woman was delivered also: and we were together; there was no stranger with us in the house, save we two in the house.

19 And this woman's child died in the night; because she overlaid it.

20 And she arose at midnight, and took my son from beside me, while thine handmaid slept, and laid it in her bosom, and laid her dead child in my bosom.

21 And when I rose in the morning to give my child suck, behold, it was dead: but when I had considered it in the morning, behold, it was not my son, which I did bear.

22 And the other woman said, Nay; but the living is my son, and the dead is thy son. And this said, No; but the dead is thy son, and the living is my son. Thus they spake before the king.

23 Then said the king, The one saith, This is my son that liveth, and thy son is the dead: and the other saith, Nay; but thy son is the dead, and my son is the living.

24 And the king said, Bring me a sword. And they brought a sword before the king.

25 And the king said, Divide the living child in two, and give half to the one, and half to the other.

26 Then spake the woman whose the living child was unto the king, for her bowels yearned upon her son, and she said, O my lord, give her the living child, and in no wise slay it. But the other said, Let it be neither mine nor thine, but divide it.

27 Then the king answered and said, Give her the living child, and in no wise slay it: she is the mother thereof.

28 And all Israel heard of the judgment which the king had judged; and they feared the king: for they saw that the wisdom of God was in him, to do judgment.

What test did Solomon devise to determine the true mother of the baby? How did this show King Solomon's wisdom? Consider the principle of wisdom, and discuss how you can develop and apply it in your life.

SOLOMON BUILDS GOD'S TEMPLE IN JERUSALEM AND OFFERS A DEDICATORY PRAYER

Solomon had been blessed by God with great wisdom, and he used that wisdom in ruling as the king of Israel. Solomon then began the massive undertaking of building a permanent temple in Jerusalem, where the same sacrifices and ordinances would take place that for nearly five hundred years had been allowed to take place only in the portable tabernacle constructed by Moses. God blessed Solomon's actions in building the temple and said: "Concerning this house which thou art in building, if thou wilt walk in my statutes, and execute my judgments, and keep all my commandments to walk in them; then will I perform my word with thee. . . . And I will dwell among the children of Israel, and will not forsake my people Israel" (1 Kings 6:12–13). Solomon built the temple using only the finest and strongest materials. When it was completed, the ark of the covenant was placed inside the temple, and the glory of the Lord filled the temple. Solomon then dedicated the temple by offering a prayer to God in the presence of a massive gathering of Israelites. Portions of that prayer are included here.

1 Kings 8:22–23, 27–30, 33–34, 37–40, 55–56, 59–62

And Solomon stood before the altar of the Lord in the presence of all the congregation of Israel, and spread forth his hands toward heaven:

23 And he said, Lord God of Israel, there is no God like thee, in heaven above, or on earth beneath, who keepest covenant and mercy with thy servants that walk before thee with all their heart:

27 But will God indeed dwell on the earth? behold, the heaven and heaven of heavens cannot contain thee; how much less this house that I have builded?

28 Yet have thou respect unto the prayer of thy servant, and to his supplication, O Lord my God, to hearken unto the cry and to the prayer, which thy servant prayeth before thee to day:

29 That thine eyes may be open toward this house night and day, even toward the place of which thou hast said, My name shall be there: that thou mayest hearken unto the prayer which thy servant shall make toward this place.

30 And hearken thou to the supplication of thy servant, and of thy people Israel, when they shall pray toward this place: and hear thou in heaven thy dwelling place: and when thou hearest, forgive.

33 When thy people Israel be smitten down before the enemy, because they have sinned against thee, and shall turn again to thee, and confess thy name, and pray, and make supplication unto thee in this house:

34 Then hear thou in heaven, and forgive the sin of thy people Israel, and bring them again unto the land which thou gavest unto their fathers.

37 If there be in the land famine, if there be pestilence, blasting, mildew, locust, or if there be caterpiller; if their enemy besiege them in the land of their cities; whatsoever plague, whatsoever sickness there be;

38 What prayer and supplication soever be made by any man, or by all thy people Israel, which shall know every man the plague of his own heart, and spread forth his hands toward this house:

39 Then hear thou in heaven thy dwelling place, and forgive, and do, and give to every man according to his ways, whose heart thou knowest; (for thou, even thou only, knowest the hearts of all the children of men;)

40 That they may fear thee all the days that they live in the land which thou gavest unto our fathers.

55 And he stood, and blessed all the congregation of Israel with a loud voice, saying,

56 Blessed be the Lord, that hath given rest unto his people Israel, according to all that he promised: there hath not failed one word of all his good promise, which he promised by the hand of Moses his servant.

59 And let these my words, wherewith I have made supplication before the Lord, be nigh unto the Lord our God day and night, that he maintain the cause of his servant, and the cause of his people Israel at all times, as the matter shall require:

60 That all the people of the earth may know that the Lord is God, and that there is none else.

61 Let your heart therefore be perfect with the Lord our God, to walk in his statutes, and to keep his commandments, as at this day.

62 And the king, and all Israel with him, offered sacrifice before the Lord.

What blessings did Solomon request of the Lord in his dedicatory prayer? In verse 56, Solomon said that the Lord "hath not failed one word of all his good promise." What good promises has the Lord given to you, and how are those promises fulfilled?

GOD ACCEPTS THE TEMPLE BUILT BY SOLOMON AND DECLARES POWERFUL PROMISES AND WARNINGS FOR THE ISRAELITES

In Jerusalem, Solomon had completed the construction of the temple using the finest and strongest materials. He then offered a lengthy dedicatory prayer in the presence of the Israelites. Then, following the prayer and the sacrifice of hundreds of thousands of animals, God appeared to Solomon.

1 KINGS 9:1–9

And it came to pass, when Solomon had finished the building of the house of the Lord, and the king's house, and all Solomon's desire which he was pleased to do,

2 That the Lord appeared to Solomon the second time, as he had appeared unto him at Gibeon.

3 And the Lord said unto him, I have heard thy prayer and thy supplication, that thou hast made before me: I have hallowed this house, which thou hast built, to put my name there for ever; and mine eyes and mine heart shall be there perpetually.

4 And if thou wilt walk before me, as David thy father walked, in integrity of heart, and in uprightness, to do according to all that I have commanded thee, and wilt keep my statutes and my judgments:

5 Then I will establish the throne of thy kingdom upon Israel for ever, as I promised to David thy father, saying, There shall not fail thee a man upon the throne of Israel.

6 But if ye shall at all turn from following me, ye or your children, and will not keep my commandments and my statutes which I have set before you, but go and serve other gods, and worship them:

7 Then will I cut off Israel out of the land which I have given them; and this house, which I have hallowed for my name, will I cast out of my sight; and Israel shall be a proverb and a byword among all people:

8 And at this house, which is high, every one that passeth by it shall be astonished, and shall hiss; and they shall say, Why hath the Lord done thus unto this land, and to this house?

9 And they shall answer, Because they forsook the Lord their God, who brought forth their fathers out of the land of Egypt, and have taken hold upon other gods, and have worshipped them, and served them: therefore hath the Lord brought upon them all this evil.

Following the completion of the temple, what was God's response to Solomon (see verse 3)? What blessings did God promise to give to Solomon if he was obedient? What blessings can you receive from having "integrity of heart"? What would happen if Solomon or his posterity turned from the Lord (see verse 7)?

ELIJAH THE PROPHET CALLS A FAMINE UPON THE LAND, PROVIDES AN UNENDING SUPPLY OF FOOD TO AN OBEDIENT WIDOW, AND RAISES A BOY FROM THE DEAD

Solomon had built and dedicated the temple in Jerusalem. Royalty from other countries came to visit him and were impressed by his wisdom and unrivaled wealth. But Solomon then began to ignore the wisdom God had given him and married non-Israelite wives, who persuaded him to build altars to false gods. God was angry with Solomon for breaking his covenants and declared that the right to rule over Israel would not be passed to Solomon's heirs. After Solomon's death, the twelve tribes of Israel once again embraced idol worship, wickedness, and political revolts, resulting in a new era in which Israel was no longer united under one king, but divided into the Northern Kingdom and the Southern Kingdom, with leaders and tribes constantly competing for political control. For a time, Ahab was a powerful and wicked ruler of the Northern Kingdom. He led his people in the worshipping of idols and the attempted killing of prophets. Contrasting Ahab's wickedness was the prophet Elijah, who preached righteousness and performed mighty miracles, including one for a starving widow.

1 KINGS 17:1–24

And Elijah the Tishbite, who was of the inhabitants of Gilead, said unto Ahab, As the Lord God of Israel liveth, before whom I stand, there shall not be dew nor rain these years, but according to my word.

2 And the word of the Lord came unto him, saying,

3 Get thee hence, and turn thee eastward, and hide thyself by the brook Cherith, that is before Jordan.

4 And it shall be, that thou shalt drink of the brook; and I have commanded the ravens to feed thee there.

5 So he went and did according unto the word of the Lord: for he went and dwelt by the brook Cherith, that is before Jordan.

6 And the ravens brought him bread and flesh in the morning, and bread and flesh in the evening; and he drank of the brook.

7 And it came to pass after a while, that the brook dried up, because there had been no rain in the land.

8 And the word of the Lord came unto him, saying,

9 Arise, get thee to Zarephath, which belongeth to Zidon, and dwell there: behold, I have commanded a widow woman there to sustain thee.

10 So he arose and went to Zarephath. And when he came to the gate of the city, behold, the widow woman was there gathering of sticks: and he called to her, and said, Fetch me, I pray thee, a little water in a vessel, that I may drink.

11 And as she was going to fetch it, he called to her, and said, Bring me, I pray thee, a morsel of bread in thine hand.

12 And she said, As the Lord thy God liveth, I have not a cake, but an handful of meal in a barrel, and a little oil in a cruse: and, behold, I am gathering two sticks, that I may go in and dress it for me and my son, that we may eat it, and die.

13 And Elijah said unto her, Fear not; go and do as thou hast said: but make me thereof a little cake first, and bring it unto me, and after make for thee and for thy son.

14 For thus saith the Lord God of Israel, The barrel of meal shall not waste, neither shall the cruse of oil fail, until the day that the Lord sendeth rain upon the earth.

15 And she went and did according to the saying of Elijah: and she, and he, and her house, did eat many days.

16 And the barrel of meal wasted not, neither did the cruse of oil fail, according to the word of the Lord, which he spake by Elijah.

17 And it came to pass after these things, that the son of the woman, the mistress of the house, fell sick; and his sickness was so sore, that there was no breath left in him.

18 And she said unto Elijah, What have I to do with thee, O thou man of God? art thou come unto me to call my sin to remembrance, and to slay my son?

19 And he said unto her, Give me thy son. And he took him out of her bosom, and carried him up into a loft, where he abode, and laid him upon his own bed.

20 And he cried unto the Lord, and said, O Lord my God, hast thou also brought evil upon the widow with whom I sojourn, by slaying her son?

21 And he stretched himself upon the child three times, and cried unto the Lord, and said, O Lord my God, I pray thee, let this child's soul come into him again.

22 And the Lord heard the voice of Elijah; and the soul of the child came into him again, and he revived.

23 And Elijah took the child, and brought him down out of the chamber into the house, and delivered him unto his mother: and Elijah said, See, thy son liveth.

24 And the woman said to Elijah, Now by this I know that thou art a man of God, and that the word of the Lord in thy mouth is truth.

What did Elijah command the widow to do? How did the widow show her faith? What blessings did she receive from being obedient? What blessings have you received from obeying modern-day prophets?

ELIJAH CONFRONTS THE FALSE PROPHETS OF BAAL AND CALLS DOWN FIRE FROM HEAVEN TO PROVE THAT JEHOVAH ALONE IS THE GOD OF ISRAEL

During a period of great wickedness, Elijah the prophet had called down a famine from heaven. During the famine he provided an unending supply of food to an obedient widow and later raised a young boy from the dead. His powerful preaching and miracles then continued as he challenged the wickedness of the powerful political leader Ahab and the wicked priests who worshipped the false god of Baal, also referred to as Baalim. In these verses, "bullocks" are young bulls or male cattle.

1 KINGS 18:17–40

And it came to pass, when Ahab saw Elijah, that Ahab said unto him, Art thou he that troubleth Israel?

18 And he answered, I have not troubled Israel; but thou, and thy father's house, in that ye have forsaken the commandments of the Lord, and thou hast followed Baalim.

19 Now therefore send, and gather to me all Israel unto mount Carmel, and the prophets of Baal four hundred and fifty, and the prophets of the groves four hundred, which eat at Jezebel's table.

20 So Ahab sent unto all the children of Israel, and gathered the prophets together unto mount Carmel.

21 And Elijah came unto all the people, and said, How long halt ye between two opinions? if the Lord be God, follow him: but if Baal, then follow him. And the people answered him not a word.

22 Then said Elijah unto the people, I, even I only, remain a prophet of the Lord; but Baal's prophets are four hundred and fifty men.

23 Let them therefore give us two bullocks; and let them choose one bullock for themselves, and cut it in pieces, and lay it on wood, and put no fire under: and I will dress the other bullock, and lay it on wood, and put no fire under:

24 And call ye on the name of your gods, and I will call on the name of the Lord: and the God that answereth by fire, let him be God. And all the people answered and said, It is well spoken.

25 And Elijah said unto the prophets of Baal, Choose you one bullock for yourselves, and dress it first; for ye are many; and call on the name of your gods, but put no fire under.

26 And they took the bullock which was given them, and they dressed it, and called on the name of Baal from morning even until noon, saying, O Baal, hear us. But there was no voice, nor any that answered. And they leaped upon the altar which was made.

27 And it came to pass at noon, that Elijah mocked them, and said, Cry aloud: for he is a god; either he is talking, or he is pursuing, or he is in a journey, or peradventure he sleepeth, and must be awaked.

28 And they cried aloud, and cut themselves after their manner with knives and lancets, till the blood gushed out upon them.

29 And it came to pass, when midday was past, and they prophesied until the time of the offering of the evening sacrifice, that there was neither voice, nor any to answer, nor any that regarded.

30 And Elijah said unto all the people, Come near unto me. And all the people came near unto him. And he repaired the altar of the Lord that was broken down.

31 And Elijah took twelve stones, according to the number of the tribes of the sons of Jacob, unto whom the word of the Lord came, saying, Israel shall be thy name:

32 And with the stones he built an altar in the name of the Lord: and he made a trench about the altar, as great as would contain two measures of seed.

33 And he put the wood in order, and cut the bullock in pieces, and laid him on the wood, and said, Fill four barrels with water, and pour it on the burnt sacrifice, and on the wood.

34 And he said, Do it the second time. And they did it the second time. And he said, Do it the third time. And they did it the third time.

35 And the water ran round about the altar; and he filled the trench also with water.

36 And it came to pass at the time of the offering of the evening sacrifice, that Elijah the prophet came near, and said, Lord God of Abraham, Isaac, and of Israel, let it be known this day that thou art God in Israel, and that I am thy servant, and that I have done all these things at thy word.

37 Hear me, O Lord, hear me, that this people may know that thou art the Lord God, and that thou hast turned their heart back again.

38 Then the fire of the Lord fell, and consumed the burnt sacrifice, and the wood, and the stones, and the dust, and licked up the water that was in the trench.

39 And when all the people saw it, they fell on their faces: and they said, The Lord, he is the God; the Lord, he is the God.

40 And Elijah said unto them, Take the prophets of Baal; let not one of them escape. And they took them: and Elijah brought them down to the brook Kishon, and slew them there.

What piercing question did Elijah ask the people in verse 21? How can you be decisive in worshipping and obeying God? In these verses, what evidence was given that God had power and the false prophets did not?

ELIJAH, WEARY AND HUNTED, IS FED BY AN ANGEL AND HEARS THE "STILL SMALL VOICE" OF GOD

In a dramatic and public display to prove that Jehovah alone was the God of Israel, the prophet Elijah had called down fire from heaven that consumed a sacrificed animal and the stone altar upon which it lay. The prophets of the false god of Baal had been unable to produce a similar feat, and Elijah executed them for leading the people astray. Elijah then called for an end of the famine, and it began to rain. At the time, Ahab was the wicked leader of the Northern Kingdom of Israel. His wife was Jezebel, a wicked woman who sent a personal letter to Elijah promising that she would have him killed for killing the false prophets of Baal.

1 KINGS 19:1–16

And Ahab told Jezebel all that Elijah had done, and withal how he had slain all the prophets with the sword.

2 Then Jezebel sent a messenger unto Elijah, saying, So let the gods do to me, and more also, if I make not thy life as the life of one of them by to morrow about this time.

3 And when he saw that, he arose, and went for his life, and came to Beer-sheba, which belongeth to Judah, and left his servant there.

4 But he himself went a day's journey into the wilderness, and came and sat down under a juniper tree: and he requested for himself that he might die; and said, It is enough; now, O Lord, take away my life; for I am not better than my fathers.

5 And as he lay and slept under a juniper tree, behold, then an angel touched him, and said unto him, Arise and eat.

6 And he looked, and, behold, there was a cake baken on the coals, and a cruse of water at his head. And he did eat and drink, and laid him down again.

7 And the angel of the Lord came again the second time, and touched him, and said, Arise and eat; because the journey is too great for thee.

8 And he arose, and did eat and drink, and went in the strength of that meat forty days and forty nights unto Horeb the mount of God.

9 And he came thither unto a cave, and lodged there; and, behold, the word of the Lord came to him, and he said unto him, What doest thou here, Elijah?

10 And he said, I have been very jealous for the Lord God of hosts: for the children of Israel have forsaken thy covenant, thrown down thine altars, and slain thy prophets with the sword; and I, even I only, am left; and they seek my life, to take it away.

11 And he said, Go forth, and stand upon the mount before the Lord. And, behold, the Lord passed by, and a great and strong wind rent the mountains, and brake in pieces the rocks before the Lord; but the Lord was not in the wind: and after the wind an earthquake; but the Lord was not in the earthquake:

12 And after the earthquake a fire; but the Lord was not in the fire: and after the fire a still small voice.

13 And it was so, when Elijah heard it, that he wrapped his face in his mantle, and went out, and stood in the entering in of the cave. And, behold, there came a voice unto him, and said, What doest thou here, Elijah?

14 And he said, I have been very jealous for the Lord God of hosts: because the children of Israel have forsaken thy covenant, thrown down thine altars, and slain thy prophets with the sword; and I, even I only, am left; and they seek my life, to take it away.

15 And the Lord said unto him, Go, return on thy way to the wilderness of Damascus: and when thou comest, anoint Hazael to be king over Syria:

16 And Jehu the son of Nimshi shalt thou anoint to be king over Israel: and Elisha the son of Shaphat of Abel-meholah shalt thou anoint to be prophet in thy room.

Who nourished Elijah when he was hungry and weary? Why was Elijah so tired and discouraged (see verse 10)? How is God's voice described in verse 12? What things make it easier or more difficult to hear the still, small voice of the Spirit?

155

ELIJAH IS TAKEN UP INTO HEAVEN IN A CHARIOT OF FIRE AND HIS MANTLE FALLS UPON ELISHA

While Elijah was hunted by wicked people, he was fed by an angel and heard the "still small voice" of God. Though he was weary and wished for his work as prophet to be over, God gave him additional duties, including calling Elisha as a new prophet in Israel. Elisha accepted the call and joined Elijah as God's work among the wicked Israelites continued. Later, Elijah prophesied that the wicked Ahab and Jezebel (who had sworn to have Elijah killed) would both be destroyed. This was brought to pass as Ahab was killed in battle, after which "the dogs licked up his blood" (1 Kings 22:38). Jezebel was later thrown from a window and trampled by a horse (see 2 Kings 9:30–37). Elijah's work as a prophet among the Israelites was now at an end. Elisha and other worthy men knew that Elijah would soon be taken from them. In preparation for this momentous event, Elijah and Elisha walked together to the edge of the river Jordan. In these verses, a mantle is a type of long scarf or cloak worn atop one's clothing, and was regarded in ancient times as a symbol of authority.

2 KINGS 2:8–15

And Elijah took his mantle, and wrapped it together, and smote the waters, and they were divided hither and thither, so that they two went over on dry ground.

9 And it came to pass, when they were gone over, that Elijah said unto Elisha, Ask what I shall do for thee, before I be taken away from thee. And Elisha said, I pray thee, let a double portion of thy spirit be upon me.

10 And he said, Thou hast asked a hard thing: nevertheless, if thou see me when I am taken from thee, it shall be so unto thee; but if not, it shall not be so.

11 And it came to pass, as they still went on, and talked, that, behold, there appeared a chariot of fire, and horses of fire, and parted them both asunder; and Elijah went up by a whirlwind into heaven.

12 And Elisha saw it, and he cried, My father, my father, the chariot of Israel, and the horsemen thereof. And he saw him no more: and he took hold of his own clothes, and rent them in two pieces.

13 He took up also the mantle of Elijah that fell from him, and went back, and stood by the bank of Jordan;

14 And he took the mantle of Elijah that fell from him, and smote the waters, and said, Where is the Lord God of Elijah? and when he also had smitten the waters, they parted hither and thither: and Elisha went over.

15 And when the sons of the prophets which were to view at Jericho saw him, they said, The spirit of Elijah doth rest on Elisha. And they came to meet him, and bowed themselves to the ground before him.

Though Elijah's work among the ancient Israelites was completed, his earthly ministry continued during two pivotal times. About nine hundred years later, he appeared to Jesus, Peter, James, and John on the Mount of Transfiguration. And about 2,700 years later—in 1836—he appeared to Joseph Smith in the Kirtland Temple, laid his hands on the prophet's head, and conferred upon him the sealing power.

What blessing did Elisha seek from Elijah? What sign confirmed that blessing was given to him? After Elijah departed, how did the people know that Elisha was God's prophet? Who leads God's Church today? What direction has God recently given to us through him?

NAAMAN IS HEALED FROM LEPROSY BY FOLLOWING ELISHA'S SIMPLE INSTRUCTIONS

Elijah had been taken into heaven by a chariot of flames. His mantle fell upon Elisha, who used it to strike the river Jordan, parting its waters. Elisha went on to perform many other miracles—some of them similar to those of Elijah, including providing food for a widow and raising a child from the dead. It was a time of continued turmoil and wickedness as various kings ruled Israel and only periodically heeded the words of the prophets. These verses describe a young Israelite woman (a "little maid") who had been taken captive by the neighboring Syrians and later served in the house of a nobleman named Naaman. Naaman was sick with leprosy, a painful skin disease, and would plead with Elisha to heal him.

2 KINGS 5:1–14

Now Naaman, captain of the host of the king of Syria, was a great man with his master, and honourable, because by him the Lord had given deliverance unto Syria: he was also a mighty man in valour, but he was a leper.

2 And the Syrians had gone out by companies, and had brought away captive out of the land of Israel a little maid; and she waited on Naaman's wife.

3 And she said unto her mistress, Would God my lord were with the prophet that is in Samaria! for he would recover him of his leprosy.

4 And one went in, and told his lord, saying, Thus and thus said the maid that is of the land of Israel.

5 And the king of Syria said, Go to, go, and I will send a letter unto the king of Israel. And he departed, and took with him ten talents of silver, and six thousand pieces of gold, and ten changes of raiment.

6 And he brought the letter to the king of Israel, saying, Now when this letter is come unto thee, behold, I have therewith sent Naaman my servant to thee, that thou mayest recover him of his leprosy.

7 And it came to pass, when the king of Israel had read the letter, that he rent his clothes, and said, Am I God, to kill and to make alive, that this man doth send unto me to recover a man of his leprosy? wherefore consider, I pray you, and see how he seeketh a quarrel against me.

8 And it was so, when Elisha the man of God had heard that the king of Israel had rent his clothes, that he sent to the king, saying, Wherefore hast thou rent thy clothes? let him come now to me, and he shall know that there is a prophet in Israel.

9 So Naaman came with his horses and with his chariot, and stood at the door of the house of Elisha.

10 And Elisha sent a messenger unto him, saying, Go and wash in Jordan seven times, and thy flesh shall come again to thee, and thou shalt be clean.

11 But Naaman was wroth, and went away, and said, Behold, I thought, He will surely come out to me, and stand, and call on the name of the Lord his God, and strike his hand over the place, and recover the leper.

12 Are not Abana and Pharpar, rivers of Damascus, better than all the waters of Israel? may I not wash in them, and be clean? So he turned and went away in a rage.

13 And his servants came near, and spake unto him, and said, My father, if the prophet had bid thee do some great thing, wouldest thou not have done it? how much rather then, when he saith to thee, Wash, and be clean?

14 Then went he down, and dipped himself seven times in Jordan, according to the saying of the man of God: and his flesh came again like unto the flesh of a little child, and he was clean.

How did Naaman learn of a prophet in Israel who could heal him? Even though she is described as a "little maid," how did this girl share her great faith in the Lord? What direction did Elisha give to Naaman to be healed? Why was Naaman initially reluctant to obey? What simple guidance have we received from the Lord's living prophets in our day?

QUEEN ESTHER LEARNS OF THE KING'S DECREE TO KILL ALL JEWS AND ASKS THE JEWS TO FAST FOR DELIVERANCE

During the two hundred years following the ministries of Elijah and Elisha, many other prophets would serve in Israel as the Northern and Southern Kingdoms continued to vie for power. The Israelites were again guilty of disobedience, idol worship, and the unauthorized altering of sacred temple ordinances. Neighboring nations battled with the Israelites and took many Israelite citizens captive to the lands of Assyria and Babylon. This was in fulfillment of the "scattering of Israel" that had been foretold by prophets and was brought about by the Israelites' disobedience. Finally, Jerusalem and the temple itself were destroyed—only to be slowly rebuilt by Israelites returning from lands of their captivity. At this point in the Old Testament record (about 500 B.C.), Israelites were often referred to as Jews, after the tribe of Judah. Esther was a beautiful woman, and one of many Jews who were taken captive to the neighboring kingdom of Persia, ruled by King Ahasuerus (see Map #5). The king had been displeased with his former queen and sought a woman to replace her. Mordecai, Esther's uncle, presented Esther to the king, and the king fell in love with her and made her his queen. All the while, the king and his servants remained unaware that Mordecai and Esther were Jews. Haman, a high-ranking official in the king's court, hated the Jews and soon learned that Mordecai was one of them. At Haman's request, the king decreed that all Jews in the land would be executed on a specific day.

When Mordecai perceived all that was done, Mordecai rent his clothes, and put on sackcloth with ashes, and went out into the midst of the city, and cried with a loud and a bitter cry;

2 And came even before the king's gate: for none might enter into the king's gate clothed with sackcloth.

3 And in every province, whithersoever the king's commandment and his decree came, there was great mourning among the Jews, and fasting, and weeping, and wailing; and many lay in sackcloth and ashes.

4 So Esther's maids and her chamberlains came and told it her. Then was the queen exceedingly grieved; and she sent raiment to clothe Mordecai, and to take away his sackcloth from him: but he received it not.

5 Then called Esther for Hatach, one of the king's chamberlains, whom he had appointed to attend upon her, and gave him a commandment to Mordecai, to know what it was, and why it was.

6 So Hatach went forth to Mordecai unto the street of the city, which was before the king's gate.

7 And Mordecai told him of all that had happened unto him, and of the sum of the money that Haman had promised to pay to the king's treasuries for the Jews, to destroy them.

8 Also he gave him the copy of the writing of the decree that was given at Shushan to destroy them, to shew it unto Esther, and to declare it unto her, and to charge her that she should go in unto the king, to make supplication unto him, and to make request before him for her people.

9 And Hatach came and told Esther the words of Mordecai.

10 Again Esther spake unto Hatach, and gave him commandment unto Mordecai;

11 All the king's servants, and the people of the king's provinces, do know, that whosoever, whether man or woman, shall come unto the king into the inner court, who is not called, there is one law of his to put him to death, except such to whom the king shall hold out the golden sceptre, that he may live: but I have not been called to come in unto the king these thirty days.

12 And they told to Mordecai Esther's words.

13 Then Mordecai commanded to answer Esther, Think not with thyself that thou shalt escape in the king's house, more than all the Jews.

14 For if thou altogether holdest thy peace at this time, then shall there enlargement and deliverance arise to the Jews from another place; but thou and thy father's house shall be destroyed: and who knoweth whether thou art come to the kingdom for such a time as this?

15 Then Esther bade them return Mordecai this answer,

16 Go, gather together all the Jews that are present in Shushan, and fast ye for me, and neither eat nor drink three days, night or day: I also and my maidens will fast likewise; and so will I go in unto the king, which is not according to the law: and if I perish, I perish.

17 So Mordecai went his way, and did according to all that Esther had commanded him.

According to verse 8, what did Mordecai want Esther to do for the Jewish people? In verse 14, Mordecai told Esther that perhaps she was "come to the kingdom for such a time as this." What could Esther do for her people that no one else could do? What unique things can you do to serve in God's kingdom today?

ESTHER RISKS HER LIFE BY ENTERING THE KING'S PRESENCE TO PLEAD FOR THE JEWS

Many Jewish citizens had been integrated into the kingdom of Persia, ruled by Ahasuerus. Esther was a beautiful woman who had been taken as the king's new queen, though he was unaware of her Jewish heritage. Haman, an evil servant of the king, knew that Esther and her uncle Mordecai were both Jews, and he convinced the king to decree that all Jews would be killed on a certain day. Haman also privately prepared gallows upon which Mordecai would be hanged. The Jews feared they would soon be destroyed, and Esther secretly called for them to fast for deliverance. She planned to approach the king without having been called by him—an action that was punishable by death unless the king indicated his approval by holding out his scepter to the person entering his presence. Esther knew this could result in her death, but was determined to plead for her people, saying, "If I perish, I perish" (Esther 4:16).

ESTHER 5:1–4

Now it came to pass on the third day, that Esther put on her royal apparel, and stood in the inner court of the king's house, over against the king's house: and the king sat upon his royal throne in the royal house, over against the gate of the house.

2 And it was so, when the king saw Esther the queen standing in the court, that she obtained favour in his sight: and the king held out to Esther the golden sceptre that was in his hand. So Esther drew near, and touched the top of the sceptre.

3 Then said the king unto her, What wilt thou, queen Esther? and what is thy request? it shall be even given thee to the half of the kingdom.

4 And Esther answered, If it seem good unto the king, let the king and Haman come this day unto the banquet that I have prepared for him.

ESTHER 7:1–6, 9–10

1 So the king and Haman came to banquet with Esther the queen.

2 And the king said again unto Esther on the second day at the banquet of wine, What is thy petition, queen Esther? and it shall be granted thee: and what is thy request? and it shall be performed, even to the half of the kingdom.

3 Then Esther the queen answered and said, If I have found favour in thy sight, O king, and if it please the king, let my life be given me at my petition, and my people at my request:

4 For we are sold, I and my people, to be destroyed, to be slain, and to perish. But if we had been sold for bondmen and bondwomen, I had held my tongue, although the enemy could not countervail the king's damage.

5 Then the king Ahasuerus answered and said unto Esther the queen, Who is he, and where is he, that durst presume in his heart to do so?

6 And Esther said, The adversary and enemy is this wicked Haman. Then Haman was afraid before the king and the queen.

9 And Harbonah, one of the chamberlains, said before the king, Behold also, the gallows fifty cubits high, which Haman had made for Mordecai, who had spoken good for the king, standeth in the house of Haman. Then the king said, Hang him thereon.

10 So they hanged Haman on the gallows that he had prepared for Mordecai. Then was the king's wrath pacified.

Why did Esther need courage to approach the king? When have you shown courage in standing up for someone? How did Esther's courage save her people?

IN THE MIDST OF HIS AFFLICTIONS, JOB DECLARES, "I KNOW THAT MY REDEEMER LIVETH"

Many people in the Old Testament faced severe trials, even though they loved God and lived righteously. Job is perhaps the most famous example of this. He is described as being "perfect and upright, and one that feared God, and eschewed [shunned] evil" (Job 1:1). Job enjoyed some of the greatest blessings a person could hope for: a large family, good health, and great wealth. But these blessings were then taken from him in a series of calamities that forced him to carefully consider his relationship with God and the purpose of suffering. His children and property were suddenly destroyed and he was afflicted with boils—large and painful blisters that covered his entire body. His friends visited him and told him he should curse God for allowing these trials to come upon him. But Job maintained his reverence for God. Though he was in great pain and anguish and didn't understand all the reasons for his suffering, he tried to focus on God's promised blessings. Ultimately, Job was rewarded for his patience and reverence as God later restored to him his health, his property, and children—even "twice as much as he had before" (Job 42:10). Many of Job's thoughts and words are recorded in the Old Testament, and some of the most powerful are those he spoke when his suffering was the greatest. In these verses he admits that God has allowed him to suffer greatly, but declares that he finds strength in his Redeemer.

JOB 19:7–27

Behold, I cry out of wrong, but I am not heard: I cry aloud, but there is no judgment.

8 He hath fenced up my way that I cannot pass, and he hath set darkness in my paths.

9 He hath stripped me of my glory, and taken the crown from my head.

10 He hath destroyed me on every side, and I am gone: and mine hope hath he removed like a tree.

11 He hath also kindled his wrath against me, and he counteth me unto him as one of his enemies.

12 His troops come together, and raise up their way against me, and encamp round about my tabernacle.

13 He hath put my brethren far from me, and mine acquaintance are verily estranged from me.

14 My kinsfolk have failed, and my familiar friends have forgotten me.

15 They that dwell in mine house, and my maids, count me for a stranger: I am an alien in their sight.

16 I called my servant, and he gave me no answer; I entreated him with my mouth.

17 My breath is strange to my wife, though I entreated for the children's sake of mine own body.

18 Yea, young children despised me; I arose, and they spake against me.

19 All my inward friends abhorred me: and they whom I loved are turned against me.

20 My bone cleaveth to my skin and to my flesh, and I am escaped with the skin of my teeth.

21 Have pity upon me, have pity upon me, O ye my friends; for the hand of God hath touched me.

22 Why do ye persecute me as God, and are not satisfied with my flesh?

23 Oh that my words were now written! oh that they were printed in a book!

24 That they were graven with an iron pen and lead in the rock for ever!

25 For I know that my redeemer liveth, and that he shall stand at the latter day upon the earth:

26 And though after my skin worms destroy this body, yet in my flesh shall I see God:

27 Whom I shall see for myself, and mine eyes shall behold, and not another; though my reins be consumed within me.

Despite his great trials, what testimony did Job share in verses 25–27? How does Job's testimony give you hope? What challenges have you had in your life? How can you righteously endure even when you suffer? How have your challenges drawn you closer to God?

A PSALM DESCRIBES THE BLESSINGS AND PROTECTION OFFERED BY THE LORD TO THE RIGHTEOUS

Most of the books that form the Old Testament are historical records of spiritual and political events. One exception is the book of Psalms. A psalm is a sacred song or hymn. Many of Psalms' 150 hymns contain specific instructions for how they are to be performed. In one sense, the book of Psalms is like a hymnbook in the middle of the Old Testament. The purpose of these psalms is to praise God's might, majesty, and mercy through poetry and metaphorical references to God's creations, such as mighty rivers, green pastures, and bounteous feasts, and to direct the listener to receive God's blessings by wisely obeying His laws. Who exactly wrote these psalms remains a matter of debate, though many of them are attributed to King David. In his youth, David was known as a skillful player of the harp and was often called upon to soothe King Saul by playing for him when he was angry or worried (see 1 Samuel 16). Later, David offered a song of thanksgiving to God that was similar in tone and subject matter to many of the psalms (see 2 Samuel 22). In the following verses, the word "chaff" refers to the dry outer husk that is separated from a seed or kernel, then blown away during the harvesting process. The word "Selah" appears in many psalms. Though its exact meaning is unknown, it is likely a simple bit of direction (such as "rest" or "pause") given to singers or musicians as they performed the psalms.

PSALM 1:1–6

Blessed is the man that walketh not in the counsel of the ungodly, nor standeth in the way of sinners, nor sitteth in the seat of the scornful.

2 But his delight is in the law of the Lord; and in his law doth he meditate day and night.

3 And he shall be like a tree planted by the rivers of water, that bringeth forth his fruit in his season; his leaf also shall not wither; and whatsoever he doeth shall prosper.

4 The ungodly are not so: but are like the chaff which the wind driveth away.

5 Therefore the ungodly shall not stand in the judgment, nor sinners in the congregation of the righteous.

6 For the Lord knoweth the way of the righteous: but the way of the ungodly shall perish.

PSALM 3:1–8

1 Lord, how are they increased that trouble me! many are they that rise up against me.

2 Many there be which say of my soul, There is no help for him in God. Selah.

3 But thou, O Lord, art a shield for me; my glory, and the lifter up of mine head.

4 I cried unto the Lord with my voice, and he heard me out of his holy hill. Selah.

5 I laid me down and slept; I awaked; for the Lord sustained me.

6 I will not be afraid of ten thousands of people, that have set themselves against me round about.

7 Arise, O Lord; save me, O my God: for thou hast smitten all mine enemies upon the cheek bone; thou hast broken the teeth of the ungodly.

8 Salvation belongeth unto the Lord: thy blessing is upon thy people. Selah.

How can we find "delight" in the Lord's law, as referred to in Psalm 1:2? Consider Psalm 1:3. What are some of the fruits—or blessings—the Lord has given you for obeying His law? Consider Psalm 3:3. In what ways can God be a "shield" for you?

PSALMS OF PRAISE HONOR GOD'S MARVELOUS CREATIONS AND HIS WILLINGNESS TO BE A "REFUGE FOR THE OPPRESSED"

These two psalms are written from the point of view of someone considering God's towering creations and the loving concern He has for each of His children.

PSALM 8:1–6, 9

O Lord our Lord, how excellent is thy name in all the earth! who hast set thy glory above the heavens.

2 Out of the mouth of babes and sucklings hast thou ordained strength because of thine enemies, that thou mightest still the enemy and the avenger.

3 When I consider thy heavens, the work of thy fingers, the moon and the stars, which thou hast ordained;

4 What is man, that thou art mindful of him? and the son of man, that thou visitest him?

5 For thou hast made him a little lower than the angels, and hast crowned him with glory and honour.

6 Thou madest him to have dominion over the works of thy hands; thou hast put all things under his feet:

9 O Lord our Lord, how excellent is thy name in all the earth!

PSALM 9:1–14

1 I will praise thee, O Lord, with my whole heart; I will shew forth all thy marvellous works.

2 I will be glad and rejoice in thee: I will sing praise to thy name, O thou most High.

3 When mine enemies are turned back, they shall fall and perish at thy presence.

4 For thou hast maintained my right and my cause; thou satest in the throne judging right.

5 Thou hast rebuked the heathen, thou hast destroyed the wicked, thou hast put out their name for ever and ever.

6 O thou enemy, destructions are come to a perpetual end: and thou hast destroyed cities; their memorial is perished with them.

7 But the Lord shall endure for ever: he hath prepared his throne for judgment.

8 And he shall judge the world in righteousness, he shall minister judgment to the people in uprightness.

9 The Lord also will be a refuge for the oppressed, a refuge in times of trouble.

10 And they that know thy name will put their trust in thee: for thou, Lord, hast not forsaken them that seek thee.

11 Sing praises to the Lord, which dwelleth in Zion: declare among the people his doings.

12 When he maketh inquisition for blood, he remembereth them: he forgetteth not the cry of the humble.

13 Have mercy upon me, O Lord; consider my trouble which I suffer of them that hate me, thou that liftest me up from the gates of death:

14 That I may shew forth all thy praise in the gates of the daughter of Zion: I will rejoice in thy salvation.

What are some of your favorite "works" and creations of God? Psalm 9:11 says, "Sing praises to the Lord." What are some of your favorite songs of praise? Why do you think we are commanded to praise God? How can you offer praise to Him?

A PSALM PROCLAIMS, "THE LORD IS MY SHEPHERD; I SHALL NOT WANT"

Psalm 23 is perhaps the best known of all the psalms. These gentle and encouraging words were repurposed into a modern-day hymn (see *Hymns*, no. 108)—a fitting tribute to lyrics that were originally intended for that very purpose.

Psalm 23:1–6

The Lord is my shepherd; I shall not want.

2 He maketh me to lie down in green pastures: he leadeth me beside the still waters.

3 He restoreth my soul: he leadeth me in the paths of righteousness for his name's sake.

4 Yea, though I walk through the valley of the shadow of death, I will fear no evil: for thou art with me; thy rod and thy staff they comfort me.

5 Thou preparest a table before me in the presence of mine enemies: thou anointest my head with oil; my cup runneth over.

6 Surely goodness and mercy shall follow me all the days of my life: and I will dwell in the house of the Lord for ever.

According to these verses, what blessings are offered by the Lord? Why is the Lord often referred to as a shepherd? In what ways does the Savior restore your soul, as described in verse 3?

PSALMS OF PRAISE REJOICE IN GOD'S MIGHT AND ENCOURAGE ALL TO "WAIT ON THE LORD" AND "BE OF GOOD COURAGE"

Some psalms contained prayer-like passages that lamented the temptations and follies that come upon all people. Many others, like these two, rejoiced in God's ability to lift mankind out of sin and guide all to salvation.

PSALM 24:1–10

The earth is the Lord's, and the fulness thereof; the world, and they that dwell therein.

2 For he hath founded it upon the seas, and established it upon the floods.

3 Who shall ascend into the hill of the Lord? or who shall stand in his holy place?

4 He that hath clean hands, and a pure heart; who hath not lifted up his soul unto vanity, nor sworn deceitfully.

5 He shall receive the blessing from the Lord, and righteousness from the God of his salvation.

6 This is the generation of them that seek him, that seek thy face, O Jacob. Selah.

7 Lift up your heads, O ye gates; and be ye lift up, ye everlasting doors; and the King of glory shall come in.

8 Who is this King of glory? The Lord strong and mighty, the Lord mighty in battle.

9 Lift up your heads, O ye gates; even lift them up, ye everlasting doors; and the King of glory shall come in.

10 Who is this King of glory? The Lord of hosts, he is the King of glory. Selah.

PSALM 27:1–14

1 The Lord is my light and my salvation; whom shall I fear? the Lord is the strength of my life; of whom shall I be afraid?

2 When the wicked, even mine enemies and my foes, came upon me to eat up my flesh, they stumbled and fell.

3 Though an host should encamp against me, my heart shall not fear: though war should rise against me, in this will I be confident.

4 One thing have I desired of the Lord, that will I seek after; that I may dwell in the house of the Lord all the days of my life, to behold the beauty of the Lord, and to inquire in his temple.

5 For in the time of trouble he shall hide me in his pavilion: in the secret of his tabernacle shall he hide me; he shall set me up upon a rock.

6 And now shall mine head be lifted up above mine enemies round about me: therefore will I offer in his tabernacle sacrifices of joy; I will sing, yea, I will sing praises unto the Lord.

7 Hear, O Lord, when I cry with my voice: have mercy also upon me, and answer me.

8 When thou saidst, Seek ye my face; my heart said unto thee, Thy face, Lord, will I seek.

9 Hide not thy face far from me; put not thy servant away in anger: thou hast been my help; leave me not, neither forsake me, O God of my salvation.

10 When my father and my mother forsake me, then the Lord will take me up.

11 Teach me thy way, O Lord, and lead me in a plain path, because of mine enemies.

12 Deliver me not over unto the will of mine enemies: for false witnesses are risen up against me, and such as breathe out cruelty.

13 I had fainted, unless I had believed to see the goodness of the Lord in the land of the living.

14 Wait on the Lord: be of good courage, and he shall strengthen thine heart: wait, I say, on the Lord.

Psalm 24:3–5 speaks of the blessings of having clean hands and a pure heart. What do you think it means to have clean hands and a pure heart? Consider Psalm 27:14. How can you wait on the Lord and be of good courage?

A PSALM OF WARNING DECLARES THAT THE WICKED WILL BE DESTROYED AND THE MEEK WILL INHERIT THE EARTH

The book of Psalms covered a wide range of topics that are highly applicable to our day. In these verses, the eternal rewards of two groups are compared: the wicked (who often have temporary success) and the righteous (who often temporarily suffer).

PSALM 37:1–24, 37–40

Fret not thyself because of evildoers, neither be thou envious against the workers of iniquity.

2 For they shall soon be cut down like the grass, and wither as the green herb.

3 Trust in the Lord, and do good; so shalt thou dwell in the land, and verily thou shalt be fed.

4 Delight thyself also in the Lord; and he shall give thee the desires of thine heart.

5 Commit thy way unto the Lord; trust also in him; and he shall bring it to pass.

6 And he shall bring forth thy righteousness as the light, and thy judgment as the noonday.

7 Rest in the Lord, and wait patiently for him: fret not thyself because of him who prospereth in his way, because of the man who bringeth wicked devices to pass.

8 Cease from anger, and forsake wrath: fret not thyself in any wise to do evil.

9 For evildoers shall be cut off: but those that wait upon the Lord, they shall inherit the earth.

10 For yet a little while, and the wicked shall not be: yea, thou shalt diligently consider his place, and it shall not be.

11 But the meek shall inherit the earth; and shall delight themselves in the abundance of peace.

12 The wicked plotteth against the just, and gnasheth upon him with his teeth.

13 The Lord shall laugh at him: for he seeth that his day is coming.

14 The wicked have drawn out the sword, and have bent their bow, to cast down the poor and needy, and to slay such as be of upright conversation.

15 Their sword shall enter into their own heart, and their bows shall be broken.

16 A little that a righteous man hath is better than the riches of many wicked.

17 For the arms of the wicked shall be broken: but the Lord upholdeth the righteous.

18 The Lord knoweth the days of the upright: and their inheritance shall be for ever.

19 They shall not be ashamed in the evil time: and in the days of famine they shall be satisfied.

20 But the wicked shall perish, and the enemies of the Lord shall be as the fat of lambs: they shall consume; into smoke shall they consume away.

21 The wicked borroweth, and payeth not again: but the righteous sheweth mercy, and giveth.

22 For such as be blessed of him shall inherit the earth; and they that be cursed of him shall be cut off.

23 The steps of a good man are ordered by the Lord: and he delighteth in his way.

24 Though he fall, he shall not be utterly cast down: for the Lord upholdeth him with his hand.

37 Mark the perfect man, and behold the upright: for the end of that man is peace.

38 But the transgressors shall be destroyed together: the end of the wicked shall be cut off.

39 But the salvation of the righteous is of the Lord: he is their strength in the time of trouble.

40 And the Lord shall help them, and deliver them: he shall deliver them from the wicked, and save them, because they trust in him.

Consider verse 11. To be meek means to be righteous, submissive to God's commands, and teachable. Who are some people you know who are meek? Verse 23 states, "The steps of a good man are ordered by the Lord." What does that mean to you? When has the Lord given you direction as you have tried to do what is right?

DAVID PLEADS WITH GOD FOR FORGIVENESS FROM HIS SIN WITH BATHSHEBA

This psalm is attributed to David and contains a prayer of repentance he may have offered after committing the sin of adultery with Bathsheba. David had been a man of honor, faith, and righteousness, but later he gave in to temptation. In this prayer, he takes responsibility for his actions, shows godly sorrow, and pleads sincerely for forgiveness of his grave error. David's repentance is especially significant considering that it was through his line that eventually the Savior Jesus Christ would be born.

Psalm 51:1–17

Have mercy upon me, O God, according to thy lovingkindness: according unto the multitude of thy tender mercies blot out my transgressions.

2 Wash me throughly from mine iniquity, and cleanse me from my sin.

3 For I acknowledge my transgressions: and my sin is ever before me.

4 Against thee, thee only, have I sinned, and done this evil in thy sight: that thou mightest be justified when thou speakest, and be clear when thou judgest.

5 Behold, I was shapen in iniquity; and in sin did my mother conceive me.

6 Behold, thou desirest truth in the inward parts: and in the hidden part thou shalt make me to know wisdom.

7 Purge me with hyssop, and I shall be clean: wash me, and I shall be whiter than snow.

8 Make me to hear joy and gladness; that the bones which thou hast broken may rejoice.

9 Hide thy face from my sins, and blot out all mine iniquities.

10 Create in me a clean heart, O God; and renew a right spirit within me.

11 Cast me not away from thy presence; and take not thy holy spirit from me.

12 Restore unto me the joy of thy salvation; and uphold me with thy free spirit.

13 Then will I teach transgressors thy ways; and sinners shall be converted unto thee.

14 Deliver me from bloodguiltiness, O God, thou God of my salvation: and my tongue shall sing aloud of thy righteousness.

15 O Lord, open thou my lips; and my mouth shall shew forth thy praise.

16 For thou desirest not sacrifice; else would I give it: thou delightest not in burnt offering.

17 The sacrifices of God are a broken spirit: a broken and a contrite heart, O God, thou wilt not despise.

What evidence of a repentant heart is found in these verses? According to verse 17, what sacrifice does God require of us when we repent? What do you think it means to have a "broken and a contrite heart"? How have you been blessed by the gift of repentance?

171

A PSALM OF PRAISE DECLARES THAT "THE FEAR OF THE LORD IS THE BEGINNING OF WISDOM" AND THAT GOD'S WORD IS "A LAMP UNTO MY FEET"

Many psalms, such as this one, included both declarations of praise and earnest pleadings for God's guidance.

PSALM 111:1–10, 33–37, 105–6, 127, 174–75

Praise ye the Lord. I will praise the Lord with my whole heart, in the assembly of the upright, and in the congregation.

2 The works of the Lord are great, sought out of all them that have pleasure therein.

3 His work is honourable and glorious: and his righteousness endureth for ever.

4 He hath made his wonderful works to be remembered: the Lord is gracious and full of compassion.

5 He hath given meat unto them that fear him: he will ever be mindful of his covenant.

6 He hath shewed his people the power of his works, that he may give them the heritage of the heathen.

7 The works of his hands are verity and judgment; all his commandments are sure.

8 They stand fast for ever and ever, and are done in truth and uprightness.

9 He sent redemption unto his people: he hath commanded his covenant for ever: holy and reverend is his name.

10 The fear of the Lord is the beginning of wisdom: a good understanding have all they that do his commandments: his praise endureth for ever.

33 Teach me, O Lord, the way of thy statutes; and I shall keep it unto the end.

34 Give me understanding, and I shall keep thy law; yea, I shall observe it with my whole heart.

35 Make me to go in the path of thy commandments; for therein do I delight.

36 Incline my heart unto thy testimonies, and not to covetousness.

37 Turn away mine eyes from beholding vanity; and quicken thou me in thy way.

105 Thy word is a lamp unto my feet, and a light unto my path.

106 I have sworn, and I will perform it, that I will keep thy righteous judgments.

127 Therefore I love thy commandments above gold; yea, above fine gold.

174 I have longed for thy salvation, O Lord; and thy law is my delight.

175 Let my soul live, and it shall praise thee; and let thy judgments help me.

Verse 10 speaks of the "fear of the Lord"—a form of reverence or respect for God. How does respect for God and His laws lead you to wisdom? How do God's laws and commandments "light" the way for you? What are some of God's laws you have grown to love?

PSALMS OF PRAISE DESCRIBE THE BLESSINGS AND HAPPINESS FOUND IN EMBRACING GOD

As you read these final passages from Psalms, look for specific blessings promised to those who put their trust in the Lord.

PSALM 138:1–8

I will praise thee with my whole heart: before the gods will I sing praise unto thee.

2 I will worship toward thy holy temple, and praise thy name for thy lovingkindness and for thy truth: for thou hast magnified thy word above all thy name.

3 In the day when I cried thou answeredst me, and strengthenedst me with strength in my soul.

4 All the kings of the earth shall praise thee, O Lord, when they hear the words of thy mouth.

5 Yea, they shall sing in the ways of the Lord: for great is the glory of the Lord.

6 Though the Lord be high, yet hath he respect unto the lowly: but the proud he knoweth afar off.

7 Though I walk in the midst of trouble, thou wilt revive me: thou shalt stretch forth thine hand against the wrath of mine enemies, and thy right hand shall save me.

8 The Lord will perfect that which concerneth me: thy mercy, O Lord, endureth for ever: forsake not the works of thine own hands.

PSALM 146:1–10

1 Praise ye the Lord. Praise the Lord, O my soul.

2 While I live will I praise the Lord: I will sing praises unto my God while I have any being.

3 Put not your trust in princes, nor in the son of man, in whom there is no help.

4 His breath goeth forth, he returneth to his earth; in that very day his thoughts perish.

5 Happy is he that hath the God of Jacob for his help, whose hope is in the Lord his God:

6 Which made heaven, and earth, the sea, and all that therein is: which keepeth truth for ever:

7 Which executeth judgment for the oppressed: which giveth food to the hungry. The Lord looseth the prisoners:

8 The Lord openeth the eyes of the blind: the Lord raiseth them that are bowed down: the Lord loveth the righteous:

9 The Lord preserveth the strangers; he relieveth the fatherless and widow: but the way of the wicked he turneth upside down.

10 The Lord shall reign for ever, even thy God, O Zion, unto all generations. Praise ye the Lord.

Consider Psalm 138:7. What do you think it means to be revived by the Lord as we walk in "the midst of trouble"? What troubles has the Lord helped you through? According to Psalm 146:6–10, what can the Lord do for His people?

A PROVERB DECLARES THAT "THE FEAR OF THE LORD IS THE BEGINNING OF KNOWLEDGE" AND WARNS TO "LEAN NOT UNTO THINE OWN UNDERSTANDING"

The next book in the Old Testament is titled the Proverbs. A proverb is a short saying or piece of advice that offers wisdom or warning. Similar to the book of Psalms, it is unclear who wrote Proverbs or when this book was recorded. Unlike the psalms, the proverbs were not intended to be set to music. Many of the proverbs focus on everyday wisdom such as how to get along with other people, the importance of patience, and the dangers of sexual temptations. Some proverbs, including those contained in the next three sections, are more spiritual in nature and are especially applicable to our day.

PROVERBS 3:5–18

Trust in the Lord with all thine heart; and lean not unto thine own understanding.

6 In all thy ways acknowledge him, and he shall direct thy paths.

7 Be not wise in thine own eyes: fear the Lord, and depart from evil.

8 It shall be health to thy navel, and marrow to thy bones.

9 Honour the Lord with thy substance, and with the firstfruits of all thine increase:

10 So shall thy barns be filled with plenty, and thy presses shall burst out with new wine.

11 My son, despise not the chastening of the Lord; neither be weary of his correction:

12 For whom the Lord loveth he correcteth; even as a father the son in whom he delighteth.

13 Happy is the man that findeth wisdom, and the man that getteth understanding.

14 For the merchandise of it is better than the merchandise of silver, and the gain thereof than fine gold.

15 She is more precious than rubies: and all the things thou canst desire are not to be compared unto her.

16 Length of days is in her right hand; and in her left hand riches and honour.

17 Her ways are ways of pleasantness, and all her paths are peace.

18 She is a tree of life to them that lay hold upon her: and happy is every one that retaineth her.

Consider verse 5. How can you show that you trust in the Lord with all your heart? How has the Lord directed your path? Has there been a time in your life when you have needed correction (see verse 12)? How did that correction benefit you? Consider Proverbs 3:13–18. What do you think are some of the blessings of obtaining wisdom and understanding?

PROVERBS WARN OF PRIDE, MISCHIEF, AND LIES AND DECLARE THAT WISDOM, LOVE, AND A GOOD NAME ARE BETTER THAN SILVER AND GOLD

As you read the following proverbs, look for behavior that displeases God and the blessings promised to the wise and righteous.

PROVERBS 6:16–19

These six things doth the Lord hate: yea, seven are an abomination unto him:

17 A proud look, a lying tongue, and hands that shed innocent blood,

18 An heart that deviseth wicked imaginations, feet that be swift in running to mischief,

19 A false witness that speaketh lies, and he that soweth discord among brethren.

PROVERBS 15:1

1 A soft answer turneth away wrath: but grievous words stir up anger.

PROVERBS 16:16, 18–19

16 How much better is it to get wisdom than gold! and to get understanding rather to be chosen than silver!

18 Pride goeth before destruction, and an haughty spirit before a fall.

19 Better it is to be of an humble spirit with the lowly, than to divide the spoil with the proud.

PROVERBS 22:1–6

1 A good name is rather to be chosen than great riches, and loving favour rather than silver and gold.

2 The rich and poor meet together: the Lord is the maker of them all.

3 A prudent man foreseeth the evil, and hideth himself: but the simple pass on, and are punished.

4 By humility and the fear of the Lord are riches, and honour, and life.

5 Thorns and snares are in the way of the froward: he that doth keep his soul shall be far from them.

6 Train up a child in the way he should go: and when he is old, he will not depart from it.

How can you avoid the seven things that are an abomination to the Lord, as described in Proverbs 6:16–19? Proverbs 16:18–19 contrasts the attributes of pride and humility. Share an example of someone that has demonstrated humility and how this blesses both the person and others. What does it mean to "train up a child in the way he should go" (Proverbs 22:6)? What do you think are some important things to teach a child?

A PROVERB DESCRIBES THE TRAITS OF A VIRTUOUS WOMAN: CHARITY, WISDOM, SERVICE, AND STRENGTH

Additional bits of wisdom from the Proverbs include the statements, "For as [a person] thinketh in his heart, so is he" (Proverbs 23:7) and, "Where there is no vision, the people perish: but he that keepeth the law, happy is he" (Proverbs 29:18). In this final chapter, the traits and behavior of a virtuous woman are given. To be virtuous means to have high moral standards.

PROVERBS 31:10–18, 20, 25–31

Who can find a virtuous woman? for her price is far above rubies.

11 The heart of her husband doth safely trust in her, so that he shall have no need of spoil.

12 She will do him good and not evil all the days of her life.

13 She seeketh wool, and flax, and worketh willingly with her hands.

14 She is like the merchants' ships; she bringeth her food from afar.

15 She riseth also while it is yet night, and giveth meat to her household, and a portion to her maidens.

16 She considereth a field, and buyeth it: with the fruit of her hands she planteth a vineyard.

17 She girdeth her loins with strength, and strengtheneth her arms.

18 She perceiveth that her merchandise is good: her candle goeth not out by night.

20 She stretcheth out her hand to the poor; yea, she reacheth forth her hands to the needy.

25 Strength and honour are her clothing; and she shall rejoice in time to come.

26 She openeth her mouth with wisdom; and in her tongue is the law of kindness.

27 She looketh well to the ways of her household, and eateth not the bread of idleness.

28 Her children arise up, and call her blessed; her husband also, and he praiseth her.

29 Many daughters have done virtuously, but thou excellest them all.

30 Favour is deceitful, and beauty is vain: but a woman that feareth the Lord, she shall be praised.

31 Give her of the fruit of her hands; and let her own works praise her in the gates.

What are some good qualities you see in the women around you? Which of the qualities mentioned in Proverbs 31 would you like to develop? What can you do to reach out to the poor and needy (see verse 20)?

THE BOOK OF ECCLESIASTES DECLARES, "TO EVERYTHING THERE IS A SEASON, AND A TIME TO EVERY PURPOSE UNDER HEAVEN"

Directly following the book of Proverbs is Ecclesiastes or, the Preacher. Similar to Psalms and Proverbs, Ecclesiastes offers observations and counsel on a variety of worldly and spiritual matters. The following passage offers a reminder that mortal life is filled with a variety of experiences that will come upon all people and that God's works are eternal.

ECCLESIASTES 3:1–8, 14, 17

To every thing there is a season, and a time to every purpose under the heaven:

2 A time to be born, and a time to die; a time to plant, and a time to pluck up that which is planted;

3 A time to kill, and a time to heal; a time to break down, and a time to build up;

4 A time to weep, and a time to laugh; a time to mourn, and a time to dance;

5 A time to cast away stones, and a time to gather stones together; a time to embrace, and a time to refrain from embracing;

6 A time to get, and a time to lose; a time to keep, and a time to cast away;

7 A time to rend, and a time to sew; a time to keep silence, and a time to speak;

8 A time to love, and a time to hate; a time of war, and a time of peace.

14 I know that, whatsoever God doeth, it shall be for ever: nothing can be put to it, nor any thing taken from it: and God doeth it, that men should fear before him.

17 I said in mine heart, God shall judge the righteous and the wicked: for there is a time there for every purpose and for every work.

What seasons of life have you recently experienced? Consider verse 2. What is it time for you to be doing now, that you can't do later? Consider verse 17: "For there is a time there for every purpose and for every work." What might be some of the purposes for difficult times in your life?

ISAIAH PROPHESIES OF TEMPLES IN THE LATTER DAYS AND WARNS THOSE WHO "CALL EVIL GOOD, AND GOOD EVIL"

The remaining seventeen books of the Old Testament are named after individual prophets, with each book containing a record of that prophet's works and prophecies (the book of Lamentations is the exception, though it was written by the prophet Jeremiah). These books are not chronological. The earliest of the prophets was Obadiah, whose works occurred around 845 B.C., directly following the prophets Elijah and Elisha. The last was Malachi, around 430 B.C. At times there were many prophets who ministered and prophesied in Israel during the same time period. Isaiah ministered in Jerusalem from 740–701 B.C. Concerning Isaiah, the Bible Dictionary states: "Isaiah is the most quoted of all the prophets, being more frequently quoted by Jesus, Paul, Peter, and John (in his Revelation) than any other Old Testament prophet. Likewise, the Book of Mormon and the Doctrine and Covenants quote from Isaiah more than from any other prophet. The Lord told the Nephites that 'great are the words of Isaiah,' and that all things Isaiah spoke of the house of Israel and of the Gentiles would be fulfilled (3 Ne. 23:1–3)." In prophesying of future events (some of which are now past, some of which are now occurring, and some of which have yet to occur), Isaiah used a unique writing style that included much symbolism and poetry. In these verses, a "plowshare" and a "pruninghook" both refer to tools used for planting and harvesting food.

Isaiah 2:1–5

The word that Isaiah the son of Amoz saw concerning Judah and Jerusalem.

2 And it shall come to pass in the last days, that the mountain of the Lord's house shall be established in the top of the mountains, and shall be exalted above the hills; and all nations shall flow unto it.

3 And many people shall go and say, Come ye, and let us go up to the mountain of the Lord, to the house of the God of Jacob; and he will teach us of his ways, and we will walk in his paths: for out of Zion shall go forth the law, and the word of the Lord from Jerusalem.

4 And he shall judge among the nations, and shall rebuke many people: and they shall beat their swords into plowshares, and their spears into pruninghooks: nation shall not lift up sword against nation, neither shall they learn war any more.

5 O house of Jacob, come ye, and let us walk in the light of the Lord.

Isaiah 5:20–25

20 Woe unto them that call evil good, and good evil; that put darkness for light, and light for darkness; that put bitter for sweet, and sweet for bitter!

21 Woe unto them that are wise in their own eyes, and prudent in their own sight!

22 Woe unto them that are mighty to drink wine, and men of strength to mingle strong drink:

23 Which justify the wicked for reward, and take away the righteousness of the righteous from him!

24 Therefore as the fire devoureth the stubble, and the flame consumeth the chaff, so their root shall be as rottenness, and their blossom shall go up as dust: because they have cast away the law of the Lord of hosts, and despised the word of the Holy One of Israel.

25 Therefore is the anger of the Lord kindled against his people, and he hath stretched forth his hand against them, and hath smitten them: and the hills did tremble, and their carcases were torn in the midst of the streets. For all this his anger is not turned away, but his hand is stretched out still.

Consider Isaiah 2:2. Where can the Lord's house be found today? What specific warnings are given in Isaiah 5? According to Isaiah 5:24, what happens to people who "cast away the law of the Lord"? How can we uphold the law of the Lord and not cast it away?

ISAIAH PROPHESIES OF CHRIST'S MORTAL UPBRINGING AND OF THE MIRACULOUS PEACE TO BE FOUND DURING HIS MILLENNIAL REIGN

The following verses contain some of Isaiah's most famous prophecies of Jesus Christ. Isaiah 9:6–7 and 11:1–5 refer to Christ's birth, early life, and mortal ministry. Isaiah 11:6–9 refers to events that will occur during Christ's Millennial reign upon the earth.

ISAIAH 9:6–7

For unto us a child is born, unto us a son is given: and the government shall be upon his shoulder: and his name shall be called Wonderful, Counsellor, The mighty God, The everlasting Father, The Prince of Peace.

7 Of the increase of his government and peace there shall be no end, upon the throne of David, and upon his kingdom, to order it, and to establish it with judgment and with justice from henceforth even for ever. The zeal of the Lord of hosts will perform this.

ISAIAH 11:1–9

1 And there shall come forth a rod out of the stem of Jesse, and a Branch shall grow out of his roots:

2 And the spirit of the Lord shall rest upon him, the spirit of wisdom and understanding, the spirit of counsel and might, the spirit of knowledge and of the fear of the Lord;

3 And shall make him of quick understanding in the fear of the Lord: and he shall not judge after the sight of his eyes, neither reprove after the hearing of his ears:

4 But with righteousness shall he judge the poor, and reprove with equity for the meek of the earth: and he shall smite the earth with the rod of his mouth, and with the breath of his lips shall he slay the wicked.

5 And righteousness shall be the girdle of his loins, and faithfulness the girdle of his reins.

6 The wolf also shall dwell with the lamb, and the leopard shall lie down with the kid; and the calf and the young lion and the fatling together; and a little child shall lead them.

7 And the cow and the bear shall feed; their young ones shall lie down together: and the lion shall eat straw like the ox.

8 And the sucking child shall play on the hole of the asp, and the weaned child shall put his hand on the cockatrice' den.

9 They shall not hurt nor destroy in all my holy mountain: for the earth shall be full of the knowledge of the Lord, as the waters cover the sea.

Of all the Lord's titles given in Isaiah 9:6, which ones have special meaning to you and why? What characteristics of the Savior are identified in Isaiah 11:2–4? What can you do to develop these Christlike qualities? According to Isaiah 11:6–9, what will conditions on the earth be like during the Millennium?

JEHOVAH DECLARES THAT BESIDES HIM "THERE IS NO SAVIOUR"

As Isaiah's many prophecies about Jesus Christ continued, he often used a writing style in which he spoke for the Savior, emphasizing His many roles as Creator, Judge, and Redeemer.

Isaiah 43:1–3, 8–11, 15

But now thus saith the Lord that created thee, O Jacob, and he that formed thee, O Israel, Fear not: for I have redeemed thee, I have called thee by thy name; thou art mine.

2 When thou passest through the waters, I will be with thee; and through the rivers, they shall not overflow thee: when thou walkest through the fire, thou shalt not be burned; neither shall the flame kindle upon thee.

3 For I am the Lord thy God, the Holy One of Israel, thy Saviour: I gave Egypt for thy ransom, Ethiopia and Seba for thee.

8 Bring forth the blind people that have eyes, and the deaf that have ears.

9 Let all the nations be gathered together, and let the people be assembled: who among them can declare this, and shew us former things? let them bring forth their witnesses, that they may be justified: or let them hear, and say, It is truth.

10 Ye are my witnesses, saith the Lord, and my servant whom I have chosen: that ye may know and believe me, and understand that I am he: before me there was no God formed, neither shall there be after me.

11 I, even I, am the Lord; and beside me there is no saviour.

15 I am the Lord, your Holy One, the creator of Israel, your King.

Isaiah 44:21–24

21 Remember these, O Jacob and Israel; for thou art my servant: I have formed thee; thou art my servant: O Israel, thou shalt not be forgotten of me.

22 I have blotted out, as a thick cloud, thy transgressions, and, as a cloud, thy sins: return unto me; for I have redeemed thee.

23 Sing, O ye heavens; for the Lord hath done it: shout, ye lower parts of the earth: break forth into singing, ye mountains, O forest, and every tree therein: for the Lord hath redeemed Jacob, and glorified himself in Israel.

24 Thus saith the Lord, thy redeemer, and he that formed thee from the womb, I am the Lord that maketh all things; that stretcheth forth the heavens alone; that spreadeth abroad the earth by myself;

What promises does the Lord make to Israel in these verses? Which of those promises are particularly meaningful to you? Consider Isaiah 43:11. What does it mean to be a savior? In what ways is Jesus Christ the Savior for the entire world?

THE SAVIOR DECLARES THAT HE WILL NEVER FORGET THOSE WHO BELIEVE IN HIM

In the following verses, Isaiah again speaks for the Savior. The Lord's unwavering commitment to His children is emphasized as He is compared to a loving mother.

ISAIAH 49:13–16, 22–26

Sing, O heavens; and be joyful, O earth; and break forth into singing, O mountains: for the Lord hath comforted his people, and will have mercy upon his afflicted.

14 But Zion said, The Lord hath forsaken me, and my Lord hath forgotten me.

15 Can a woman forget her sucking child, that she should not have compassion on the son of her womb? yea, they may forget, yet will I not forget thee.

16 Behold, I have graven thee upon the palms of my hands; thy walls are continually before me.

22 Thus saith the Lord God, Behold, I will lift up mine hand to the Gentiles, and set up my standard to the people: and they shall bring thy sons in their arms, and thy daughters shall be carried upon their shoulders.

23 And kings shall be thy nursing fathers, and their queens thy nursing mothers: they shall bow down to thee with their face toward the earth, and lick up the dust of thy feet; and thou shalt know that I am the Lord: for they shall not be ashamed that wait for me.

24 Shall the prey be taken from the mighty, or the lawful captive delivered?

25 But thus saith the Lord, Even the captives of the mighty shall be taken away, and the prey of the terrible shall be delivered: for I will contend with him that contendeth with thee, and I will save thy children.

26 And I will feed them that oppress thee with their own flesh; and they shall be drunken with their own blood, as with sweet wine: and all flesh shall know that I the Lord am thy Saviour and thy Redeemer, the mighty One of Jacob.

According to verse 13, what cause do people have to sing and be joyful? Consider verse 16. "Graven" is another word for "carved" or "deeply impressed." How has the Savior graven us upon the palms of His hands? How can we continually remember the Savior and His sacrifice for us?

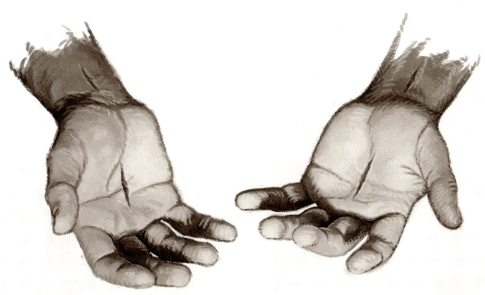

ISAIAH SPEAKS FOR JESUS CHRIST, WHO CALLS ALL PEOPLE TO LOOK UNTO HIM FOR COMFORT AND SALVATION

In speaking for Jesus Christ, Isaiah had compared the Lord's affection for His children to that of a loving mother. The following verses have specific application to the latter days, when God's power and salvation will be available to those who seek Him.

ISAIAH 51:1–6, 12–16

Hearken to me, ye that follow after righteousness, ye that seek the Lord: look unto the rock whence ye are hewn, and to the hole of the pit whence ye are digged.

2 Look unto Abraham your father, and unto Sarah that bare you: for I called him alone, and blessed him, and increased him.

3 For the Lord shall comfort Zion: he will comfort all her waste places; and he will make her wilderness like Eden, and her desert like the garden of the Lord; joy and gladness shall be found therein, thanksgiving, and the voice of melody.

4 Hearken unto me, my people; and give ear unto me, O my nation: for a law shall proceed from me, and I will make my judgment to rest for a light of the people.

5 My righteousness is near; my salvation is gone forth, and mine arms shall judge the people; the isles shall wait upon me, and on mine arm shall they trust.

6 Lift up your eyes to the heavens, and look upon the earth beneath: for the heavens shall vanish away like smoke, and the earth shall wax old like a garment, and they that dwell therein shall die in like manner: but my salvation shall be for ever, and my righteousness shall not be abolished.

12 I, even I, am he that comforteth you: who art thou, that thou shouldest be afraid of a man that shall die, and of the son of man which shall be made as grass;

13 And forgettest the Lord thy maker, that hath stretched forth the heavens, and laid the foundations of the earth; and hast feared continually every day because of the fury of the oppressor, as if he were ready to destroy? and where is the fury of the oppressor?

14 The captive exile hasteneth that he may be loosed, and that he should not die in the pit, nor that his bread should fail.

15 But I am the Lord thy God, that divided the sea, whose waves roared: The Lord of hosts is his name.

16 And I have put my words in thy mouth, and I have covered thee in the shadow of mine hand, that I may plant the heavens, and lay the foundations of the earth, and say unto Zion, Thou art my people.

Consider verse 1. How can you be someone who follows after righteousness? How has the Lord comforted you as you have tried to be obedient? According to verse 6, what will last forever?

JEHOVAH COMMANDS HIS PEOPLE TO REJOICE IN THE REDEMPTION MADE POSSIBLE BY HIM

Through Isaiah, the Lord declared His willingness and ability to grant salvation. Additional prophecies concerning the last days then continued as the Lord commanded His people to rejoice and live worthy of eternal blessings.

Isaiah 52:1–3, 7–12

Awake, awake; put on thy strength, O Zion; put on thy beautiful garments, O Jerusalem, the holy city: for henceforth there shall no more come into thee the uncircumcised and the unclean.

2 Shake thyself from the dust; arise, and sit down, O Jerusalem: loose thyself from the bands of thy neck, O captive daughter of Zion.

3 For thus saith the Lord, Ye have sold yourselves for nought; and ye shall be redeemed without money.

7 How beautiful upon the mountains are the feet of him that bringeth good tidings, that publisheth peace; that bringeth good tidings of good, that publisheth salvation; that saith unto Zion, Thy God reigneth!

8 Thy watchmen shall lift up the voice; with the voice together shall they sing: for they shall see eye to eye, when the Lord shall bring again Zion.

9 Break forth into joy, sing together, ye waste places of Jerusalem: for the Lord hath comforted his people, he hath redeemed Jerusalem.

10 The Lord hath made bare his holy arm in the eyes of all the nations; and all the ends of the earth shall see the salvation of our God.

11 Depart ye, depart ye, go ye out from thence, touch no unclean thing; go ye out of the midst of her; be ye clean, that bear the vessels of the Lord.

12 For ye shall not go out with haste, nor go by flight: for the Lord will go before you; and the God of Israel will be your rearward.

Consider verse 7. What are some examples of those who "publisheth peace" and "bringeth good tidings of good" today? What can you do to bring more peace and good into the world? How do you feel knowing that the Lord "will go before you," as promised in verse 12?

ISAIAH PROPHESIES OF JESUS CHRIST'S GREAT HUMILITY AS HE ENDURED HIS ATONING SACRIFICE

Many prophets prophesied of Jesus Christ's atoning sacrifice, which included His suffering in the Garden of Gethsemane and His death upon the cross. But Isaiah was unique in the way he described these events. He used words and phrases that help us better understand many of the individual pains Jesus Christ endured, such as, "I gave my back to the smiters, and my cheeks to them that plucked off the hair: I hid not my face from shame and spitting" (Isaiah 50:6). As you read the following verses, look for descriptions of some of the specific events that occurred during the last week of Christ's mortal life.

ISAIAH 53:1–12

Who hath believed our report? and to whom is the arm of the Lord revealed?

2 For he shall grow up before him as a tender plant, and as a root out of a dry ground: he hath no form nor comeliness; and when we shall see him, there is no beauty that we should desire him.

3 He is despised and rejected of men; a man of sorrows, and acquainted with grief: and we hid as it were our faces from him; he was despised, and we esteemed him not.

4 Surely he hath borne our griefs, and carried our sorrows: yet we did esteem him stricken, smitten of God, and afflicted.

5 But he was wounded for our transgressions, he was bruised for our iniquities: the chastisement of our peace was upon him; and with his stripes we are healed.

6 All we like sheep have gone astray; we have turned every one to his own way; and the Lord hath laid on him the iniquity of us all.

7 He was oppressed, and he was afflicted, yet he opened not his mouth: he is brought as a lamb to the slaughter, and as a sheep before her shearers is dumb, so he openeth not his mouth.

8 He was taken from prison and from judgment: and who shall declare his generation? for he was cut off out of the land of the living: for the transgression of my people was he stricken.

9 And he made his grave with the wicked, and with the rich in his death; because he had done no violence, neither was any deceit in his mouth.

10 Yet it pleased the Lord to bruise him; he hath put him to grief: when thou shalt make his soul an offering for sin, he shall see his seed, he shall prolong his days, and the pleasure of the Lord shall prosper in his hand.

11 He shall see of the travail of his soul, and shall be satisfied: by his knowledge shall my righteous servant justify many; for he shall bear their iniquities.

12 Therefore will I divide him a portion with the great, and he shall divide the spoil with the strong; because he hath poured out his soul unto death: and he was numbered with the transgressors; and he bare the sin of many, and made intercession for the transgressors.

According to these verses, what are some of the specific pains Jesus Christ endured as part of His atoning sacrifice? Consider verse 4. How has Christ "carried" sorrows? How are God's children like sheep who have gone astray? How has the Savior made it possible for us to be brought back to His fold?

ISAIAH SPEAKS OF THE JOY, PEACE, AND SALVATION OFFERED BY GOD FREELY TO ALL PEOPLE

Isaiah had prophesied in great detail of Jesus Christ's birth, upbringing, atoning sacrifice, and continuing works on behalf of all mankind. He spoke poetically of the incredible humility Christ showed while enduring the tormenting pains of His atoning sacrifice. In these verses, Isaiah again speaks for the Lord, declaring the eternal purpose and blessings of His Atonement.

Isaiah 55:1–3, 6–13

Ho, every one that thirsteth, come ye to the waters, and he that hath no money; come ye, buy, and eat; yea, come, buy wine and milk without money and without price.

2 Wherefore do ye spend money for that which is not bread? and your labour for that which satisfieth not? hearken diligently unto me, and eat ye that which is good, and let your soul delight itself in fatness.

3 Incline your ear, and come unto me: hear, and your soul shall live; and I will make an everlasting covenant with you, even the sure mercies of David.

6 Seek ye the Lord while he may be found, call ye upon him while he is near:

7 Let the wicked forsake his way, and the unrighteous man his thoughts: and let him return unto the Lord, and he will have mercy upon him; and to our God, for he will abundantly pardon.

8 For my thoughts are not your thoughts, neither are your ways my ways, saith the Lord.

9 For as the heavens are higher than the earth, so are my ways higher than your ways, and my thoughts than your thoughts.

10 For as the rain cometh down, and the snow from heaven, and returneth not thither, but watereth the earth, and maketh it bring forth and bud, that it may give seed to the sower, and bread to the eater:

11 So shall my word be that goeth forth out of my mouth: it shall not return unto me void, but it shall accomplish that which I please, and it shall prosper in the thing whereto I sent it.

12 For ye shall go out with joy, and be led forth with peace: the mountains and the hills shall break forth before you into singing, and all the trees of the field shall clap their hands.

13 Instead of the thorn shall come up the fir tree, and instead of the brier shall come up the myrtle tree: and it shall be to the Lord for a name, for an everlasting sign that shall not be cut off.

How does Christ fill those who are hungry and thirsty? What has Christ given you that cannot be bought with money? Consider verses 8–9. How are God's thoughts different from our thoughts? How does knowing this help you?

GOD DECLARES TO JEREMIAH THAT HE WAS FOREORDAINED TO BE A PROPHET IN ISRAEL

About one hundred years after the life of Isaiah, God raised up another powerful prophet in Jerusalem. His name was Jeremiah. Like Isaiah, Jeremiah labored for about forty years during a time of great wickedness among the children of Israel. He recorded many prophecies and warnings, both to people of his day and of our day. Jeremiah's ministry occurred about six hundred years before the birth of Jesus Christ—the same time period when Lehi and his family were led by God out of Jerusalem to a promised land in the ancient Americas, as recorded in the Book of Mormon. The challenges and temptations faced by the Israelites at that time were similar to those faced by Church members today: Would they turn from the pride, vanity, and wickedness of the world and embrace God? Would they shun wicked traditions and honor their sacred covenants with the one true God who had repeatedly saved them? Would their conversion to God sink deep into their hearts and truly change them, or would they stubbornly regard God's commandments and covenants as a list of annoying requirements? The internal wickedness and strife within Israel was compounded by external troubles as neighboring nations made war with Israel, destroyed much of their property, and carried many Israelites away into bondage. During this deeply challenging time, God called Jeremiah to perform mighty works, as recorded here in Jeremiah's own words.

JEREMIAH 1:4–10, 17–19

Then the word of the Lord came unto me, saying,

5 Before I formed thee in the belly I knew thee; and before thou camest forth out of the womb I sanctified thee, and I ordained thee a prophet unto the nations.

6 Then said I, Ah, Lord God! behold, I cannot speak: for I am a child.

7 But the Lord said unto me, Say not, I am a child: for thou shalt go to all that I shall send thee, and whatsoever I command thee thou shalt speak.

8 Be not afraid of their faces: for I am with thee to deliver thee, saith the Lord.

9 Then the Lord put forth his hand, and touched my mouth. And the Lord said unto me, Behold, I have put my words in thy mouth.

10 See, I have this day set thee over the nations and over the kingdoms, to root out, and to pull down, and to destroy, and to throw down, to build, and to plant.

17 Thou therefore gird up thy loins, and arise, and speak unto them all that I command thee: be not dismayed at their faces, lest I confound thee before them.

18 For, behold, I have made thee this day a defenced city, and an iron pillar, and brasen walls against the whole land, against the kings of Judah,

against the princes thereof, against the priests thereof, and against the people of the land.

19 And they shall fight against thee; but they shall not prevail against thee; for I am with thee, saith the Lord, to deliver thee.

What do these verses say about how long God had known Jeremiah? How does Jeremiah react to being called a a prophet? In these verses, what does the Lord say to Jeremiah to encourage him in his calling? How can you apply the Lord's encouragement to Jeremiah when you are asked to do difficult things?

190

JEREMIAH OFFERS THE BLESSING OF REPENTANCE TO THE GROSSLY WICKED ISRAELITES

Jeremiah was a righteous prophet who knew the goodness of God and witnessed the ongoing wickedness of the Israelites. This caused Jeremiah great sorrow. At God's command, he scolded the Israelites for turning away from God, then extended an invitation to repent. In these verses, the word "backsliding" means to slowly return to old habits and wicked actions. As you read, look for the specific actions Jeremiah told the Israelites to take in order to receive forgiveness.

JEREMIAH 3:12–15, 17–19

Go and proclaim these words toward the north, and say, Return, thou backsliding Israel, saith the Lord; and I will not cause mine anger to fall upon you: for I am merciful, saith the Lord, and I will not keep anger for ever.

13 Only acknowledge thine iniquity, that thou hast transgressed against the Lord thy God, and hast scattered thy ways to the strangers under every green tree, and ye have not obeyed my voice, saith the Lord.

14 Turn, O backsliding children, saith the Lord; for I am married unto you: and I will take you one of a city, and two of a family, and I will bring you to Zion:

15 And I will give you pastors according to mine heart, which shall feed you with knowledge and understanding.

17 At that time they shall call Jerusalem the throne of the Lord; and all the nations shall be gathered unto it, to the name of the Lord, to Jerusalem: neither shall they walk any more after the imagination of their evil heart.

18 In those days the house of Judah shall walk with the house of Israel, and they shall come together out of the land of the north to the land that I have given for an inheritance unto your fathers.

19 But I said, How shall I put thee among the children, and give thee a pleasant land, a goodly heritage of the hosts of nations? and I said, Thou shalt call me, My father; and shalt not turn away from me.

JEREMIAH 7:3–7

3 Thus saith the Lord of hosts, the God of Israel, Amend your ways and your doings, and I will cause you to dwell in this place.

4 Trust ye not in lying words, saying, The temple of the Lord, The temple of the Lord, The temple of the Lord, are these.

5 For if ye throughly amend your ways and your doings; if ye throughly execute judgment between a man and his neighbour;

6 If ye oppress not the stranger, the fatherless, and the widow, and shed not innocent blood in this place, neither walk after other gods to your hurt:

7 Then will I cause you to dwell in this place, in the land that I gave to your fathers, for ever and ever.

In these verses, what specific actions did Jeremiah tell the Israelites to take? What did the Lord promise to do if the Israelites repented (see Jeremiah 3:14–15, 17)? Consider Jeremiah 3:15. What "pastors" or leaders in Christ's Church have been a blessing to you? In what specific ways have they blessed you? Consider Jeremiah 7:6–7. How can you view "the stranger, the fatherless, and the widow" with love and seek to serve them?

JEREMIAH PROPHESIES OF THE GATHERING OF ISRAEL IN THE LATTER DAYS

While ministering as a prophet in Jerusalem for about forty years, Jeremiah had repeatedly witnessed God's mercy and the ongoing wickedness of the Israelites. He was valiant in delivering God's word to the people, prophesying boldly that Israel would soon be destroyed and scattered by the neighboring kingdom of Babylon. The gift of repentance was offered to the Israelites, but instead of repenting, the people became angry and put Jeremiah in prison. As Jeremiah had prophesied, Israel was then overrun by Babylon. Jerusalem was destroyed, and the people—the twelve tribes of Israel—were scattered from the lands of their inheritance to nations throughout the world. But even then—around 600 B.C.—Jeremiah knew of God's enduring mercy. He prophesied that God would continue to extend the blessing of repentance to the Israelites and would gather them together as one people in the latter days. These verses speak of that gathering, which is presently taking place throughout the world.

JEREMIAH 31:1, 4–13, 31–34

At the same time, saith the Lord, will I be the God of all the families of Israel, and they shall be my people.

4 Again I will build thee, and thou shalt be built, O virgin of Israel: thou shalt again be adorned with thy tabrets, and shalt go forth in the dances of them that make merry.

5 Thou shalt yet plant vines upon the mountains of Samaria: the planters shall plant, and shall eat them as common things.

6 For there shall be a day, that the watchmen upon the mount Ephraim shall cry, Arise ye, and let us go up to Zion unto the Lord our God.

7 For thus saith the Lord; Sing with gladness for Jacob, and shout among the chief of the nations: publish ye, praise ye, and say, O Lord, save thy people, the remnant of Israel.

8 Behold, I will bring them from the north country, and gather them from the coasts of the earth, and with them the blind and the lame, the woman with child and her that travaileth with child together: a great company shall return thither.

9 They shall come with weeping, and with supplications will I lead them: I will cause them to walk by the rivers of waters in a straight way, wherein they shall not stumble: for I am a father to Israel, and Ephraim is my firstborn.

10 Hear the word of the Lord, O ye nations, and declare it in the isles afar off, and say, He that scattered Israel will gather him, and keep him, as a shepherd doth his flock.

11 For the Lord hath redeemed Jacob, and ransomed him from the hand of him that was stronger than he.

12 Therefore they shall come and sing in the height of Zion, and shall flow together to the goodness of the Lord, for wheat, and for wine, and for oil, and for the young of the flock and of the herd: and their soul shall be as a watered garden; and they shall not sorrow any more at all.

13 Then shall the virgin rejoice in the dance, both young men and old together: for I will turn their mourning into joy, and will comfort them, and make them rejoice from their sorrow.

31 Behold, the days come, saith the Lord, that I will make a new covenant with the house of Israel, and with the house of Judah:

32 Not according to the covenant that I made with their fathers in the day that I took them by the hand to bring them out of the land of Egypt; which my covenant they brake, although I was an husband unto them, saith the Lord:

33 But this shall be the covenant that I will make with the house of Israel; After those days, saith the Lord, I will put my law in their inward parts, and write it in their hearts; and will be their God, and they shall be my people.

34 And they shall teach no more every man his neighbour, and every man his brother, saying, Know the Lord: for they shall all know me, from the least of them unto the greatest of them, saith the Lord: for I will forgive their iniquity, and I will remember their sin no more.

How will the children of Israel feel when they are gathered in the latter days (see verses 12–13)? How can you have the law of God written in your heart, as it says in verse 33? What is the gathering of Israel, and what opportunities do you have to participate in that work?

EZEKIEL IS CALLED BY GOD TO PREACH REPENTANCE AND IS WARNED THAT FAILURE TO DO SO WILL PLACE ISRAEL'S SINS UPON HIM

Ezekiel was another prophet called to preach to the Israelites during an extended period of great wickedness and disarray. Ezekiel's ministry—occurring from 592 to 570 B.C.—briefly overlapped that of Jeremiah's. For hundreds of years, various kings came and went, but the words of the prophets remained consistent: Repent or Israel will be destroyed and its people will be scattered. Ezekiel would be commanded by God to boldly and publicly declare this message many times. The following verses contain Ezekiel's description of being called by God to preach and prophesy—and the serious personal consequences if he failed to do so.

EZEKIEL 2:1–8

And he said unto me, Son of man, stand upon thy feet, and I will speak unto thee.

2 And the spirit entered into me when he spake unto me, and set me upon my feet, that I heard him that spake unto me.

3 And he said unto me, Son of man, I send thee to the children of Israel, to a rebellious nation that hath rebelled against me: they and their fathers have transgressed against me, even unto this very day.

4 For they are impudent children and stiff-hearted. I do send thee unto them; and thou shalt say unto them, Thus saith the Lord God.

5 And they, whether they will hear, or whether they will forbear, (for they are a rebellious house,) yet shall know that there hath been a prophet among them.

6 And thou, son of man, be not afraid of them, neither be afraid of their words, though briers and thorns be with thee, and thou dost dwell among scorpions: be not afraid of their words, nor be dismayed at their looks, though they be a rebellious house.

7 And thou shalt speak my words unto them, whether they will hear, or whether they will forbear: for they are most rebellious.

8 But thou, son of man, hear what I say unto thee; Be not thou rebellious like that rebellious house: open thy mouth, and eat that I give thee.

EZEKIEL 3:16–21

16 And it came to pass at the end of seven days, that the word of the Lord came unto me, saying,

17 Son of man, I have made thee a watchman unto the house of Israel: therefore hear the word at my mouth, and give them warning from me.

18 When I say unto the wicked, Thou shalt surely die; and thou givest him not warning, nor speakest to warn the wicked from his wicked way, to save his life; the same wicked man shall die in his iniquity; but his blood will I require at thine hand.

19 Yet if thou warn the wicked, and he turn not from his wickedness, nor from his wicked way, he shall die in his iniquity; but thou hast delivered thy soul.

20 Again, When a righteous man doth turn from his righteousness, and commit iniquity, and I lay a stumblingblock before him, he shall die: because thou hast not given him warning, he shall die in his sin, and his righteousness which he hath done shall not be remembered; but his blood will I require at thine hand.

21 Nevertheless if thou warn the righteous man, that the righteous sin not, and he doth not sin, he shall surely live, because he is warned; also thou hast delivered thy soul.

What specific things was Ezekiel told to not be afraid of in Ezekiel 2:6? How can that guidance pertain to you today? What consequences did Ezekiel face if he failed to call the people to repentance (see Ezekiel 3:18)? Consider the Lord's description of Ezekiel as a "watchman." What is the purpose of a watchman? Who are the Lord's watchmen today?

GOD TEACHES EZEKIEL THAT PEOPLE ARE PUNISHED FOR THEIR OWN SINS—NOT THE SINS OF THOSE WHO COME BEFORE OR AFTER THEM

Ezekiel was shown many visions and was fully aware of the gross iniquity practiced by the Israelites and the Lord's anger at their disobedience. He chastised false prophets who spoke lies, and he repeatedly and powerfully told the Israelites that if they did not repent, they would face the consequences of being smitten and scattered. At that time, a saying was commonly repeated in Israel: "The parents ate the sour grapes, but the children got the sour taste" (see Ezekiel 18:2). This saying referred to the mistaken belief that the Israelites' current challenges were due to the sins of their ancestors. In these verses, God commanded that this saying be done away with, as God taught Ezekiel the principle that each person is accountable for his or her own sins—not the sins of those who came before or come after.

 EZEKIEL 18:19–32

Yet say ye, Why? doth not the son bear the iniquity of the father? When the son hath done that which is lawful and right, and hath kept all my statutes, and hath done them, he shall surely live.

20 The soul that sinneth, it shall die. The son shall not bear the iniquity of the father, neither shall the father bear the iniquity of the son: the righteousness of the righteous shall be upon him, and the wickedness of the wicked shall be upon him.

21 But if the wicked will turn from all his sins that he hath committed, and keep all my statutes, and do that which is lawful and right, he shall surely live, he shall not die.

22 All his transgressions that he hath committed, they shall not be mentioned unto him: in his righteousness that he hath done he shall live.

23 Have I any pleasure at all that the wicked should die? saith the Lord God: and not that he should return from his ways, and live?

24 But when the righteous turneth away from his righteousness, and committeth iniquity, and doeth according to all the abominations that the wicked man doeth, shall he live? All his righteousness that he hath done shall not be mentioned: in his trespass that he hath trespassed, and in his sin that he hath sinned, in them shall he die.

25 Yet ye say, The way of the Lord is not equal. Hear now, O house of Israel; Is not my way equal? are not your ways unequal?

26 When a righteous man turneth away from his righteousness, and committeth iniquity, and dieth in them; for his iniquity that he hath done shall he die.

27 Again, when the wicked man turneth away from his wickedness that he hath committed, and doeth that which is lawful and right, he shall save his soul alive.

28 Because he considereth, and turneth away from all his transgressions that he hath committed, he shall surely live, he shall not die.

29 Yet saith the house of Israel, The way of the Lord is not equal. O house of Israel, are not my ways equal? are not your ways unequal?

30 Therefore I will judge you, O house of Israel, every one according to his ways, saith the Lord God. Repent, and turn yourselves from all your transgressions; so iniquity shall not be your ruin.

31 Cast away from you all your transgressions, whereby ye have transgressed; and make you a new heart and a new spirit: for why will ye die, O house of Israel?

32 For I have no pleasure in the death of him that dieth, saith the Lord God: wherefore turn yourselves, and live ye.

What does verse 20 teach about the consequences of sin—and those who are accountable for sin? What do verses 26–27 teach about the righteous who turn to sin and sinners who repent and turn to righteousness? How can you show that you take personal responsibility for your sins and shortcomings?

GOD CONDEMNS LEADERS OF HIS PEOPLE WHO LOOK AFTER ONLY THEMSELVES AND FAIL TO CARE FOR HIS FLOCK

Ezekiel continued to obey God's command to declare Israel's sins and invite the people to repent. But the Israelites did not repent. As had been prophesied, their cities were slowly destroyed and the people began again to be scattered to other nations. Though the nation of Israel itself was in decline, God spoke to Ezekiel about His tender concern for each of His individual children. In these verses, God chastises those in Israel who had been called to lead and minister to their fellow Israelites but instead focused only on themselves. As you read, consider your own responsibilities in the Lord's Church and the expectations God has for you as a leader, minister, and friend to His children.

EZEKIEL 34:1–6, 10–16, 25, 30

And the word of the Lord came unto me, saying,

2 Son of man, prophesy against the shepherds of Israel, prophesy, and say unto them, Thus saith the Lord God unto the shepherds; Woe be to the shepherds of Israel that do feed themselves! should not the shepherds feed the flocks?

3 Ye eat the fat, and ye clothe you with the wool, ye kill them that are fed: but ye feed not the flock.

4 The diseased have ye not strengthened, neither have ye healed that which was sick, neither have ye bound up that which was broken, neither have ye brought again that which was driven away, neither have ye sought that which was lost; but with force and with cruelty have ye ruled them.

5 And they were scattered, because there is no shepherd: and they became meat to all the beasts of the field, when they were scattered.

6 My sheep wandered through all the mountains, and upon every high hill: yea, my flock was scattered upon all the face of the earth, and none did search or seek after them.

10 Thus saith the Lord God; Behold, I am against the shepherds; and I will require my flock at their

hand, and cause them to cease from feeding the flock; neither shall the shepherds feed themselves any more; for I will deliver my flock from their mouth, that they may not be meat for them.

11 For thus saith the Lord God; Behold, I, even I, will both search my sheep, and seek them out.

12 As a shepherd seeketh out his flock in the day that he is among his sheep that are scattered; so will I seek out my sheep, and will deliver them out of all places where they have been scattered in the cloudy and dark day.

13 And I will bring them out from the people, and gather them from the countries, and will bring them to their own land, and feed them upon the mountains of Israel by the rivers, and in all the inhabited places of the country.

14 I will feed them in a good pasture, and upon the high mountains of Israel shall their fold be:

there shall they lie in a good fold, and in a fat pasture shall they feed upon the mountains of Israel.

15 I will feed my flock, and I will cause them to lie down, saith the Lord God.

16 I will seek that which was lost, and bring again that which was driven away, and will bind up that which was broken, and will strengthen that which was sick: but I will destroy the fat and the strong; I will feed them with judgment.

25 And I will make with them a covenant of peace, and will cause the evil beasts to cease out of the land: and they shall dwell safely in the wilderness, and sleep in the woods.

30 Thus shall they know that I the Lord their God am with them, and that they, even the house of Israel, are my people, saith the Lord God.

According to these verses, what specific things had the spiritual shepherds in Israel failed to do? In verses 11–16, what actions did the Lord promise to take as a shepherd to His flock? How has He "sought" and "delivered" and "fed" you? What specific direction and counsel have modern-day prophets given in regard to caring for one another's physical and spiritual needs?

EZEKIEL DESCRIBES THE CLEANSING EFFECT OF GOD AS HE RESTORES THE RIGHTEOUS IN THE LAST DAYS

Ezekiel was shown both the awful state of the Israelites of his day and the glorious work of God in the latter days. He recorded many of these visions and prophecies, including the following revelation from God that poetically describes the Lord's merciful cleansing of His people to save them from sin.

EZEKIEL 36:16–18, 21–36

Moreover the word of the Lord came unto me, saying,

17 Son of man, when the house of Israel dwelt in their own land, they defiled it by their own way and by their doings: their way was before me as the uncleanness of a removed woman.

18 Wherefore I poured my fury upon them for the blood that they had shed upon the land, and for their idols wherewith they had polluted it:

21 But I had pity for mine holy name, which the house of Israel had profaned among the heathen, whither they went.

22 Therefore say unto the house of Israel, Thus saith the Lord God; I do not this for your sakes, O house of Israel, but for mine holy name's sake, which ye have profaned among the heathen, whither ye went.

23 And I will sanctify my great name, which was profaned among the heathen, which ye have profaned in the midst of them; and the heathen shall know that I am the Lord, saith the Lord God, when I shall be sanctified in you before their eyes.

24 For I will take you from among the heathen, and gather you out of all countries, and will bring you into your own land.

25 Then will I sprinkle clean water upon you, and ye shall be clean: from all your filthiness, and from all your idols, will I cleanse you.

26 A new heart also will I give you, and a new spirit will I put within you: and I will take away the stony heart out of your flesh, and I will give you an heart of flesh.

27 And I will put my spirit within you, and cause you to walk in my statutes, and ye shall keep my judgments, and do them.

28 And ye shall dwell in the land that I gave to your fathers; and ye shall be my people, and I will be your God.

29 I will also save you from all your uncleannesses: and I will call for the corn, and will increase it, and lay no famine upon you.

30 And I will multiply the fruit of the tree, and the increase of the field, that ye shall receive no more reproach of famine among the heathen.

31 Then shall ye remember your own evil ways, and your doings that were not good, and shall lothe yourselves in your own sight for your iniquities and for your abominations.

32 Not for your sakes do I this, saith the Lord God, be it known unto you: be ashamed and confounded for your own ways, O house of Israel.

33 Thus saith the Lord God; In the day that I shall have cleansed you from all your iniquities I will also cause you to dwell in the cities, and the wastes shall be builded.

34 And the desolate land shall be tilled, whereas it lay desolate in the sight of all that passed by.

35 And they shall say, This land that was desolate is become like the garden of Eden; and the waste and desolate and ruined cities are become fenced, and are inhabited.

36 Then the heathen that are left round about you shall know that I the Lord build the ruined places, and plant that that was desolate: I the Lord have spoken it, and I will do it.

Consider verses 25–27. How does the Lord promise to change those who believe in Him? What changes have you noticed in yourself as you have tried to keep God's commandments? How has the Lord changed your heart?

EZEKIEL IS SHOWN THE COMBINED EFFECT OF THE HOLY BIBLE AND THE BOOK OF MORMON UPON PEOPLE IN THE LATTER DAYS

In this concluding selection of Ezekiel's words, he describes the miraculous coming forth of both the Holy Bible and the Book of Mormon in the latter days. In Ezekiel's time (around 580 B.C.), the words of the prophets were carefully written on animal skins or papyrus and then rolled up around a stick or scroll for safekeeping and portability. In these verses, the Lord uses this term—a stick—to describe two collections of scriptures that would come from two branches of the house of Israel. The stick of Judah refers to what would become the Holy Bible, as recorded by prophets such as Moses, Isaiah, and Ezekiel, who lived in and around the Holy Land. The stick of Joseph (also called the stick of Ephraim) refers to what would become the Book of Mormon, as recorded by prophets such as Nephi, Alma, and Mormon, who lived in the ancient Americas. The coming forth of these two volumes of scripture was no accident. God carefully prepared a way for His children in ancient days and modern days to be able to read and know of God's existence, the Atoning sacrifice of Jesus Christ, and God's saving covenants available to all people.

EZEKIEL 37:15–28

The word of the Lord came again unto me, saying,

16 Moreover, thou son of man, take thee one stick, and write upon it, For Judah, and for the children of Israel his companions: then take another stick, and write upon it, For Joseph, the stick of Ephraim, and for all the house of Israel his companions:

17 And join them one to another into one stick; and they shall become one in thine hand.

18 And when the children of thy people shall speak unto thee, saying, Wilt thou not shew us what thou meanest by these?

19 Say unto them, Thus saith the Lord God; Behold, I will take the stick of Joseph, which is in the hand of Ephraim, and the tribes of Israel his fellows, and will put them with him, even with the stick of Judah, and make them one stick, and they shall be one in mine hand.

20 And the sticks whereon thou writest shall be in thine hand before their eyes.

21 And say unto them, Thus saith the Lord God; Behold, I will take the children of Israel from among the heathen, whither they be gone, and will gather them on every side, and bring them into their own land:

22 And I will make them one nation in the land upon the mountains of Israel; and one king shall be king to them all: and they shall be no more two nations, neither shall they be divided into two kingdoms any more at all:

23 Neither shall they defile themselves any more with their idols, nor with their detestable things, nor with any of their transgressions: but I will save them out of all their dwellingplaces, wherein they have sinned, and will cleanse them: so shall they be my people, and I will be their God.

24 And David my servant shall be king over them; and they all shall have one shepherd: they shall also walk in my judgments, and observe my statutes, and do them.

25 And they shall dwell in the land that I have given unto Jacob my servant, wherein your fathers have dwelt; and they shall dwell therein, even they, and their children, and their children's children for ever: and my servant David shall be their prince for ever.

26 Moreover I will make a covenant of peace with them; it shall be an everlasting covenant with them: and I will place them, and multiply them, and will set my sanctuary in the midst of them for evermore.

27 My tabernacle also shall be with them: yea, I will be their God, and they shall be my people.

28 And the heathen shall know that I the Lord do sanctify Israel, when my sanctuary shall be in the midst of them for evermore.

What knowledge do you have because of the Bible and Book of Mormon? What promise does the Lord make to the house of Israel in verses 21 and 22? In verse 26, the Lord promises to make a "covenant of peace" with Israel. How do your covenants with the Lord bring you peace?

DANIEL AND HIS THREE ISRAELITE COMPANIONS ARE DETERMINED TO HONOR GOD AND REFUSE TO EAT FORBIDDEN FOOD OFFERED BY THE KING OF BABYLON

Jeremiah and Ezekiel's prophetic ministries among the Israelites briefly overlapped. Both men boldly preached repentance, but most people continued in wickedness, leading to another wave of destruction and scattering. Nebuchadnezzar was the king of Babylon. His mighty nation invaded Jerusalem and took many Israelites back to Babylon (see Map #4, C3). Among the Israelites taken to Babylon were four young men who feared God and were determined to keep His commandments, even if it meant offending the powerful king who could quickly order that the disobedient be executed. Previously, as part of the law of Moses, the Israelites had been commanded to never eat certain foods. Some of these forbidden foods—referred to in these verses as "the king's meat"—would be offered to these young men. Also in these verses, a "eunuch" was a royal servant in the king's court, and "pulse" was most likely a type of vegetable or bean that was permitted in the law of Moses.

In the third year of the reign of Jehoiakim king of Judah came Nebuchadnezzar king of Babylon unto Jerusalem, and besieged it.

2 And the Lord gave Jehoiakim king of Judah into his hand, with part of the vessels of the house of God: which he carried into the land of Shinar to the house of his god; and he brought the vessels into the treasure house of his god.

3 And the king spake unto Ashpenaz the master of his eunuchs, that he should bring certain of the children of Israel, and of the king's seed, and of the princes;

4 Children in whom was no blemish, but well favoured, and skilful in all wisdom, and cunning in knowledge, and understanding science, and such as had ability in them to stand in the king's palace, and whom they might teach the learning and the tongue of the Chaldeans.

5 And the king appointed them a daily provision of the king's meat, and of the wine which he drank: so nourishing them three years, that at the end thereof they might stand before the king.

6 Now among these were of the children of Judah, Daniel, Hananiah, Mishael, and Azariah:

7 Unto whom the prince of the eunuchs gave names: for he gave unto Daniel the name of Belteshazzar; and to Hananiah, of Shadrach; and to Mishael, of Meshach; and to Azariah, of Abednego.

8 But Daniel purposed in his heart that he would not defile himself with the portion of the king's meat, nor with the wine which he drank: therefore he requested of the prince of the eunuchs that he might not defile himself.

9 Now God had brought Daniel into favour and tender love with the prince of the eunuchs.

10 And the prince of the eunuchs said unto Daniel, I fear my lord the king, who hath appointed your meat and your drink: for why should he see your faces worse liking than the children which are of your sort? then shall ye make me endanger my head to the king.

11 Then said Daniel to Melzar, whom the prince of the eunuchs had set over Daniel, Hananiah, Mishael, and Azariah,

12 Prove thy servants, I beseech thee, ten days; and let them give us pulse to eat, and water to drink.

13 Then let our countenances be looked upon before thee, and the countenance of the children that eat of the portion of the king's meat: and as thou seest, deal with thy servants.

14 So he consented to them in this matter, and proved them ten days.

15 And at the end of ten days their countenances appeared fairer and fatter in flesh than all the children which did eat the portion of the king's meat.

16 Thus Melzar took away the portion of their meat, and the wine that they should drink; and gave them pulse.

17 As for these four children, God gave them knowledge and skill in all learning and wisdom: and Daniel had understanding in all visions and dreams.

18 Now at the end of the days that the king had said he should bring them in, then the prince of the eunuchs brought them in before Nebuchadnezzar.

19 And the king communed with them; and among them all was found none like Daniel, Hananiah, Mishael, and Azariah: therefore stood they before the king.

20 And in all matters of wisdom and understanding, that the king inquired of them, he found them ten times better than all the magicians and astrologers that were in all his realm.

What were the names of the four young men who refused to eat the forbidden food? Consider verse 8. What do you think it meant that Daniel "purposed in his heart" that he would not disobey God's commandments? What can you do to prepare to keep the commandments when you face temptation?

DANIEL PREPARES TO USE HIS SPIRITUAL GIFTS AND ACKNOWLEDGES GOD AS THE SOURCE OF THOSE GIFTS

Four righteous young men from Israel had been taken captive to Babylon. They were referred to by both their Israelite names and the new names given them by the Babylonians. Daniel was Belteshazzar; Hananiah was Shadrach; Mishael was Meshach; Azariah was Abed-nego. Led by Daniel, these four young men were determined to honor God and refused to eat forbidden foods that were forcefully given to them by the powerful King Nebuchadnezzar. God rewarded their integrity and provided them health and "knowledge and skill in all learning and wisdom: and Daniel had understanding in all visions and dreams" (Daniel 1:17). These four were part of a larger group of "wise men" who were to serve King Nebuchadnezzar. The king then had a dream that disturbed him, and he demanded that someone tell him the interpretation of the dream. Magicians and sorcerers offered to interpret it only after the king described the dream itself, but the king refused and made a decree: If someone could tell him what he had dreamed *and* interpret the dream he would honor him with rewards and honor. But if they could not, they would be killed. The magicians and sorcerers protested, saying what the king desired was impossible.

DANIEL 2:12–30

For this cause the king was angry and very furious, and commanded to destroy all the wise men of Babylon.

13 And the decree went forth that the wise men should be slain; and they sought Daniel and his fellows to be slain.

14 Then Daniel answered with counsel and wisdom to Arioch the captain of the king's guard, which was gone forth to slay the wise men of Babylon:

15 He answered and said to Arioch the king's captain, Why is the decree so hasty from the king? Then Arioch made the thing known to Daniel.

16 Then Daniel went in, and desired of the king that he would give him time, and that he would shew the king the interpretation.

17 Then Daniel went to his house, and made the thing known to Hananiah, Mishael, and Azariah, his companions:

18 That they would desire mercies of the God of heaven concerning this secret; that Daniel and his fellows should not perish with the rest of the wise men of Babylon.

19 Then was the secret revealed unto Daniel in a night vision. Then Daniel blessed the God of heaven.

20 Daniel answered and said, Blessed be the name of God for ever and ever: for wisdom and might are his:

21 And he changeth the times and the seasons: he removeth kings, and setteth up kings: he giveth wisdom unto the wise, and knowledge to them that know understanding:

22 He revealeth the deep and secret things: he knoweth what is in the darkness, and the light dwelleth with him.

23 I thank thee, and praise thee, O thou God of my fathers, who hast given me wisdom and might, and hast made known unto me now what we desired of thee: for thou hast now made known unto us the king's matter.

24 Therefore Daniel went in unto Arioch, whom the king had ordained to destroy the wise men of Babylon: he went and said thus unto him; Destroy not the wise men of Babylon: bring me in before the king, and I will shew unto the king the interpretation.

25 Then Arioch brought in Daniel before the king in haste, and said thus unto him, I have found a man of the captives of Judah, that will make known unto the king the interpretation.

26 The king answered and said to Daniel, whose name was Belteshazzar, Art thou able to make

known unto me the dream which I have seen, and the interpretation thereof?

27 Daniel answered in the presence of the king, and said, The secret which the king hath demanded cannot the wise men, the astrologers, the magicians, the soothsayers, shew unto the king;

28 But there is a God in heaven that revealeth secrets, and maketh known to the king Nebuchadnezzar what shall be in the latter days. Thy dream, and the visions of thy head upon thy bed, are these;

29 As for thee, O king, thy thoughts came into thy mind upon thy bed, what should come to pass hereafter: and he that revealeth secrets maketh known to thee what shall come to pass.

30 But as for me, this secret is not revealed to me for any wisdom that I have more than any living, but for their sakes that shall make known the interpretation to the king, and that thou mightest know the thoughts of thy heart.

What did Daniel ask his companions to do in order to secure God's blessings (see verses 17–18)? Even though Daniel had been blessed with spiritual gifts, he had to remain worthy of those gifts and prepare to use them. What are some ways you can prepare to use spiritual gifts you have been given? Consider Daniel 2:19–23. What was Daniel's response when the king's dream was revealed to him in a vision? How did Daniel show humility to God when he talked with the king?

DANIEL INTERPRETS KING NEBUCHADNEZZAR'S DREAM—A LATTER-DAY PROPHECY OF GOD'S KINGDOM FILLING THE WHOLE EARTH

King Nebuchadnezzar had had a disturbing dream and demanded that his wise men tell him what he had dreamed and interpret the meaning of the dream. After magicians and sorcerers were unable to do so, the king declared that all the wise men in his kingdom be killed. Daniel intervened and promised to reveal all the king desired to know. He commanded his companions to call upon God for mercy, and Daniel was blessed with a vision in which he was shown what the king had dreamed and what it meant. He then appeared before the king, acknowledged that his gift of interpretation came from God, and described the king's dream.

DANIEL 2:31–49

Thou, O king, sawest, and behold a great image. This great image, whose brightness was excellent, stood before thee; and the form thereof was terrible.

32 This image's head was of fine gold, his breast and his arms of silver, his belly and his thighs of brass,

33 His legs of iron, his feet part of iron and part of clay.

34 Thou sawest till that a stone was cut out without hands, which smote the image upon his feet that were of iron and clay, and brake them to pieces.

35 Then was the iron, the clay, the brass, the silver, and the gold, broken to pieces together, and became like the chaff of the summer threshing-floors; and the wind carried them away, that no place was found for them: and the stone that smote the image became a great mountain, and filled the whole earth.

36 This is the dream; and we will tell the interpretation thereof before the king.

37 Thou, O king, art a king of kings: for the God of heaven hath given thee a kingdom, power, and strength, and glory.

38 And wheresoever the children of men dwell, the beasts of the field and the fowls of the heaven hath he given into thine hand, and hath made thee ruler over them all. Thou art this head of gold.

39 And after thee shall arise another kingdom inferior to thee, and another third kingdom of brass, which shall bear rule over all the earth.

40 And the fourth kingdom shall be strong as iron: forasmuch as iron breaketh in pieces and subdueth all things: and as iron that breaketh all these, shall it break in pieces and bruise.

41 And whereas thou sawest the feet and toes, part of potters' clay, and part of iron, the kingdom shall be divided; but there shall be in it of the strength of the iron, forasmuch as thou sawest the iron mixed with miry clay.

42 And as the toes of the feet were part of iron, and part of clay, so the kingdom shall be partly strong, and partly broken.

43 And whereas thou sawest iron mixed with miry clay, they shall mingle themselves with the seed of men: but they shall not cleave one to another, even as iron is not mixed with clay.

44 And in the days of these kings shall the God of heaven set up a kingdom, which shall never be destroyed: and the kingdom shall not be left to other people, but it shall break in pieces and consume all these kingdoms, and it shall stand for ever.

45 Forasmuch as thou sawest that the stone was cut out of the mountain without hands, and that it brake in pieces the iron, the brass, the clay, the silver, and the gold; the great God hath made known to the king what shall come to pass

hereafter: and the dream is certain, and the interpretation thereof sure.

46 Then the king Nebuchadnezzar fell upon his face, and worshipped Daniel, and commanded that they should offer an oblation and sweet odours unto him.

47 The king answered unto Daniel, and said, Of a truth it is, that your God is a God of gods, and a Lord of kings, and a revealer of secrets, seeing thou couldest reveal this secret.

48 Then the king made Daniel a great man, and gave him many great gifts, and made him ruler over the whole province of Babylon, and chief of the governors over all the wise men of Babylon.

49 Then Daniel requested of the king, and he set Shadrach, Meshach, and Abed-nego, over the affairs of the province of Babylon: but Daniel sat in the gate of the king.

In 1831, Joseph Smith received a revelation from God that declared: "The keys of the kingdom of God are committed unto man on the earth, and from thence shall the gospel roll forth unto the ends of the earth, as the stone which is cut out of the mountain without hands shall roll forth, until it has filled the whole earth" (Doctrine and Covenants 65:2).

According to Daniel's interpretation, what did the different images in the king's dream represent? What prophecy was made in verse 44 concerning God's kingdom? How is that prophecy being fulfilled today? What responsibilities do you have to help spread the gospel to the whole earth? Why do you think so many latter-day events were revealed to prophets of the Old Testament?

SHADRACH, MESHACH, AND ABED-NEGO ARE CAST INTO A FIERY FURNACE FOR REFUSING TO BOW DOWN TO FALSE GODS AND ARE SAVED BY THE TRUE AND LIVING GOD

Daniel had greatly impressed Nebuchadnezzar by revealing and interpreting the king's dream. In response, Nebuchadnezzar made Daniel the "chief of the governors over all the wise men of Babylon" (Daniel 2:48). Daniel then requested that his fellow Israelites Shadrach, Meshach, and Abed-nego be given positions of status, and they were set "over the affairs of the province of Babylon" (v. 49). But though Daniel's friends had been given positions of power, they were still regarded by some in Babylon as different and inferior, on account of their unique religion and their determination to worship only their God. This posed a great problem when King Nebuchadnezzar built an enormous idol of gold and commanded that when certain music was played, all people were to fall down and worship it. Daniel's three friends refused to worship the idol, and their disobedience was brought to the attention of the king.

DANIEL 3:13–30

Then Nebuchadnezzar in his rage and fury commanded to bring Shadrach, Meshach, and Abed-nego. Then they brought these men before the king.

14 Nebuchadnezzar spake and said unto them, Is it true, O Shadrach, Meshach, and Abed-nego, do not ye serve my gods, nor worship the golden image which I have set up?

15 Now if ye be ready that at what time ye hear the sound of the cornet, flute, harp, sackbut, psaltery, and dulcimer, and all kinds of musick, ye fall down and worship the image which I have made; well: but if ye worship not, ye shall be cast the same hour into the midst of a burning fiery furnace; and who is that God that shall deliver you out of my hands?

16 Shadrach, Meshach, and Abed-nego, answered and said to the king, O Nebuchadnezzar, we are not careful to answer thee in this matter.

17 If it be so, our God whom we serve is able to deliver us from the burning fiery furnace, and he will deliver us out of thine hand, O king.

18 But if not, be it known unto thee, O king, that we will not serve thy gods, nor worship the golden image which thou hast set up.

19 Then was Nebuchadnezzar full of fury, and the form of his visage was changed against Shadrach, Meshach, and Abed-nego: therefore he spake, and commanded that they should heat the furnace one seven times more than it was wont to be heated.

20 And he commanded the most mighty men that were in his army to bind Shadrach, Meshach, and Abed-nego, and to cast them into the burning fiery furnace.

21 Then these men were bound in their coats, their hosen, and their hats, and their other garments, and were cast into the midst of the burning fiery furnace.

22 Therefore because the king's commandment was urgent, and the furnace exceeding hot, the flame of the fire slew those men that took up Shadrach, Meshach, and Abed-nego.

23 And these three men, Shadrach, Meshach, and Abed-nego, fell down bound into the midst of the burning fiery furnace.

24 Then Nebuchadnezzar the king was astonied, and rose up in haste, and spake, and said unto his counsellors, Did not we cast three men bound into the midst of the fire? They answered and said unto the king, True, O king.

25 He answered and said, Lo, I see four men loose, walking in the midst of the fire, and they have no hurt; and the form of the fourth is like the Son of God.

26 Then Nebuchadnezzar came near to the mouth of the burning fiery furnace, and spake, and said, Shadrach, Meshach, and Abed-nego, ye

servants of the most high God, come forth, and come hither. Then Shadrach, Meshach, and Abed-nego, came forth of the midst of the fire.

27 And the princes, governors, and captains, and the king's counsellors, being gathered together, saw these men, upon whose bodies the fire had no power, nor was an hair of their head singed, neither were their coats changed, nor the smell of fire had passed on them.

28 Then Nebuchadnezzar spake, and said, Blessed be the God of Shadrach, Meshach, and Abed-nego, who hath sent his angel, and delivered his servants that trusted in him, and have changed the king's word, and yielded their bodies, that they might not serve nor worship any god, except their own God.

29 Therefore I make a decree, That every people, nation, and language, which speak any thing amiss against the God of Shadrach, Meshach, and Abed-nego, shall be cut in pieces, and their houses shall be made a dunghill: because there is no other God that can deliver after this sort.

30 Then the king promoted Shadrach, Meshach, and Abed-nego, in the province of Babylon.

Consider the three friends' response to the king in verses 16–18. How did they show faith in God's ability to deliver them? How did they show a willingness to accept the outcome if they were not delivered from the fiery furnace? What experiences have you had in which God has protected and prospered you for your obedience? When have you had to show faith even if the outcome to a challenge wasn't what you wanted? How can you remember those experiences as you face new challenges?

KING BELSHAZZAR IS STRICKEN WITH FEAR AS A HEAVENLY HAND WRITES A MESSAGE UPON THE WALL

Daniel and his three friends Shadrach, Meshach, and Abed-nego had been carried captive into Babylon, where they remained determined to obey only the God of Israel—even if it meant punishment or death. Their actions greatly impressed the powerful King Nebuchadnezzar, and the young men were promoted to positions of influence and power in Babylon. Nebuchadnezzar was then succeeded by his son Belshazzar, who one day threw a lavish feast for his princes, their wives, and their concubines. At the feast, the people drank wine from containers of gold and silver that the Babylonians had stolen from the Lord's temple when they destroyed the city of Jerusalem. The people also praised the gods of gold, silver, and other earthly materials. Suddenly, in the middle of the feast, King Belshazzar saw something that struck him with great fear: A hand appearing in the air, writing words on the wall in a language he could not understand. All present were astonished, and the queen called for Daniel to interpret the writing.

DANIEL 5:13–30

Then was Daniel brought in before the king. And the king spake and said unto Daniel, Art thou that Daniel, which art of the children of the captivity of Judah, whom the king my father brought out of Jewry?

14 I have even heard of thee, that the spirit of the gods is in thee, and that light and understanding and excellent wisdom is found in thee.

15 And now the wise men, the astrologers, have been brought in before me, that they should read this writing, and make known unto me the interpretation thereof: but they could not shew the interpretation of the thing:

16 And I have heard of thee, that thou canst make interpretations, and dissolve doubts: now if thou canst read the writing, and make known

212

to me the interpretation thereof, thou shalt be clothed with scarlet, and have a chain of gold about thy neck, and shalt be the third ruler in the kingdom.

17 Then Daniel answered and said before the king, Let thy gifts be to thyself, and give thy rewards to another; yet I will read the writing unto the king, and make known to him the interpretation.

18 O thou king, the most high God gave Nebuchadnezzar thy father a kingdom, and majesty, and glory, and honour:

19 And for the majesty that he gave him, all people, nations, and languages, trembled and feared before him: whom he would he slew; and whom he would he kept alive; and whom he would he set up; and whom he would he put down.

20 But when his heart was lifted up, and his mind hardened in pride, he was deposed from his kingly throne, and they took his glory from him:

21 And he was driven from the sons of men; and his heart was made like the beasts, and his dwelling was with the wild asses: they fed him with grass like oxen, and his body was wet with the dew of heaven; till he knew that the most high God ruled in the kingdom of men, and that he appointeth over it whomsoever he will.

22 And thou his son, O Belshazzar, hast not humbled thine heart, though thou knewest all this;

23 But hast lifted up thyself against the Lord of heaven; and they have brought the vessels of his house before thee, and thou, and thy lords, thy wives, and thy concubines, have drunk wine in them; and thou hast praised the gods of silver, and gold, of brass, iron, wood, and stone, which see not, nor hear, nor know: and the God in whose hand thy breath is, and whose are all thy ways, hast thou not glorified:

24 Then was the part of the hand sent from him; and this writing was written.

25 And this is the writing that was written, MENE, MENE, TEKEL, UPHARSIN.

26 This is the interpretation of the thing: MENE; God hath numbered thy kingdom, and finished it.

27 TEKEL; Thou art weighed in the balances, and art found wanting.

28 PERES; Thy kingdom is divided, and given to the Medes and Persians.

29 Then commanded Belshazzar, and they clothed Daniel with scarlet, and put a chain of gold about his neck, and made a proclamation concerning him, that he should be the third ruler in the kingdom.

30 In that night was Belshazzar the king of the Chaldeans slain.

The phrase "Thou art weighed in the balances, and art found wanting" refers to the ancient custom of using a scale (also called "balances") to compare the weight of two objects. In this sense, King Belshazzar was being told that his life and actions were being weighed—or judged—by God, and Belshazzar had fallen short of what was expected of him.

In these verses, what description did Daniel give of King Nebuchadnezzar's fall from power (see verses 18–21)? What did the writing on the wall say, and how did it apply to King Belshazzar? How was the writing on the wall fulfilled? Consider your own life and the expectations the Lord has for you. What steps can you take now to help ensure you are not "found wanting" when you are judged by God?

DANIEL IS CAST INTO A DEN OF LIONS FOR PRAYING TO THE GOD OF ISRAEL, THEN IS MIRACULOUSLY SAVED BY ANGELS

The powerful King Nebuchadnezzar had been driven from his throne due to his pride. His son Belshazzar reigned in his stead, and during a lavish feast, Daniel interpreted the miraculous writing on the wall that told Belshazzar: "Thou art weighed in the balances, and art found wanting" (Daniel 5:27). The writing on the wall further explained that Belshazzar's kingdom would be divided, and he was killed that night. Daniel was again recognized as a great man, and Darius became the new king.

DANIEL 6:1–23

It pleased Darius to set over the kingdom an hundred and twenty princes, which should be over the whole kingdom;

2 And over these three presidents; of whom Daniel was first: that the princes might give accounts unto them, and the king should have no damage.

3 Then this Daniel was preferred above the presidents and princes, because an excellent spirit was in him; and the king thought to set him over the whole realm.

4 Then the presidents and princes sought to find occasion against Daniel concerning the kingdom; but they could find none occasion nor fault; forasmuch as he was faithful, neither was there any error or fault found in him.

5 Then said these men, We shall not find any occasion against this Daniel, except we find it against him concerning the law of his God.

6 Then these presidents and princes assembled together to the king, and said thus unto him, King Darius, live for ever.

7 All the presidents of the kingdom, the governors, and the princes, the counsellors, and the captains, have consulted together to establish a royal statute, and to make a firm decree, that whosoever shall ask a petition of any God or man for thirty days, save of thee, O king, he shall be cast into the den of lions.

8 Now, O king, establish the decree, and sign the writing, that it be not changed, according to the law of the Medes and Persians, which altereth not.

9 Wherefore king Darius signed the writing and the decree.

10 Now when Daniel knew that the writing was signed, he went into his house; and his windows being open in his chamber toward Jerusalem, he kneeled upon his knees three times a day, and prayed, and gave thanks before his God, as he did aforetime.

11 Then these men assembled, and found Daniel praying and making supplication before his God.

12 Then they came near, and spake before the king concerning the king's decree; Hast thou not signed a decree, that every man that shall ask a petition of any God or man within thirty days, save of thee, O king, shall be cast into the den of lions? The king answered and said, The thing is true, according to the law of the Medes and Persians, which altereth not.

13 Then answered they and said before the king, That Daniel, which is of the children of the captivity of Judah, regardeth not thee, O king, nor the decree that thou hast signed, but maketh his petition three times a day.

14 Then the king, when he heard these words, was sore displeased with himself, and set his heart on Daniel to deliver him: and he laboured till the going down of the sun to deliver him.

15 Then these men assembled unto the king, and said unto the king, Know, O king, that the law of the Medes and Persians is, That no decree nor statute which the king establisheth may be changed.

16 Then the king commanded, and they brought Daniel, and cast him into the den of lions. Now the king spake and said unto Daniel, Thy God whom thou servest continually, he will deliver thee.

17 And a stone was brought, and laid upon the mouth of the den; and the king sealed it with his own signet, and with the signet of his lords; that the purpose might not be changed concerning Daniel.

18 Then the king went to his palace, and passed the night fasting: neither were instruments of musick brought before him: and his sleep went from him.

19 Then the king arose very early in the morning, and went in haste unto the den of lions.

20 And when he came to the den, he cried with a lamentable voice unto Daniel: and the king spake and said to Daniel, O Daniel, servant of the living God, is thy God, whom thou servest continually, able to deliver thee from the lions?

21 Then said Daniel unto the king, O king, live for ever.

22 My God hath sent his angel, and hath shut the lions' mouths, that they have not hurt me: forasmuch as before him innocency was found in me; and also before thee, O king, have I done no hurt.

23 Then was the king exceeding glad for him, and commanded that they should take Daniel up out of the den. So Daniel was taken up out of the den, and no manner of hurt was found upon him, because he believed in his God.

What did King Darius believe about the God of Israel (see verse 16)? Daniel had been given gifts and authority both from God and from the king. How did he regard those gifts and those two types of authority? What did King Darius do to invite God's blessings upon Daniel? Consider Daniel's life and the many pressures he faced to turn away from God. What pressures exist in the world today that persuade us to turn away from God? How can you follow Daniel's example today as you face similar pressures?

THE PROPHET JONAH ATTEMPTS TO FLEE HIS RESPONSIBILITIES AND IS SWALLOWED BY A WHALE

For centuries, God repeatedly called prophets to command the Israelites to repent. One of these was a prophet named Amos, who declared: "Surely the Lord God will do nothing, but he revealeth his secret unto his servants the prophets" (Amos 3:7). This pattern began in the days of Adam and continues today as God reveals His truths, covenants, and commandments to prophets who then declare them to the world. Jonah was another prophet tasked with these duties. He lived around the time of Amos (about 800 B.C.). Jonah was initially reluctant to obey God's commandment to tell people things they probably didn't want to hear. He tried to abandon his duties—and quickly faced dangerous consequences. In these verses, a "mariner" is a sailor.

JONAH 1:1–17

Now the word of the Lord came unto Jonah the son of Amittai, saying,

2 Arise, go to Nineveh, that great city, and cry against it; for their wickedness is come up before me.

3 But Jonah rose up to flee unto Tarshish from the presence of the Lord, and went down to Joppa; and he found a ship going to Tarshish: so he paid the fare thereof, and went down into it, to go with them unto Tarshish from the presence of the Lord.

4 But the Lord sent out a great wind into the sea, and there was a mighty tempest in the sea, so that the ship was like to be broken.

5 Then the mariners were afraid, and cried every man unto his god, and cast forth the wares that were in the ship into the sea, to lighten it of them. But Jonah was gone down into the sides of the ship; and he lay, and was fast asleep.

6 So the shipmaster came to him, and said unto him, What meanest thou, O sleeper? arise, call upon thy God, if so be that God will think upon us, that we perish not.

7 And they said every one to his fellow, Come, and let us cast lots, that we may know for whose cause this evil is upon us. So they cast lots, and the lot fell upon Jonah.

8 Then said they unto him, Tell us, we pray thee, for whose cause this evil is upon us; What is thine occupation? and whence comest thou? what is thy country? and of what people art thou?

9 And he said unto them, I am an Hebrew; and I fear the Lord, the God of heaven, which hath made the sea and the dry land.

10 Then were the men exceedingly afraid, and said unto him, Why hast thou done this? For the men knew that he fled from the presence of the Lord, because he had told them.

11 Then said they unto him, What shall we do unto thee, that the sea may be calm unto us? for the sea wrought, and was tempestuous.

12 And he said unto them, Take me up, and cast me forth into the sea; so shall the sea be calm unto you: for I know that for my sake this great tempest is upon you.

13 Nevertheless the men rowed hard to bring it to the land; but they could not: for the sea wrought, and was tempestuous against them.

14 Wherefore they cried unto the Lord, and said, We beseech thee, O Lord, we beseech thee, let us not perish for this man's life, and lay not upon us innocent blood: for thou, O Lord, hast done as it pleased thee.

15 So they took up Jonah, and cast him forth into the sea: and the sea ceased from her raging.

16 Then the men feared the Lord exceedingly, and offered a sacrifice unto the Lord, and made vows.

17 Now the Lord had prepared a great fish to swallow up Jonah. And Jonah was in the belly of the fish three days and three nights.

How did Jonah respond to God's commandment to preach to the people of Nineveh? What happened to Jonah as a result of his disobedience? What duties has God given to you? In what ways might we be tempted to abandon our responsibilities to God—and what are some consequences of failing to fulfil those responsibilities? Share an example of someone who fulfilled his or her responsibilities to God even though it was difficult.

JONAH REPENTS, IS FREED FROM THE BELLY OF THE WHALE, AND PROPHESIES IN NINEVEH, AND THE PEOPLE REPENT AND ARE SAVED

Jonah had been called by God to preach repentance to the wicked people of Nineveh, but he avoided his duties and tried to run away from them. Instead of traveling to Nineveh as commanded, he boarded a ship bound for a distant city. God then caused a great storm to come upon the sea, and the sailors searched for the cause of the storm. Jonah admitted the storm had arisen due to his disobedience, and the sailors threw Jonah into the sea, where he was swallowed by a whale.

JONAH 2:1–10

Then Jonah prayed unto the Lord his God out of the fish's belly,

2 And said, I cried by reason of mine affliction unto the Lord, and he heard me; out of the belly of hell cried I, and thou heardest my voice.

3 For thou hadst cast me into the deep, in the midst of the seas; and the floods compassed me about: all thy billows and thy waves passed over me.

4 Then I said, I am cast out of thy sight; yet I will look again toward thy holy temple.

5 The waters compassed me about, even to the soul: the depth closed me round about, the weeds were wrapped about my head.

6 I went down to the bottoms of the mountains; the earth with her bars was about me for ever: yet hast thou brought up my life from corruption, O Lord my God.

7 When my soul fainted within me I remembered the Lord: and my prayer came in unto thee, into thine holy temple.

8 They that observe lying vanities forsake their own mercy.

9 But I will sacrifice unto thee with the voice of thanksgiving; I will pay that that I have vowed. Salvation is of the Lord.

10 And the Lord spake unto the fish, and it vomited out Jonah upon the dry land.

JONAH 3:1–10; JOSEPH SMITH TRANSLATION, JONAH 3:9–10

1 And the word of the Lord came unto Jonah the second time, saying,

2 Arise, go unto Nineveh, that great city, and preach unto it the preaching that I bid thee.

3 So Jonah arose, and went unto Nineveh, according to the word of the Lord. Now Nineveh was an exceeding great city of three days' journey.

4 And Jonah began to enter into the city a day's journey, and he cried, and said, Yet forty days, and Nineveh shall be overthrown.

5 So the people of Nineveh believed God, and proclaimed a fast, and put on sackcloth, from the greatest of them even to the least of them.

6 For word came unto the king of Nineveh, and he arose from his throne, and he laid his robe from him, and covered him with sackcloth, and sat in ashes.

7 And he caused it to be proclaimed and published through Nineveh by the decree of the king and his nobles, saying, Let neither man nor beast, herd nor flock, taste any thing: let them not feed, nor drink water:

8 But let man and beast be covered with sackcloth, and cry mightily unto God: yea, let them turn every one from his evil way, and from the violence that is in their hands.

9 Who can tell if *we will repent, and turn unto God, but he will turn away from us his fierce anger.*

10 And God saw their works, that they turned from their evil way *and repented; and God turned away the evil that he had said he would bring upon them.*

How did Jonah show he was repentant? While in the belly of the whale, what promises did he make to God? What was God's response? What was the result of Jonah's preaching to the people of Nineveh? What lessons can Jonah's actions teach us about duty, repentance, and God's mercy?

MICAH PROPHESIES OF THE LATTER DAYS WHEN GOD WILL DESTROY THE WICKED AND LOVINGLY GATHER THE RIGHTEOUS UPON MOUNT ZION

Around 720 B.C., Micah served as a prophet in Israel—after Jonah and at the same time as Isaiah. Like other prophets from this era, he boldly chastised the Israelites for their many wicked habits and prophesied that their gross sins would lead to the destruction of their cities and the scattering of their people. Sadly, the people did not repent, and Micah was an eyewitness to both the Israelites' sins and their destructive consequences. But Micah also prophesied of the latter days, when God would restore His covenants to His righteous children. As you read, look for descriptions of some events that are occurring now and others that will occur in the future.

MICAH 4:1–7

But in the last days it shall come to pass, that the mountain of the house of the Lord shall be established in the top of the mountains, and it shall be exalted above the hills; and people shall flow unto it.

2 And many nations shall come, and say, Come, and let us go up to the mountain of the Lord, and to the house of the God of Jacob; and he will teach us of his ways, and we will walk in his paths: for the law shall go forth of Zion, and the word of the Lord from Jerusalem.

3 And he shall judge among many people, and rebuke strong nations afar off; and they shall beat their swords into plowshares, and their spears into pruninghooks: nation shall not lift up a sword against nation, neither shall they learn war any more.

4 But they shall sit every man under his vine and under his fig tree; and none shall make them afraid: for the mouth of the Lord of hosts hath spoken it.

5 For all people will walk every one in the name of his god, and we will walk in the name of the Lord our God for ever and ever.

6 In that day, saith the Lord, will I assemble her that halteth, and I will gather her that is driven out, and her that I have afflicted;

7 And I will make her that halted a remnant, and her that was cast far off a strong nation: and the Lord shall reign over them in mount Zion from henceforth, even for ever.

Micah 5:8–15

8 And the remnant of Jacob shall be among the Gentiles in the midst of many people as a lion among the beasts of the forest, as a young lion among the flocks of sheep: who, if he go through, both treadeth down, and teareth in pieces, and none can deliver.

9 Thine hand shall be lifted up upon thine adversaries, and all thine enemies shall be cut off.

10 And it shall come to pass in that day, saith the Lord, that I will cut off thy horses out of the midst of thee, and I will destroy thy chariots:

11 And I will cut off the cities of thy land, and throw down all thy strong holds:

12 And I will cut off witchcrafts out of thine hand; and thou shalt have no more soothsayers:

13 Thy graven images also will I cut off, and thy standing images out of the midst of thee; and thou shalt no more worship the work of thine hands.

14 And I will pluck up thy groves out of the midst of thee: so will I destroy thy cities.

15 And I will execute vengeance in anger and fury upon the heathen, such as they have not heard.

What are some events listed in these verses that have already occurred? What are some events that have yet to occur? Consider Micah 4:1–2. What opportunities do you have—now and in the future—to make covenants with God in His temple? What do we learn in the temple? What warnings did God give to the wicked in these verses?

MALACHI PROPHESIES OF CHRIST'S RETURN AND SAYS, "WILL A MAN ROB GOD?"

The prophet Micah had prophesied powerfully of the latter days, when God will destroy the wicked and lovingly gather the righteous upon Mount Zion. He was joined by many other prophets who arose in the five hundred–year era that followed the time of Saul, David, and Solomon. The final prophet of the Old Testament record was Malachi, who lived about 430 years before the birth of Christ. The following prophecy of Malachi speaks of the Savior's latter-day return, the cleansing effect He will have upon those who believe in Him, and the importance of paying tithing. When Jesus Christ appeared to the Nephites, He commanded them to record the very same words included in the entire chapters of Malachi 3–4. Later, in 1823, the resurrected Book of Mormon prophet Moroni appeared to Joseph Smith and quoted portions of Malachi's words found in these same two chapters (see Joseph Smith—History 1:36–39). Note: Verse 2 refers to "fullers' soap." In ancient times, a fuller was someone who made soap through a complex and intense process.

Malachi 3:1–18

Behold, I will send my messenger, and he shall prepare the way before me: and the Lord, whom ye seek, shall suddenly come to his temple, even the messenger of the covenant, whom ye delight in: behold, he shall come, saith the Lord of hosts.

2 But who may abide the day of his coming? and who shall stand when he appeareth? for he is like a refiner's fire, and like fullers' soap:

3 And he shall sit as a refiner and purifier of silver: and he shall purify the sons of Levi, and purge them as gold and silver, that they may offer unto the Lord an offering in righteousness.

4 Then shall the offering of Judah and Jerusalem be pleasant unto the Lord, as in the days of old, and as in former years.

5 And I will come near to you to judgment; and I will be a swift witness against the sorcerers, and against the adulterers, and against false swearers, and against those that oppress the hireling in his wages, the widow, and the fatherless, and that turn aside the stranger from his right, and fear not me, saith the Lord of hosts.

6 For I am the Lord, I change not; therefore ye sons of Jacob are not consumed.

7 Even from the days of your fathers ye are gone away from mine ordinances, and have not kept them. Return unto me, and I will return unto you, saith the Lord of hosts. But ye said, Wherein shall we return?

8 Will a man rob God? Yet ye have robbed me. But ye say, Wherein have we robbed thee? In tithes and offerings.

9 Ye are cursed with a curse: for ye have robbed me, even this whole nation.

10 Bring ye all the tithes into the storehouse, that there may be meat in mine house, and prove me now herewith, saith the Lord of hosts, if I will not open you the windows of heaven, and pour you out a blessing, that there shall not be room enough to receive it.

11 And I will rebuke the devourer for your sakes, and he shall not destroy the fruits of your ground; neither shall your vine cast her fruit before the time in the field, saith the Lord of hosts.

12 And all nations shall call you blessed: for ye shall be a delightsome land, saith the Lord of hosts.

13 Your words have been stout against me, saith the Lord. Yet ye say, What have we spoken so much against thee?

14 Ye have said, It is vain to serve God: and what profit is it that we have kept his ordinance, and that we have walked mournfully before the Lord of hosts?

15 And now we call the proud happy; yea, they that work wickedness are set up; yea, they that tempt God are even delivered.

16 Then they that feared the Lord spake often one to another: and the Lord hearkened, and

heard it, and a book of remembrance was written before him for them that feared the Lord, and that thought upon his name.

17 And they shall be mine, saith the Lord of hosts, in that day when I make up my jewels; and I will spare them, as a man spareth his own son that serveth him.

18 Then shall ye return, and discern between the righteous and the wicked, between him that serveth God and him that serveth him not.

Consider verse 6. In what ways does God "change not"? According to these verses, how has man robbed God? In these verses, what blessings are promised to those who pay tithing? How have you seen those blessings in your own life?

MALACHI PROPHESIES THAT ELIJAH WILL RETURN IN THE LATTER DAYS TO "TURN THE HEART OF THE FATHERS TO THE CHILDREN, AND THE HEART OF THE CHILDREN TO THEIR FATHERS"

The following verses contain the concluding words of the Old Testament record. For four thousand years God had called prophets to teach His children the principles of repentance, obedience, and covenants. He taught them of the atoning sacrifice of Jesus Christ and the promised blessing of eternal life with Heavenly Father and Jesus Christ. In these final verses, many of those principles are referred to as Malachi prophesies of events of the latter days. Note again the fact that these verses were quoted word for word by Jesus Christ to the Nephites and were referred to in detail by Moroni when he appeared to the Prophet Joseph Smith (see Joseph Smith—History 1:36–39).

MALACHI 4:1–6

For, behold, the day cometh, that shall burn as an oven; and all the proud, yea, and all that do wickedly, shall be stubble: and the day that cometh shall burn them up, saith the Lord of hosts, that it shall leave them neither root nor branch.

2 But unto you that fear my name shall the Sun of righteousness arise with healing in his wings; and ye shall go forth, and grow up as calves of the stall.

3 And ye shall tread down the wicked; for they shall be ashes under the soles of your feet in the day that I shall do this, saith the Lord of hosts.

4 Remember ye the law of Moses my servant, which I commanded unto him in Horeb for all Israel, with the statutes and judgments.

5 Behold, I will send you Elijah the prophet before the coming of the great and dreadful day of the Lord:

6 And he shall turn the heart of the fathers to the children, and the heart of the children to their fathers, lest I come and smite the earth with a curse.

In fulfillment of the prophecy given in verses 5–6, Elijah appeared to the Prophet Joseph Smith and Oliver Cowdery on April 3, 1836, shortly after the dedication of the Kirtland Temple. Prior to Elijah's appearance, Moses and Elias appeared and bestowed the keys of the gathering of Israel and committed to them "the dispensation of the gospel of Abraham." Elijah then appeared, quoted from Malachi 4:5–6, and conferred upon Joseph and Oliver the priesthood authority to seal families together for eternity (see Doctrine and Covenants 110:11–16).

According to these verses, what will happen to the wicked at the last day? Who did God promise to send to the earth prior to the return of Jesus Christ? When was that prophecy fulfilled? What effect would Elijah's return have upon the people in the last days? How have you seen that promise fulfilled?

About the Editors

Tyler McKellar was born and raised in Teton Valley, Idaho, where he now lives with his wife, Stephanie, and their six children. He served a mission for The Church of Jesus Christ of Latter-day Saints in South Korea and graduated from Brigham Young University with a degree in advertising. He presently works as a freelance writer and screenwriter. He likes college football, golf, milkshakes, and mountain biking.

Stephanie O'Brien McKellar was born and raised in Teton Valley, Idaho. She served a mission for The Church of Jesus Christ of Latter-day Saints in Jackson, Mississippi, and graduated from Brigham Young University with a degree in English. For the last twenty-three years she has been raising six children, reading and writing poetry, and taking long morning walks. She loves her family and has a special place in her heart for her cats.

About the Illustrator

Dan Burr, an award-winning illustrator, earned a bachelor of fine arts degree from Utah State University and a master's degree in illustration from Syracuse University. He and his wife, Patti, are the parents of two children and live in Tetonia, Idaho. Dan has illustrated many children's books, including *One Little Match, The Miracle of the Wooden Shoes, I Heard the Bells on Christmas Day,* and *The Christmas Train.*